AF172550

Communications
in Computer and Information Science   2623

Series Editors

Gang Li , *School of Information Technology, Deakin University, Burwood, VIC,*
Australia
Joaquim Filipe , *Polytechnic Institute of Setúbal, Setúbal, Portugal*
Zhiwei Xu, *Chinese Academy of Sciences, Beijing, China*

Rationale

The CCIS series is devoted to the publication of proceedings of computer science conferences. Its aim is to efficiently disseminate original research results in informatics in printed and electronic form. While the focus is on publication of peer-reviewed full papers presenting mature work, inclusion of reviewed short papers reporting on work in progress is welcome, too. Besides globally relevant meetings with internationally representative program committees guaranteeing a strict peer-reviewing and paper selection process, conferences run by societies or of high regional or national relevance are also considered for publication.

Topics

The topical scope of CCIS spans the entire spectrum of informatics ranging from foundational topics in the theory of computing to information and communications science and technology and a broad variety of interdisciplinary application fields.

Information for Volume Editors and Authors

Publication in CCIS is free of charge. No royalties are paid, however, we offer registered conference participants temporary free access to the online version of the conference proceedings on SpringerLink (http://link.springer.com) by means of an http referrer from the conference website and/or a number of complimentary printed copies, as specified in the official acceptance email of the event.

CCIS proceedings can be published in time for distribution at conferences or as post-proceedings, and delivered in the form of printed books and/or electronically as USBs and/or e-content licenses for accessing proceedings at SpringerLink. Furthermore, CCIS proceedings are included in the CCIS electronic book series hosted in the SpringerLink digital library at http://link.springer.com/bookseries/7899. Conferences publishing in CCIS are allowed to use our online conference service (Meteor) for managing the whole proceedings lifecycle (from submission and reviewing to preparing for publication) free of charge.

Publication process

The language of publication is exclusively English. Authors publishing in CCIS have to sign the Springer CCIS copyright transfer form, however, they are free to use their material published in CCIS for substantially changed, more elaborate subsequent publications elsewhere. For the preparation of the camera-ready papers/files, authors have to strictly adhere to the Springer CCIS Authors' Instructions and are strongly encouraged to use the CCIS LaTeX style files or templates.

Abstracting/Indexing

CCIS is abstracted/indexed in DBLP, Google Scholar, EI-Compendex, Mathematical Reviews, SCImago, Scopus. CCIS volumes are also submitted for the inclusion in ISI Proceedings.

How to start

To start the evaluation of your proposal for inclusion in the CCIS series, please send an e-mail to ccis@springer.com

Ticianne Darin · Kamila Rios · Georgia Cruz ·
Leonardo Tórtoro · Diego Ricca
Editors

Interaction and Player Research in Game Development

4th International Workshop, WIPlay 2025
Belo Horizonte, Brazil, September 8, 2025
Proceedings

 Springer

Editors
Ticianne Darin ⓘD
Federal University of Ceará
Fortaleza, Brazil

Kamila Rios ⓘD
University of São Paulo
São Carlos - SP, Brazil

Georgia Cruz ⓘD
Federal University of Ceará
Fortaleza, Brazil

Leonardo Tórtoro ⓘD
São Paulo State University
São Paulo, Brazil

Diego Ricca ⓘD
Federal University of Ceará
Fortaleza, Brazil

ISSN 1865-0929   ISSN 1865-0937 (electronic)
Communications in Computer and Information Science
ISBN 978-3-032-01425-2   ISBN 978-3-032-01426-9 (eBook)
https://doi.org/10.1007/978-3-032-01426-9

This Springer imprint is published by the registered company Springer Nature Switzerland AG
The registered company address is: Gewerbestrasse 11, 6330 Cham, Switzerland

If disposing of this product, please recycle the paper.

Preface

This volume contains the papers presented at the IV Workshop on Interaction and Player Research in Game Development (WIPlay). The workshop was held in Belo Horizonte, Brazil, on September 8, 2025, as part of the 20th IFIP TC13 International Conference on Human-Computer Interaction (INTERACT 2025).

WIPlay was founded in Brazil on the conviction that, as digital games become a significant global medium, the Human-Computer Interaction (HCI) community has a crucial role in shaping their future. The workshop's primary goal was to foster cross-cultural collaboration, using the presented papers as a foundation for discussing a shared research agenda in human-centered game design. This event represents a deliberate evolution from its origins as three successful national workshops at the Brazilian Symposium on Human-Computer Interaction (IHC). The move to an international stage at INTERACT was intended to amplify discussions and connect with the international community.

The accepted papers had to be sound and spark discussions. They involved ongoing research, position papers, and experience reports, coalescing into three distinct thematic areas that reflected the workshop's core goals. The most prominent theme was socially conscious and inclusive game design, with contributions addressing accessibility for players with visual or hearing impairments, sound design for autistic players, and gender equity in games. The second focused on ethical design, with work examining deceptive game design and proposing strategies to enhance player well-being. The third provided practical methods, tools, and frameworks for user research, offering tangible guidance for the community.

Submissions underwent a double-blind peer review by two experts, with a third arbitrating disagreements. Following a meta-review, two non-conflicted chairs made final decisions after authors incorporated feedback into their submissions. From 15 submissions, we accepted 12 papers: 10 full and 2 short. The acceptance rate reflects a deliberate editorial decision. Each paper was judged on its scientific merit through our peer-review process. We chose to publish all work deemed a substantial contribution, rather than rejecting papers simply to achieve a lower acceptance rate. The result is a cohesive volume that accurately represents the work of a focused, growing community.

We express our sincere gratitude to the members of the Program Committee for their diligent and insightful evaluations. We thank all the authors for submitting their research to WIPlay, and the participants for the engaging discussions during the workshop. We are grateful to the organizing committee of INTERACT 2025 for their support.

September 2025

Ticianne Darin
Kamila Rios
Georgia Cruz
Leonardo Tórtoro
Diego Ricca

Organization

Program Committee Chairs

Ticianne Darin	Federal University of Ceará, Brazil
Kamila Rodrigues	University of São Paulo, Brazil
Georgia Cruz	Federal University of Ceará, Brazil
Leonardo Tórtoro	University of São Paulo, Brazil
Diego Ricca	Federal University of Ceará, Brazil

Program Committee

Alcides Teixeira	Mackenzie Presbyterian University, Brazil
Thiago Barcelos	Federal Institute of Education, Science and Technology of São Paulo, Brazil
Nayana Carneiro	Federal University of Ceará, Brazil
Bruna Cunha	University of São Paulo, Brazil
Guilherme Derenievicz	Federal University of Paraná, Brazil
Sandra Gama	University of Lisbon, Portugal
Wilk Oliveira	Tampere University, Finland
Gustavo Sato	State University of Maringá, Brazil
Matheus Serafim	Federal University of Ceará, Brazil
Marcos Seruffo	Federal University of Pará, Brazil
Windson Viana	Federal University of Ceará, Brazil
Claudia Werner	Federal University of Rio de Janeiro, Brazil

Contents

Practical Methods and Frameworks for Game Design and Evaluation

Socially Conscious and Inclusive Game Design

Lost Memories: Developing an Accessible Game for Visually Impaired Players

Hondenis Santos Garcia(✉) [iD], Pedro Marcos Alves[iD],
João Victor Pimenta Neves[iD], Guilherme Konzen[iD],
Ludmilla Fernandes Oliveira Galvão[iD], and Paulo Guilherme Paes da Silva[iD]

Federal University of Mato Grosso, Cuiabá, MT, Brazil
{hondenis.garcia,pedro.alves2,joao.neves2,guilherme.konzen}@sou.ufmt.br,
{ludmilla.galvao,paulo.silva27}@ufmt.br

Abstract. This paper explores accessibility in digital games for visually impaired players, with a focus on the development of a 3D Role-
Playing Game (RPG). To inform the design process, a questionnaire
was applied to gather insights into players perceptions of RPGs and
accessibility, alongside an interview with a blind player to identify specific challenges and preferences. The development process was guided
by the Design Thinking methodology, selected for its emphasis on user
empathy and problem-solving grounded in real user needs. This approach
was integrated with the use of the Unity engine, chosen for its flexibility and widespread use in accessible game development. Data analysis
informed the creation of a player profile and personas, which, combined
with the Game Accessibility Guidelines (GAG), supported design decisions throughout the project. The findings suggest that, despite broad
recognition of the importance of accessibility, its practical implementation in digital games remains limited. This underscores the need for
Information Technology (IT) degree programs to incorporate accessibility into their curricula, fostering the training of professionals equipped
to create more inclusive digital experiences.

Keywords: Design Thinking · Visually Impaired People · Digital
Games · Accessibility

1   Introduction

According to the World Health Organization (WHO), approximately 285 million people worldwide have impaired vision [11]. The exclusion of people with
disabilities, especially those with visual impairments, occurs due to society's
lack of information about blindness. This is a prejudice that does not manifest
itself aggressively, but this rejection reinforces social exclusion. The ideology of
deficit sustains this discrimination, which links the value of the individual to
their productivity [6]. In this context, the Brazilian Law for the Inclusion of
People with Disabilities [4] establishes guidelines to guarantee accessibility and

T. Darin et al. (Eds.): WIPlay 2025, CCIS 2623, pp. 3–18, 2026.
https://doi.org/10.1007/978-3-032-01426-9_1

social inclusion, reinforcing the importance of eliminating barriers that hinder their participation in numerous spheres, including digital entertainment.

Accessibility in games has gained greater attention in the gaming market, through initiatives such as *The Game Awards*[1], which developed a specific category to reward games that bring innovations in accessibility. Another initiative is the association *AbleGamers*[2], which is dedicated to creating opportunities to reduce social isolation for people with disabilities, such as donating adaptive video game controls to this audience. In addition, the organization offers courses and guidelines for game developers to create more accessible games. However, even with these incentives, there are still few titles developed with the visually impaired audience in mind, especially when we consider the Brazilian scenario. Games like *Breu*[3], a horror audio game with the premise of involving visually impaired players in an investigative narrative, is an exception to the rule.

When analyzing the context of game genres with a strong narrative, RPG stands out. Initially a type of board game, it was adapted for computers between 1974 and 1975 [9]. This genre stands out for promoting emotional involvement with the characters by the players [13], having a shared and changing narrative [15], and encouraging meaningful playful interaction [17]. Even though it promotes all these aspects, there are few examples of RPG games that are accessible to people with visual impairments, mainly due to their high dependence on texts.

Thus, this study aimed to understand which aspects should be taken into consideration for the development of an RPG game aiming at accessibility for people with visual impairments. To this end, it is necessary that the game be inclusive for all players, with and without visual impairments, without compromising gameplay. Thus, it is considered in this work that an accessible game should provide an equitable experience for all audiences, ensuring that no player has an advantage over the other, regardless of their limitations.

This work is organized as follows: Sect. 2 presents the theoretical basis of this research. Section 3 presents the methodology adopted. Section 4 presents the results obtained and their discussions. Section 5 presents the game development process. Section 6 presents the lessons learned throughout the research. Finally, Sect. 7 presents the conclusions of this study, its limitations, and future works.

2   Theoretical Basis

According to Ottaiano et al. [2019], visual function is classified into four levels: normal vision, moderate visual impairment, severe visual impairment, and blindness. Individuals who are unable to perform everyday tasks due to significant visual impairment - whether they have some residual vision or are completely without sight - are considered blind. In addition to these levels of visual impairment, there are also visual dysfunctions such as color blindness, which interferes

---

[1] https://thegameawards.com/, Accessed on: May 18, 2025.
[2] https://ablegamers.org.br/, Accessed on: May 18, 2025.
[3] https://store.steampowered.com/app/2213890/Breu_Ataque_das_Sombras/, Accessed on: May 18, 2025.

with the perception and distinction of certain colors, predominantly affecting men [16].

This research focuses on accessibility in games according to GAG (*Game Accessibility Guidelines*), a set of guidelines which helps game developers produce content that can prevent players from being excluded due to lack of accessibility [7]. GAG provides game developers with guidelines, tools, and examples that cover aspects of vision, hearing, cognition, and motor skills, divided into 3 levels of implementation difficulty: basic, intermediate, and advanced. This way, game development teams can choose the guidelines that make sense in their contexts.

Regarding visual accessibility, GAG presents guidelines that assist in the development of solutions for people with different degrees of visual impairment and visual dysfunctions. An example of a game compliant with GAG guidelines is *The Last of Us Part II*[4], winner of the "Innovation in Accessibility" category at *The Game Awards 2020*. The game stood out for offering a comprehensive set of settings aimed at people with visual impairments, including high contrast display, colorblind interface mode, and audio-based navigation assistance. In the Brazilian context, examples of accessible games for people with visual impairments are scarce, with most falling into the category of serious or educational games rather than entertainment games [1], which is the focus of this research.

3 Methodology

This research was developed during a "Projects in Computer Engineering" course at Federal University of Mato Grosso (UFMT), which involves planning, prototyping, validating, and testing software solutions involving technological trends. It was based on the *Design Thinking* (DT) methodology, an iterative process that software development teams use to understand their users and implement innovative solutions to relevant problems [10].

DT is divided into 5 stages: I) Empathize, in which the goal is to define a target audience and understand them; II) Define, in which the target audience's problem(s) that will be addressed in the application are defined; III) Ideate, in which possible ideas for the application to be developed are raised; IV) Prototype, in which a prototype of the application is developed based on the knowledge acquired; and V) Test, in which the developed prototype is evaluated by experts or the target audience.

The research reported in this paper is part of the Empathize, Define, Ideate and Prototype stages. Its objective was to develop a deeper understanding of the target audience and to create an initial prototype. To understand the target audience of the game, two techniques were used: I) **User profile** (here referred to as player), which consists of developing a detailed description of the characteristics of users [2]; and II) **Personas,** which consists of developing one or more fictional characters, hypothetical archetypes of a group of real users, created to describe a typical user [2].

---

[4] https://www.playstation.com/pt-br/games/the-last-of-us-part-ii-remastered/, Accessed on: May 18, 2025.

In order to execute the aforementioned techniques, it was necessary to collect data from potential users. A questionnaire was applied [2], targeting different profiles, via *Google Forms*[5] and contained 14 questions aimed at understanding users' experiences with games, the most commonly used gaming platforms, their preferences in game styles, and their perceptions of accessibility. Thirty students from UFMT participated by completing the questionnaire.

Data collected from the questionnaire was analyzed by identifying patterns in responses and reviewing the charts generated by *Google Forms*. This process allowed us to classify reported preferences and challenges, which then informed the game's development plan to cater to both target audiences.

In addition to the questionnaire, an interview [2] was also conducted with a visually impaired person, to obtain a more in-depth account of the difficulties faced in this context. The interview analysis was carried out through thematic analysis, whereby the data were analyzed and grouped into categories [3]. Initially, the material was read in full to familiarize ourselves with the data. Then, units of meaning related to accessibility challenges in games were identified. The information collected was essential to understand the main limitations faced by visually impaired players and, thus, implement more appropriate solutions in the development of the game.

All the questions, both from the questionnaire and the interview, were designed to provide insights that could support the process of requirements elicitation for the game. In this way, the results would inform decisions in the game's planning phase, such as the choice of development platform, which types of accessibility settings would be relevant, and whether the target audience would be receptive to an RPG-style game, as well as which RPG mechanics they prefer (combat, puzzles, or branching narrative).

Although the data collection procedures were not submitted to the Ethics Committee of UFMT, there were concerns about the ethics of the research. Before the questionnaire and interview were applied, all participants were informed about the objectives of the research, the voluntary nature of participation, and the use of data for academic purposes only. In the case of the questionnaire, consent was obtained digitally through *Google Forms*, where participants agreed before proceeding. During the interview, consent was recorded through verbal authorization, ensuring that the participant was aware of and agreed to their participation.

4   Results and Discussions

This section will present the data obtained from both the questionnaire (Subsect. 4.1) and the interview (Subsect. 4.2), as well as the player profile and personas developed (Subsect. 4.3).

---

[5] https://drive.google.com/file/d/1E1wgK-o9GHG5xZTYe9vcXfXm9FP00emO/view?usp=sharing, Accessed on: May 18,2025.

4.1   Questionnaire

To better understand the game's target audience, a questionnaire was applied to 30 participants, most of whom were students at UFMT. The questionnaire addressed the following information: I) Average age and gender of participants; II) Frequency with which they usually play; III) Platforms they use (e.g., cell phone, computer); IV) Game genres they like the most; V) If they have ever played RPG games; VI) If they like games focused on narrative; VII) If they have ever used or use accessibility features, and if possible, give an example; and VIII) If they use a narration feature during the game and consider this feature useful for casual players.

The results indicated that most participants (36.7%) are in the 18 to 24 age group, which reflects an expected university bias. Regarding the frequency with which they usually play, most of them play every day (46.7%). Regarding the most used platforms, computers (53.3%) and cell phones (30%) stood out, indicating consumption trends among this audience and influencing decisions about the development and distribution of the game proposed.

Regarding game genre preferences, RPG was the most cited (19 respondents), followed by adventure games (18 respondents) and simulation (16 respondents). This result reinforces the acceptance of narrative mechanics and suggests a potential interest in the RPG game to be developed. Regarding having played RPG games, half of the participants said they had played (50%), which suggests familiarity with this genre. In addition, the majority of them prefer games with more complex narratives (80%), with puzzles and challenges on the maps (96.7%). Participants cited examples of this genre, with emphasis on the game *Chrono Trigger*[6], a title recognized for offering great freedom of exploration, an engaging narrative and a striking soundtrack. Among the list of games cited, no Brazilian RPG was mentioned, which suggests that these games have less visibility among participants. These data suggest a potential challenge for the proposed game, particularly in identifying factors that affect the recognition and dissemination of national games within this genre.

Regarding accessibility, only a small portion of participants reported having used this kind of feature (16.7%). These data align with the findings of the Game Brazil Survey [2025], which reported that only 25.5% of respondents stated they used some form of accessibility feature in games. This result can be interpreted in two ways: either there is a lack of knowledge on the part of players about what constitutes an accessibility feature, such as subtitles and contrast adjustments, or, in fact, there is a lack of games that offer features to make the experience more inclusive and accessible. This scenario reinforces the importance of raising awareness about accessibility in games, both among developers and among players themselves.

Among the accessibility resources used by the interviewees, we have: I) Fonts for people with dyslexia; II) Subtitles; III) Automatic collection of items; IV)

---

[6]   https://store.steampowered.com/app/613830/CHRONO_TRIGGER/, Accessed on: May 18, 2025.

Redundancy of *feedback*, that is, it is presented in audio and visual form; and V) Visualization of sound on the map. Some interviewees mentioned the games in which they use these accessibility resources, highlighting titles such as *The Last of Us Part II*.

Finally, when asked whether a narration resource would be useful for casual players, that is, a voice narrating aspects such as the story and the player's actions, the majority responded in favor (66.7%). However, a significant percentage (30%) showed uncertainty, which may indicate a lack of familiarity with this type of accessibility configuration. Still, the majority perception that narration can contribute to inclusion reinforces the importance of developing and implementing accessible solutions that expand the reach of games to different player profiles.

4.2   Interview

After the questionnaire was applied, an interview was conducted with a participant with total visual impairment to gain insights into the main challenges faced by him while playing and to identify potential adaptations to enhance the accessibility of digital games. During the interview, he pointed out that he had extensive experience with games, since he had been playing since he was a child. He was not born visually impaired but acquired the condition later in life, which required him to relearn how to play games. Nowadays, he works as an accessibility consultant for games, bringing a valuable perspective on the barriers faced and possible solutions to make games more inclusive.

The participant stated that he uses screen readers while playing, including a mobile application that provides screen reading on mobile devices, as well as the screen reader built into his computer's operating system. During the interview, he recommended the adoption of the *UI Accessibility Plugin* (UAP)[7], a free *plugin* that makes the game interface accessible to screen readers. This feature, he said, would be an important tool for improving accessibility in games, especially for visually impaired players.

When asked about the challenges he faces in gaming, the participant highlighted the frustration of being unable to play some titles, especially when the games are popular and his friends talk about them. He feels left out, unable to participate in conversations due to the lack of accessibility features in these games. This highlights the need for the development of more inclusive games, which can help combat the social isolation faced by many people with disabilities, allowing everyone to participate equally in gaming culture.

Regarding the difficulties he encounters during gameplay, the participant stated that the lack of accessibility limits his options, preventing him from playing certain genres of games. He believes that, although some accessibility features exist, they do not always function as intended. Among the games he can play is *Mortal Kombat*[8], since he has developed an ability to adapt to fighting games by

---

[7] https://assetstore.unity.com/packages/tools/gui/ui-accessibility-plugin-uap-87935, accessed on: May 18, 2025.

[8] https://www.mortalkombat.com/pt-br, Accessed on: May 18, 2025.

memorizing the sounds made by characters during battles. Like the interviewees in the questionnaire, the interviewee did not include any Brazilian games in the list of accessible titles that he can play, which points to a significant need in the Brazilian gaming industry. This suggests a gap in the availability of accessible games developed in Brazil, underscoring the importance of enhancing inclusion and accessibility within this market.

Finally, regarding the way he receives feedback in games, he expressed the desire to receive beeps for quick events, screen reading, navigation assistance and, in shooting games, aim assistance. When asked about his opinion on narration as an accessibility feature, he stated that, although it is not a bad option, the feature needs to be implemented in a way that improves the player experience. In his case, he values the ability to play more than detailed narration of every aspect of the game. For him, a narration that describes the environment excessively, such as "You are now inside a cave, drops of water run down the rocky stalactites of the ceiling and fall to the ground", would not be useful, but if an external narration to enhance the mechanical experience, such as in commands or important events, could be a good option.

4.3   Player Profile and Personas

The player profile, presented in Fig. 1, was developed based on the analysis of the data obtained through the questionnaire and the interview. Thus, based on this player profile, decisions related to the game design were made. The protagonist is a young adult male, in line with the player profile, which is predominantly male. The game was developed for computers, one of the platforms most used by this audience, and was set in a medieval context, in accordance with the titles mentioned by the respondents in the questionnaire.

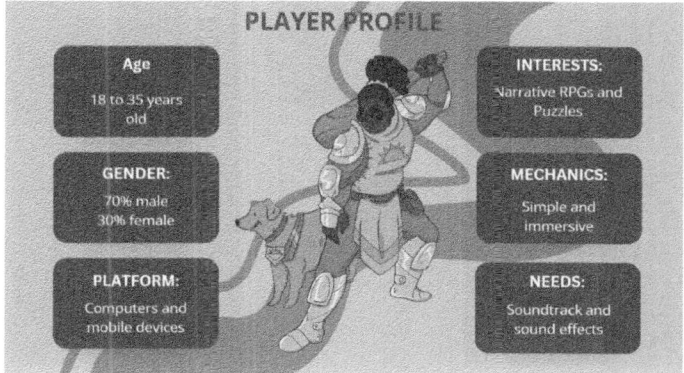

Fig. 1. Player Profile

To ensure an engaging experience, one of the team's developers specialized in building narratives and scripts, considering that the story is one of the main elements of interest to players. In addition, the game adopted traditional RPG mechanics, including puzzles, inspired by the games mentioned by the survey participants. Sound is also a key aspect, and to this end, one of the team members specialized in sound design.

With accessibility in mind, the game is compatible with screen readers and features a navigation system adapted for people with visual impairments. Interactive elements, such as items, obstacles and enemies, have distinct beeps, allowing the player to identify them intuitively. This decision was inspired by the interviewee's comments and goes against the initial idea of implementing narration throughout the game, which reinforces the commitment to inclusion in the game's design.

To create the personas, the design tool *Canva*[9] and the artificial intelligence photo generator *Random Face Generator*[10] were used. The first persona (Fig. 2) is called "Gabriel Silva", a 22-year-old Computer Science student with total blindness. He is a video game lover, always seeking new experiences in the world of games even though he faces accessibility barriers. He relies heavily on features that provide an inclusive and immersive experience, such as screen readers and haptic and audio feedback to interact with digital interfaces, and prefers to play games that support these features, such as Mortal Kombat. However, he is often frustrated when he finds games he wants to play that do not have adequate support. His experience with gaming highlights the importance of developing accessibility features in games for the inclusion of visually impaired players.

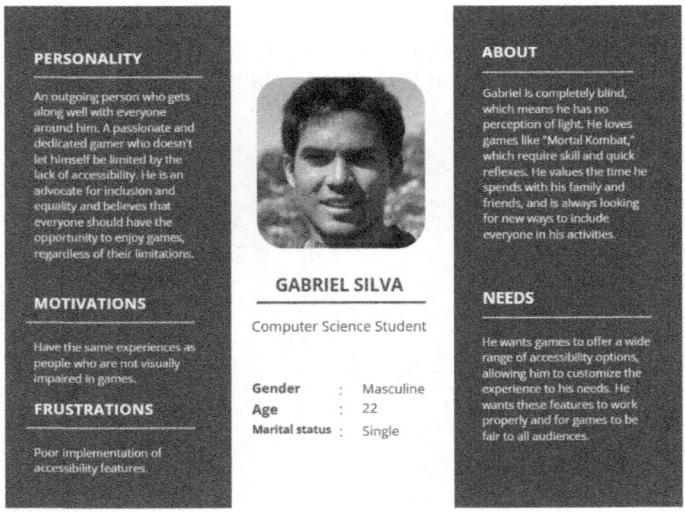

Fig. 2. Persona "Gabriel Silva"

---

[9] https://www.canva.com/, Accessed on: May 18, 2025.
[10] https://this-person-does-not-exist.com/en, Accessed on: May 18, 2025.

This persona (Fig. 2) was developed based primarily on the interview conducted with the visually impaired participant (Sec. 4.2). During the interview, he shared details about his experience with digital games, highlighting challenges related to the lack of accessibility in titles he would like to play. These frustrations were incorporated into the persona, making it more representative. In addition, the choice of the game *Mortal Kombat* was strongly influenced by the interviewee, who mentioned this title among his favorites, as well as his preference for action games that require quick reflexes. Finally, the persona's motivation to advocate for accessibility reflects the interviewee himself, who works in the development of inclusive games and reflects on the importance of having people with disabilities working in the gaming market.

The second persona (Fig. 3) is called "Mônica Ferreira", and is a 23-year-old Design student who enjoys games that can provide a relaxing and immersive experience. This persona (Fig. 3) was developed mainly inspired by the data obtained in the questionnaire (Sect. 4.1), which is why Mônica is not visually impaired. Her interest in design led her to explore the importance of accessibility in games, especially because of her younger brother, who is visually impaired. The two have always shared a strong connection through games, but over time, Mônica realized how the lack of accessibility created barriers for him, excluding him from many experiences. Her frustration led her to seek out more inclusive games. Determined and passionate about her field, Mônica wants, as a future designer, to contribute to the development of more accessible games. For her, game design should not be limited to the visual aspect, but rather allow for a complete and accessible experience for everyone.

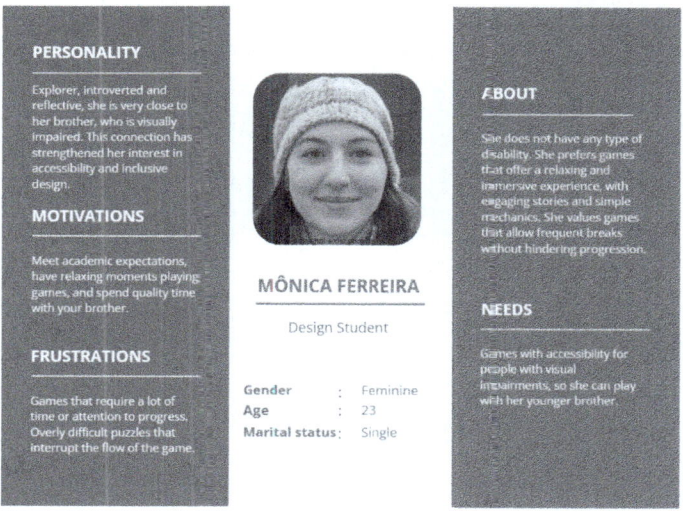

PERSONALITY

Explorer, introverted and reflective, she is very close to her brother, who is visually impaired. This connection has strengthened her interest in accessibility and inclusive design.

MOTIVATIONS

Meet academic expectations, have relaxing moments playing games, and spend quality time with your brother.

FRUSTRATIONS

Games that require a lot of time or attention to progress. Overly difficult puzzles that interrupt the flow of the game.

MÔNICA FERREIRA

Design Student

Gender   : Feminine
Age   : 23
Marital status: Single

ABOUT

She does not have any type of disability. She prefers games that offer a relaxing and immersive experience, with engaging stories and simple mechanics. She values games that allow frequent breaks without hindering progression.

NEEDS

Games with accessibility for people with visual impairments, so she can play with her younger brother.

Fig. 3. Persona "Mônica Ferreira"

This persona (Fig. 3) was developed mainly inspired by the data obtained in the questionnaire (Sect. 4.1), which is why Monica is not visually impaired. In addition, several respondents had a casual gamer profile, which was transferred to the persona. Even without a disability, she still maintains a connection with the motivation for games with greater accessibility through her brother (who is visually impaired) and her area of expertise. This persona represents all the people who live with family members who are people with disabilities, and highlights how "leisure for families of children and young people with disabilities is an important situation that favors the development, personal satisfaction and social inclusion of these people" [12, p. 13].

The third and last persona (Fig. 4) is called "Lucas Almeida", a 26-year-old Systems Analyst who is colorblind. He seeks games as a way to escape his work routine and prefers games with rich narratives and challenging puzzles, which keep him engaged for hours. As an introvert, Lucas prefers the company of games, as well as fantasy and science fiction books, which reinforces his appreciation for engaging stories. Due to his color blindness, he values games that offer accessibility filters for color blind people, ensuring a satisfactory visual experience and allowing him to appreciate the complexity of virtual worlds. However, he still faces difficulties in many games that feature indistinguishable colors and poorly synchronized subtitles, compromising his immersion.

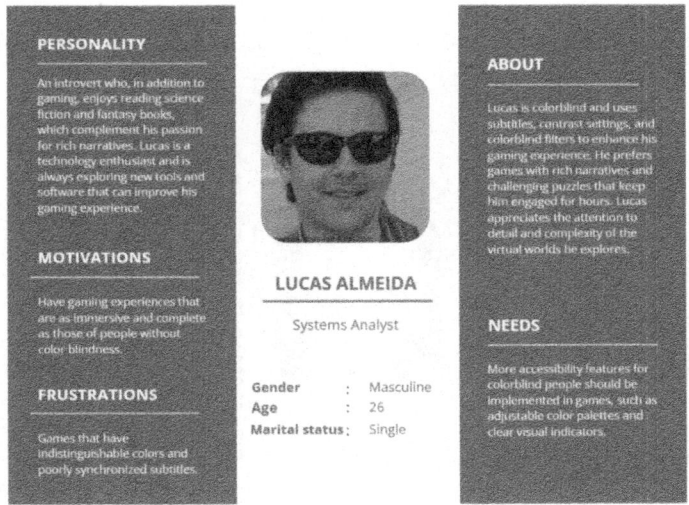

Fig. 4. Persona "Lucas Almeida"

This persona (Fig. 4) had characteristics inspired by the data obtained in the questionnaire, mainly his preference for RPG-style games and the constant use of subtitles in games. Although no participant in the survey was identified as colorblind, this characteristic was included due to the high incidence of the condition, which affects approximately 10% of the male population [2].

In short, three personas were developed, representing different profiles of possible target players: a person with total visual impairment who enjoys frenetic games, a female player without disabilities who prefers casual games, and a colorblind player who enjoys RPGs. These personas supported the development of a more inclusive and accessible game and may serve as a resource for other game development teams working on accessible game design.

5 Game Development

After collecting and analyzing the data, it was possible to continue the implementation of the game *Lost Memories*. The steps involved in this process are presented below: I) Creating the game concept; II) Selecting GAG guidelines; III) Developing the game; and IV) Testing and distributing the game.

To develop the game concept and narrative, a brainstorming session was held in which each team member presented ideas for the game, taking into account the player profile and the defined personas. After a period of consolidation, a central narrative was defined: the story of a wizard who wakes up with no memories and must explore an unknown world to recover his past. In addition, images aligned with the game's medieval theme were selected, including settings (castles, medieval cities, forests) and characters (wizards, villagers, villains). Based on these decisions, one of the team members began focusing on developing the narrative and creating the characters.

During the second stage, GAG guidelines were selected with the primary goal of addressing the needs of visually impaired players. This process took place during a meeting in which each team member presented reasoned arguments regarding the relevance of each guideline to the project, along with discussions about their technical and financial feasibility. Below are the guidelines chosen by GAG that will be part of the game project:

– **Basic Guidelines**

– **GAG1: Provide high contrast between text/UI and background.** This guideline was chosen to provide a better experience for people with low vision or color blindness who are affected by low contrast displays;
– **GAG2: Use simple and clear text formatting.** The choice of this guideline aligns with some of the questionnaire responses, which indicated that captions are the most commonly used accessibility feature;
– **GAG3: Ensure that interactive elements/virtual controls are large and well spaced, especially on small or touch-sensitive screens.** This guideline was chosen because visually impaired people can easily make mistakes in interfaces with elements/controls that are too close together;
– **GAG4: Use a standard font size that is easily readable.** This guideline was chosen because many people, with or without visual impairments, have difficulty reading very small fonts, especially in captions;

– **GAG5: Ensure that no essential information is conveyed by a fixed color alone.** This guideline is aligned with GAG1 and is essential to ensure that players with color blindness or poor color perception do not miss information during gameplay.

– **Intermediate Guidelines**

– **GAG6: Clearly indicate that interactive elements are interactive.** Using distinct visual highlights or sounds can be beneficial for both visually impaired players and those with cognitive disabilities;

– **GAG7: Ensure that sound/music choices for each key object or event are distinct from each other.** The choice of this guideline is aligned with one of the most discussed ideas during the interview: The importance of informing the player about the presence of an object in the scene. Distinct sounds are especially useful for this, making it easier to distinguish between different objects;

– **GAG8: Provide separate volume controls or mute options for effects, speech, and background music.** This guideline was chosen because this type of setup allows people with visual or hearing impairments to choose which type of sound to prioritize during gameplay.

– **Advanced Guidelines**

– **GAG9: Use a distinct sound/music design for all objects and events.** The choice of this guideline is also aligned with the conversation with the interviewee, who commented that it would be interesting to bring distinct sounds in the form of beeps for each object and event, such as, for example, to differentiate an obstacle from an enemy;

– **GAG10: Provide pre-recorded narration for all text, including menus and installers.** The initial premise of the game was to make it fully narrated. However, after interviewing the visually impaired player, it became clear that this approach could overwhelm the user. As a result, alternative guidelines were adopted, such as the use of the UAP plugin. Nevertheless, narration will still be included during character dialogues.

The project is currently in its first version, with the introduction of the game's storyline already implemented. Free visual assets previously available — such as environments and characters—were used, along with the development of a functional initial menu. The Fig. 5 shows the game's initial menu and settings screens. In this environment, the user is greeted with background music, sound effects when clicking on buttons and the screen reader already activated, which offers direct support to people with visual impairments. By selecting the settings option, it is possible to activate or deactivate the screen reader according to the user's preference (GAG10), as well as customize the volume of sound

Fig. 5. Menu and settings (portuguese version)

effects and background music (GAG8). Lastly, the game's menu is designed with high contrast (GAG1, GAG5) and utilizes a sans-serif font (Roboto) to enhance readability (GAG2, GAG4), with well spaced spaced buttons (GAG3).

Figure 6 illustrates the beginning of the game's journey. Azarion awakens in a village with no recollection of his past, holding a mysterious staff that whispers cryptic words to him. In this same village, a strange man warns him that his homeland was destroyed by the Generals—powerful warriors who rule the world with an iron fist—who are now pursuing him because of the staff. Therefore, Azarion must defeat these Generals in order to restore peace to the world, recover his lost memories, and remember who he truly is.

Fig. 6. Azarion E. in the game scenario (portuguese version)

As for the gameplay, players will engage with various classic RPG mechanics, including branching narratives based on player choices, battles against monsters and bosses, map exploration, missions, puzzle-solving for rewards, and resource management through an inventory system. Last but not least, the player will be able to upgrade Azarion E.'s combat skills by leveling up.

Beyond the visual aspects and functional programming, the game's interaction mechanics were developed to be inclusive and immersive. When the player approaches an element in the scenery, a beep sound plays. This was added to allow the identification and differentiation of elements such as houses, trees, and NPCs (Non-Playable Characters). This functionality is an essential feature that not only enriches the experience but also ensures accessibility, aligning with guidelines GAG7 and GAG9. Furthermore, interactions with NPCs include narrated dialogues by volunteer voice actors, accompanied by subtitles, following GAG10. There's also an interactive item, a diary, whose writings are also narrated. The only GAG guideline that has not been implemented so far is GAG6, as it proved to be a bit more complex than initially anticipated. During implementation, there were problems with the integration of 3D sound into interactive items and also with the light beam that was supposed to mark the item, which prevented its full functionality.

Although several GAG recommendations have been adopted and implemented, some technical limitations and challenges have emerged. For example, GAG9, which deals with the distinct use of music/sound for all in-game objects, presented implementation difficulties due to the compatibility options available in the engine's resources. In attempts to link sound to objects, compatibility issues result in some sounds having low volumes even when the overall volume is increased. Another example is GAG10, which addresses narration for all texts, including menus and installers. This generates some incompatibilities with the Portuguese language, such as the inability to pronounce words with accent marks.

Once the game is fully completed and all GAG guidelines have been implemented, it will be tested with both visually impaired and sighted users to gather feedback for further improvements. After reaching a satisfactory version, the game will be made available on a game distribution platform, to be decided.

6   Lessons Learned

Before this project, the team had limited knowledge about game accessibility, mainly due to its absence in their daily lives and academic formation. As noted by Correa et al. [2023], the lack of accessibility in software is often linked to its limited presence in IT curricula at Brazilian institutions. This reflects the context of the university where the project was developed, where accessibility is not addressed in any mandatory course. Although an HCI (Human-Computer Interaction) course is planned in the Pedagogical Project's update, it will be offered only as an elective, allowing students to graduate without exposure to accessible software development. This highlights the need to integrate accessibility into the core computing curriculum.

This context of limited academic exposure to accessibility influenced the direction of the project. While the initial idea involved developing a conventional game, early discussions led to a proposal focused on accessibility, a topic recognized as both challenging and socially relevant. The decision was also influenced by misconceptions encountered during the data collection process, such as the perception, expressed by one of the questionnaire respondents, that accessibility features make games easier. This view illustrates a common misunderstanding about the role of accessibility in interactive systems.

During an interview with a visually impaired participant, this misconception was addressed directly. The interviewee clarified that accessibility is not intended to simplify games, but rather to ensure fairness, enabling individuals with disabilities to experience games on equal terms with others. This perspective significantly influenced our design approach.

Although the development of an accessible game initially appeared complex, the process revealed that, while it does require attention, it is not impossible. Tools such as UAP, proved to be straightforward to implement. Additionally, character dialogues were narrated by volunteers from UFMT, and the integration of these audio resources was technically feasible within the scope of the project.

The experience demonstrated that developing accessible games is achievable for independent development teams, provided there is genuine commitment and awareness of the importance of inclusion. Key lessons learned include the value of actively listening to individuals with disabilities, the importance of challenging the perception of accessibility as an optional feature, and the recognition that inclusive practices can be integrated from the earliest stages of design.

7   Conclusion

This study investigated game accessibility through the development of an inclusive RPG for visually impaired players. A questionnaire and an interview helped identify key challenges and accessibility needs. The findings reveal that, despite growing awareness, accessibility is still limited in the gaming industry, especially in Brazil. The study highlights the importance of features like audio feedback, adaptive narratives, and screen reader support, and aims to inspire more developers to create accessible games in both educational and entertainment contexts.

The main limitations of this research are related to the composition of the sample and the scope of the data. The questionnaire is biased, since most respondents are students at UFMT, which may limit the diversity of perspectives. In addition, the interview was conducted with only one person, which restricts the possibility of generalizing the results. Finally, technical aspects of implementing accessibility in the game still need to be studied in greater depth.

As future work, we intend to continue producing the game, based on the data collected and the artifacts developed, as indicated in Sect. 5. Additionally, we are designing custom artwork and 3D models specifically for the game, rather than relying on free assets, in order to establish a unique visual identity. ITo ensure both accessibility and quality of experience, the game will be tested by individuals with and without visual impairments, enabling a thorough validation of its mechanics and accessibility features.

Acknowledgements. We thank UFMT for supporting and enabling this research. We are also grateful to all participants whose perspectives contributed to the development of the game. In addition, ChatGPT was used to help with the translation of this text.

References

1. Andrade, L.H.F.B.d., Da Costa, R.M.E.M., Werneck, V.M.B.: Accessibility in games: A systematic mapping. In: Brazilian Symposium on Games and Digital Entertainment (SBGames), pp. 840–848. SBC (2021). https://doi.org/10.5753/sbgames_estendido.2021.19722
2. Barbosa, S.D.J., Silva, B.d., Silveira, M.S., Gasparini, I., Darin, T., Barbosa, G.D.J.: Human-computer interaction and user experience. Self-publishing (2021)
3. Braun, V., Clarke, V.: Using thematic analysis in psychology. Qual. Res. Psychol. **3**(2), 77–101 (2006). https://doi.org/10.1191/1478088706qp063oa
4. Brazil: Law N 13,146, of July 6, 2015 - Brazilian Law for the Inclusion of Persons with Disabilities (Statute of the Person with Disabilities) (2015). https://www.planalto.gov.br/ccivil_03/_ato2015-2018/2015/lei/l13146.htm. Accessed 18 May 2025
5. Correa, R., Teixeira, N., Portilho, F., Junior, C.P., Aranha, R.: Computer science education and (lack of) accessibility in computational systems: Coincidence or outcome? In: Proceedings of the XXXI Workshop on Computer Science Education, pp. 488–498. SBC, Porto Alegre, RS, Brazil (2023).https://doi.org/10.5753/wei.2023.230244
6. Franco, J.R., Denari, F.E.: Society and blindness: Discrimination and exclusion. J. Benjamin Constant Inst. **48**(1) (2011). https://revista.ibc.gov.br/index.php/BC/article/view/414. Accessed 18 May 2025
7. Game Accessibility Guidelines: Game accessibility guidelines (2012). http://gameaccessibilityguidelines.com/. Accessed 18 May 2025
8. Game Brazil Survey: PGB free trend report (2025). https://materiais.pesquisagamebrasil.com.br/2025-painel-gratuito-pgb25. Accessed 18 May 2025
9. Grando, A., Tarouco, L.M.R.: The use of educational RPG-style games in education. RENOTE **6**(1) (2008).https://doi.org/10.22456/1679-1916.14403
10. Interaction Design Foundation: What is Design Thinking (DT)? (2016). https://www.interaction-design.org/literature/topics/design-thinking. Accessed 18 May 2025
11. Martins, F.: WHO warns that 285 million people worldwide have impaired vision (2023). https://tinyurl.com/2ambfmhw. Accessed 18 May 2025
12. Messa, A.A., et al.: Family leisure: A study on the perception of parents of children with disabilities. Postgrad. J. Dev. Dis. **5**(1) (2005)
13. Novak, J.: Game development essentials: An introduction. Cengage Learning (2011)
14. Ottaiano, J.A.A., Ávila, M.P.d., Umbelino, C.C., Taleb, A.C.: Ocular health conditions in Brazil. São Paulo: Brazilian Council of Ophthalmology (2019). http://www.cbo.com.br/novo/publicacoes/condicoes_saude_ocular_brasil2019.pdf
15. Pessini, A., Kemczinski, A., da Silva Hounsell, M.: An authoring tool for the development of serious games in the RPG genre. Proceedings of Computer on the Beach, pp. 071–080 (2015)
16. Tirloni, M., Machado, C.C.: A proposal to assist people with visual impairment and color blindness in identifying colors and their possible combinations. Symposium on Science, Innovation, and Technology, p. 9 (2018)
17. Vicente, M.P., Barna, L.A.D., Fachinetto, L.: Generic game mechanics applied across different platforms. Tech. J. Am. Fatec **4**(2), 148–152 (2016). http://ric.cps.sp.gov.br/handle/123456789/138

Revisiting and Reframing Play: Towards Incorporating Representation and Diversity in Contemporary Game Design

Virgínia Fernandes Mota[1,2]([⊠]) and Emanuel Felipe Duarte[1]

[1] Instituto de Computação, Universidade Estadual de Campinas (IC/UNICAMP),
Campinas, Brazil
virginia@teiacoltec.org, emanuel@ic.unicamp.br
[2] Colégio Técnico, Universidade Federal de Minas Gerais (COLTEC/UFMG),
Belo Horizonte, Brazil

Abstract. Digital games are more than entertainment; they are powerful cultural spaces where identities are performed, narratives contested, and communities formed. As players and developers increasingly reflect global diversity, the critical question shifts from what play is to whose play is centered, how it is shaped, and what it can become. Contemporary social movements demand that we rethink power, identity, and representation, including how games engage with these dynamics. This paper revisits and reframes play through decolonial, intersectional, and plural lenses. Drawing on linguistic, epistemological, and design-based critiques, we examine how mainstream frameworks marginalize Global South traditions of play and may not represent their theoretical-methodological value. We propose a shift from asking what play is to whose play counts, linking this reframing to six core principles—linguistic humility, epistemic pluralism, design justice, non-universality, non-neutrality, and anti-essentialism. We conclude by discussing implications for game design, emphasizing the need for co-creation, contextual sensitivity, and expanded notions of play that reflect the plurality of global player experiences.

Keywords: Digital Games · Play · Representation · Decolonialism

1 Introduction

Play is never just "play". Among its diverse manifestations, it is a conduit of cultural values, a site of negotiation, and in digital games, increasingly a battleground for representation. While game studies have productively expanded discussions of accessibility (who can play) and representation (who is depicted), we've been slower to question whose conceptions of play shape these very systems. Dominant theories—from Huizinga's formalism [7] to psychological models

T. Darin et al. (Eds.): WIPlay 2025 CCIS 2623, pp. 19–28, 2026.
https://doi.org/10.1007/978-3-032-01426-9_2

of universal play behaviors by Sutton-Smith [16]—often treat play as a transcendent category, inadvertently marginalizing traditions that don't conform to Global North Western academic constructs.

This paper contributes to an ongoing effort to explore fairness in digital games through the interrelation of access, representation, and play. Here, we revisit the play component to deepen its theoretical and cultural dimensions. Prior work within this agenda aimed to address fairness holistically, positioning access as the means to enable participation, representation as the mechanism for symbolic inclusion, and play as the experiential core of game interaction. However, while accessibility and representation have gained increasing traction in both industry and academia (e.g., the *Game Awards* introduced the Innovation in Accessibility award in 2020), the concept of play often remains narrowly understood through Global North Western lenses—privileging structured, rule-based forms and overlooking its cultural specificity and expressive plurality. In many cases, play is not explicitly theorized but rather treated as an assumed constant—an issue illustrated in Kafai *et al.* [14], where normative assumptions about what constitutes a "gamer girl" go unchallenged. This implicitness perpetuates a *status quo* in which certain forms of play—competitive, rule-governed, and system-oriented—are legitimized, while others are rendered peripheral or illegible [13,17][9, *Chapter 2*].

The concept of play is prior understood as the essential ludic experience that must be preserved even as games become more inclusive and accessible. This view is rooted on the classic definition of play by Huizinga [7] and Caillois [3]. The goal was to ensure that efforts to improve functional access—such as interface design, assistive technologies, or adaptable mechanics—would not dilute or compromise the expressive and imaginative potential that defines play itself. This positioning in the prior work emphasized the need to sustain the "essence of play" alongside technical and symbolic inclusion. However, such a formulation, while necessary, remains limited if it treats play as a neutral or universal category. What is often overlooked is that play, like access and representation, is shaped by cultural values, power dynamics, and historical narratives [5,9]. It is not only a site of interaction, but also one of meaning-making.

This paper examines what gets lost when we fail to recognize play as culturally situated: not just different ways of playing, but fundamentally different epistemologies of play itself. To meaningfully integrate representation and diversity into game design, it becomes crucial to recognize play as a politically and culturally situated practice. Expanding the notion of play requires us to move beyond functionalist or mechanical understandings and consider how different communities conceptualize, value, and enact play as a form of expression, resistance, and identity. In this position paper, therefore, we argue for an expanded view of play, not as a universal constant, but as a situated, evolving, and culturally embedded practice that intersects with identity, community, and representation. Therefore, this paper aligns with the grand challenges in Human-Computer Interaction (HCI), particularly third and fourth: Plurality and Decoloniality in HCI [11], and Sociocultural Aspects in Human-Computer Interaction [10]. Unfortunately, there are no equivalent grand challenges in game research that directly address these concerns.

The remainder of this work is structured as follows: Sect. 2 examines existing frameworks and challenges colonial biases in play theory, Sect. 3 introduces an alternative perspective and explore practical applications for game design. Finally, the Conclusion synthesizes key insights and suggests directions for future research.

2 Revisiting: Decolonizing the Concept of Play

The conceptualization of play in game studies has historically been framed by Euro-American traditions. Foundational scholars such as Huizinga [7], Caillois [3], and Sutton-Smith [16] have provided influential definitions and frameworks, yet these emerge from a Western perspective. Huizinga, for instance, defines play as a voluntary activity set apart from ordinary life, characterized by freedom, uncertainty, and order. Caillois expands on this by offering a taxonomy of play types, categorizing them into four key modes: *agon* (competition), *alea* (chance), *mimicry* (simulation), and *ilinx* (vertigo). Both authors draw from Global North historical and linguistic roots, but neither fully engages with Global South perspectives or addresses the cultural specificity of play practices from diverse global contexts. While Huizinga briefly acknowledges variations in the word "play" across languages and cultures, his analysis largely focuses on Global North traditions without considering the broader, more inclusive concept of play that might arise in other cultural and political settings.

This absence becomes particularly evident when translating the concept of play into other cultural-linguistic contexts. In Brazilian Portuguese, for instance, the terms *brincar* (associated with childlike spontaneity), *jogar* (linked to structured games), and *lúdico* (a more abstract term often used in educational discourse) only partially capture the theoretical and experiential breadth implied by "play". Similarly, in Latin American Spanish, we have the terms *jugar* (typically associated with games and structured play), *juego* (the noun form, often referring to both the activity and the object), and *lúdico* (used in educational and psychological contexts to refer to playful or creative activities). In Japanese, the word *asobi* (遊び reflects a concept of play that encompasses leisure, creativity, and aesthetic expression. Unlike Western views that often separate play from work or ritual, *asobi* can imply fluidity, improvisation, and spiritual depth. The idea of *asobi gokoro* (遊び心), or "playful spirit", is present in practices such as calligraphy and traditional performance arts, where play is embedded in disciplined form. In many African cultures, play is not isolated from community, ritual, or performance. In Yoruba, for instance, the verb *sèré* refers both to playing and to engaging in joyful, performative acts such as dancing, singing, or joking. Although these examples are not meant to be exaustive, this blurring between play, art, and social bonding reflects a more holistic and integrated view of ludic experience, where boundaries between categories like "game", "ritual", and "performance" are fluid and often inseparable.

Additionally, Salen and Zimmerman, in *Rules of Play: Game Design Fundamentals* [15], contribute to the contemporary understanding of play as a structured system within which players navigate rules and systems. They synthesize various definitions of play and explore its role within game design. However, their model remains largely grounded in design-oriented perspectives that are characteristic of the Global North and insufficiently attuned to the cultural diversity of play experiences across different regions and social contexts. For instance, their emphasis on formal rule systems does not account for ludic practices.

By offering a more holistic view of play, these works offer valuable insights, yet they also underscore the need for more inclusive frameworks that consider both symbolic and material conditions in diverse cultural settings. Combined, issues of linguistic fragmentation and hegemonic design-oriented perspectives reflect a broader epistemic gap: the notion of play, as employed in dominant game studies literature, may obscure or marginalize culturally specific ludic practices. Practices like Afro-Brazilian *capoeira* (simultaneously game, dance, and resistance) or Indigenous ceremonies that integrate play with storytelling and ecology are often marginalized as "not real play" under dominant frameworks. These limitations point to a broader need: frameworks for understanding play that do not assume universality but instead engage with local and global diversities in the practice and experience of play. This is particularly crucial as the game industry continues to globalize and incorporate varied cultural narratives, perspectives, and methodologies in design processes. Reflecting on these gaps is key to developing more inclusive and representative models of play that honor cultural diversity and reject the traditional biases that dominate current frameworks.

In this direction, there are contemporary scholars, such as Mary Flanagan, that offer critiques of this Global North-centric framework. In her work *Critical Play: Radical Game Design* [5], Flanagan argues that games are not neutral; rather, they are cultural artifacts deeply embedded in political, social, and cultural structures. She challenges the notion that play is inherently free of social and political dimensions, positioning it instead as a form of expression and critique. A more inclusive framework must, therefore, critically examine not only *what* play means, but also *whose* play is being theorized. By interrogating the Global North Western-centric assumptions that shape much of the discourse, we open space for alternative epistemologies that consider ludic experience as historically, linguistically, and culturally situated.

By recognizing these nuances we can expand our understanding of *play* and support efforts to decolonize its theoretical foundations. To do so, we must center questions of whose play counts and who gets to define it. This requires:

- **Linguistic humility**: Acknowledging that general terms like "play" (and its many variations and equivalents in different languages), although useful, are imperfect translations of culturally specific concepts.
- **Epistemic pluralism**: Valuing Global South ludic traditions as valid theoretical contributions, not just ethnographic curiosities.
- **Design justice**: Creating games that amplify through empowerment, rather than through appropriation, marginalized play practices.

By grounding play theory in this plurality, we challenge the inherent colonialism of knowledge production in game studies. This opens a space for more equitable futures, and allows play to be reframed.

3   Reframing: An Alternative Dimension for Play

In this paper we discuss play not as a universal or abstract activity bounded by rules, but as a culturally situated and politically charged practice that is inseparable from questions of identity, representation, and power. While classical theories of play—from Huizinga's magic circle to Caillois' taxonomies—have emphasized structure, competition, and voluntary detachment from ordinary life, such models often erase the specific cultural, historical, and embodied conditions under which play emerges and is experienced. What they neglect is that play is always mediated by the values, narratives, and exclusions of the worlds in which it takes place. In this expanded view, play is not neutral—it is structured by social imaginaries, shaped by who is allowed to play, and whose modes of playing are considered valid. It can be a space of agency, but also of discipline, marginalization, and resistance. Reframing play in this way allows us to see it as a site where representation is enacted, challenged, or denied. This calls for a reorientation in both theory and design: to center play as a plural, lived, and contested practice that reflects and reproduces cultural meaning. In doing so, we reposition play not outside politics, but within the ongoing negotiations of fairness, access, and visibility in games.

Play and representation are often treated as separate domains in discussions of fairness in digital games, one concerned with mechanics and interaction, the other with identity and symbolism. However, such a division risks obscuring their deep interrelation, or even inseparability. In this expanded view, play is not merely a formal system or experiential mode that exists independently of representation; rather, it is a domain where identity, culture, and meaning are continuously negotiated through interaction. Who plays, how they play, and what forms of play are legitimized or marginalized are all shaped by representational politics. Characters, mechanics, aesthetics, and narratives do not merely reflect culture, they constitute the very terms under which play becomes intelligible and accessible.

Rather than seeking to define what play is or is not, we aim to decenter dominant Euro-American frameworks and reframe play through a decolonial, intersectional, and plural lens. This approach shifts the analytical focus from fixed taxonomies to more critical questions: whose play counts, how it is culturally and politically shaped, and what it can become within the evolving landscape of digital games. By interrogating which practices are legitimized or marginalized in mainstream game design and scholarship, this perspective reveals play as a dynamic, situated act: one that is deeply entangled with issues of power, identity, and representation.

This critique is not entirely new, other scholars have similarly challenged colonial foundations in game design and representation, even if not always through the lens of play itself. Arrivabene [1] argues that colonialist values are embedded not only in the narratives of digital games but also in their mechanics and design conventions. By tracing the influence of Eurocentric ideologies, such as expansionism, anthropocentrism, and rationalist meritocracy, he reveals how even seemingly neutral game systems often reproduce extractivist logics and white-supremacist tropes. Contrasting these with pre-colonial and Indigenous ludic traditions, which emphasize community, spirituality, and ecological balance, his work advocates for alternative methods rooted in plural epistemologies. Zambrano [17] examines how video games can serve as platforms for decolonial design by challenging Western-centric narratives and representational norms embedded in mainstream game development. Analyzing eight case studies, the paper highlights how cultural specificity, community collaboration, and alternative storytelling strategies enable games to resist colonial epistemologies and promote more inclusive and empathetic perspectives. Drawing from Latin American decolonial theory, particularly the works of Quijano [12] and Mignolo and Walsh [8], the author argues that decolonial design must go beyond aesthetic representation to encompass epistemic justice, foregrounding Indigenous, Afrodescendant, and subaltern knowledge systems in game mechanics, narrative structures, and player experiences. The study affirms that digital games are not neutral artifacts but sociotechnical expressions of power, and thus, capable of subversion and transformation. Their work does not address play explicitly, but shares key affinities with our approach to decolonizing the concept of play. Flanagan and Jakobsson [6] examine how colonial ideologies are embedded in board game mechanics, such as conquest, resource extraction, and racial hierarchies, arguing that these systems normalize domination and exploitation under the guise of entertainment. Their insights help illuminate how digital games also replicate colonialist logics through mechanics like 4X (eXplore, eXpand, eXploit, eXterminate), which remain central to titles such as Civilization, Age of Empires, and Starcraft.

Therefore, our decolonial and intersectional lens shifts the focus from "what play is" to "whose play counts". It challenges three assumptions of Euro-American frameworks:

- **Non-Universality**: Play is not a transcendent or universally shared phenomenon, but is culturally and historically situated. Its meanings and forms vary across contexts, shaped by local epistemologies and social norms.
- **Non-Neutrality**: Play is not exempt from systems of power. It can reproduce, contest, or mask inequalities, such as when racialized avatars influence player behavior, or when normative mechanics exclude marginalized identities.
- **Against Essentialism:** Games are not fixed objects with inherent rule structures; rather, play emerges through social practice. Rules are negotiated, interpreted, and culturally shaped. A game is not just its software, it is a situated experience enacted by players in context.

To clarify how this proposal diverges from and dialogues with foundational theories in game studies, Table 1 compares key dimensions of play across classical and critical perspectives.

3.1   Implications for Game Design

Translating a decolonial and intersectional lens into game design practice requires more than adding representational elements or accessibility features; it involves

Table 1. Comparative overview of conceptual approaches to play across classical and critical game studies.

Aspect	Our Proposal	Huizinga [7]	Caillois [3]	Flanagan [5]
Core Question	Whose play counts, and how is it shaped by power, identity, and culture?	What is play and how does it underpin the emergence of culture?	How can play be categorized and distinguished from other activities?	How can games be used for critique, resistance, and social change?
View of Play	Play is culturally situated, plural, and shaped by systems of power	Play is universal, voluntary, and separate from 'ordinary' life	Play is classifiable (agon, alea, mimicry, ilinx); ranges from free to rule-bound	Play can be a site of resistance and transformation
Theoretical Lens	Decolonial, intersectional, critical theory	Formalist, philosophical	Structuralist, taxonomic	Feminist theory, critical theory, art history
Goal	Reframe play beyond dominant (Global North) theories to include marginalized forms	Define play's role in the development of civilization	Categorize types of play and how they evolve	Redesign games for political critique and social justice
Cultural Perspective	Emphasizes plural epistemologies, especially from the Global South	Eurocentric, universalizing	Eurocentric with anthropological lens	Western-centric with feminist and activist angles
Focus	Digital games and the politics of design and recognition	Abstract and philosophical understanding of play	Typology of play and its social function	Game design practice and historical analysis of activist play
Relation to Power/Identity	Central theme: play as a site of identity, power, and exclusion/inclusion	Implicit; culture is the main concern	Play as social behavior; less focused on identity or power	Explicitly concerned with gender, politics, ideology in play
Play as Political	Yes—play reflects and shapes systems of representation and inclusion	Rarely—more focused on cultural function than critique	Somewhat—sees social roles but not deeply political	Yes—play can critique dominant ideologies and power structures

rethinking the very foundations of how games are conceptualized and created. Each of the six principles discussed earlier—linguistic humility, epistemic pluralism, design justice, non-universality, non-neutrality, and anti-essentialism—raises important implications for how designers approach play.

- Linguistic humility draws attention to the fact that "play" is not a universally translatable concept. Designers must be cautious not to assume that dominant definitions of play—often shaped by English-speaking, Western traditions—are applicable across all contexts. Instead, play should be localized conceptually as well as linguistically, acknowledging culturally specific ludic practices.
- Epistemic pluralism reinforces the idea that Global South ludic traditions are not peripheral or folkloric, but theoretical contributions in their own

right. These traditions—ranging from Afro-Brazilian practices to Indigenous cosmologies—should inform not only aesthetic choices but also core mechanics, player goals, and feedback systems. Recognizing these epistemologies challenges designers to expand what is considered legitimate game logic or structure beyond the *status quo*.

– The concept of design justice, as articulated by Sasha Costanza-Chock in the context of architecture and design [4], can be meaningfully extended to the field of game design. It calls for a shift in who participates in the design process. Rather than extracting from marginalized communities—across axes of gender, race, and disability—for thematic inspiration or market appeal, game development should adopt co-design practices that position these communities as active agents. This includes shared authorship, participatory workshops, and sustained accountability beyond the product's release. Designing with, rather than for, fosters more ethical, inclusive, and responsive design ecosystems.

– The principle of non-universality reminds us that not all players engage with games in the same way. It encourages the creation of mechanics and systems that allow for multiple modalities of play, including improvisational, cooperative, contemplative. Moving beyond competitive or mastery-based paradigms broadens what counts as meaningful engagement and makes space for a wider diversity of players. This principle also invites us to critically examine how educational games frequently frame subjects like physics, mathematics, and biology as culturally neutral or universally structured. Such framing often masks the epistemological assumptions embedded in how these disciplines are taught and gamified. For instance, many gamified learning platforms rely heavily on behaviorist models (such as reward systems, point accumulation, or streak mechanics) that assume learning is linear, individualistic, and universally motivating. This overlooks alternative pedagogies which may prioritize process over outcome, or relational over transactional learning. A decolonial approach would reimagine educational games not as vehicles to standardize knowledge, but as opportunities to honor plural ways of knowing, playing, and becoming.

– Understanding the non-neutrality of design means acknowledging that all mechanics, interfaces, and narratives carry cultural and political weight. Games reflect and reproduce systems of power, whether in how difficulty is scaled, how bodies are represented, or how progression is rewarded. Game designers must critically assess the ideological assumptions embedded in their systems and actively work to challenge or redistribute power within the game-world. For instance, Blouin-Payer, Cook, and Gómez [2] propose decolonized mechanics that shift away from extraction, conquest, and linear mastery, suggesting instead systems based on ecological regeneration, relational progression, and reparative conflict resolution. These mechanics not only subvert colonial logics but open space for culturally grounded and plural forms of play that value care, reciprocity, and community well-being.

– Finally, rejecting essentialist views of play means understanding games not as fixed artifacts defined solely by rules or code, but as dynamic experiences that emerge in relation to players, communities and context. Designing for emergence, interpretation, and local adaptation transforms the role of the player from passive user to co-creator. It also means welcoming unintended uses, alternate readings, and fluid boundaries between play and non-play. As an example, findings from the last *Pesquisa Game Brasil* (PGB 2025)[1] highlight the diversity of gaming habits across regions, income levels, and generations in Brazil. For instance, 80.1% of Brazilians report playing digital games as their primary form of entertainment, with mobile phones being the most common platform, particularly among lower-income groups. The report also indicates that 53.2% of players are women (within a binary classification), and that 49.4% belong to the millennial generation (born between 1981 and 1996) These data underscore the importance of designing for local preferences, platforms, and player identities.

Incorporating these principles does not imply a checklist or template, but rather a reorientation of values. It challenges dominant frameworks of game design and opens space for practices that are more equitable, culturally grounded, and imaginative. Designing for plural play is not only possible, it is necessary for a more fair and inclusive future in games.

4 Conclusion

This paper has examined how dominant conceptions of play in game studies—rooted in Euro-American traditions—tend to universalize and depoliticize ludic practices. By reframing play through decolonial and intersectional perspectives, we argue that play is not a fixed or neutral category, but a culturally situated and contested domain shaped by power, identity, and historical context.

To address these limitations, we proposed six guiding principles—linguistic humility, epistemic pluralism, design justice, non-universality, non-neutrality, and anti-essentialism—that emphasize the need to reconceptualize play in both theory and practice. These principles offer pathways for more inclusive and culturally responsive game design that moves beyond representational inclusion toward deeper epistemic engagement.

As global game cultures continue to diversify, building more equitable futures for games will depend not only on who gets to play, but on how we understand what play is, what it can do, and who it can serve. Reimagining play through this lens is not just a theoretical exercise, but a necessary step toward achieving truly equity in the design of digital games. Therefore, we highlight as future work the need for frameworks, methodologies, instruments and other tools to contribute towards more concrete representation and diversity in contemporary game design.

Acknowlegments. This study was financed, in part, by the São Paulo Research Foundation (FAPESP), Brasil, Process Number #2024/16790-5; by the Universidade Estad-

---

[1] https://www.pesquisagamebrasil.com.br.

ual de Campinas (UNICAMP), Brasil, FAEPEX grant #2356/24; and by the Coordenação de Aperfeiçoamento de Pessoal de Nível Superior (CAPES), Brasil, Finance Code 001.

References

1. Arrivabene, R.M.C.: For a decolonial approach to game design methods beyond representation. Emerg. Media **3**(1), 38–48 (2025)
2. Blouin-Payer, M., Cook, J., Gómez, E.: Decolonizing play: exploring frameworks for game design free of colonial values (2023). https://polarisgamedesign.com/2023/decolonizing-play-exploring-frameworks-for-game-design-free-of-colonial-values/. Polaris Game Design Retreat
3. Caillois, R.: Man, Play and Games. University of Illinois Press (2001). Originally published in 1958
4. Costanza-Chock, S.: Design Justice: Community-Led Practices to Build the Worlds We Need. MIT Press, Cambridge (2020)
5. Flanagan, M.: Critical Play: Radical Game Design. MIT Press (2009)
6. Flanagan, M., Jakobsson, M.: Playing Oppression: The Legacy of Conquest and Empire in Colonialist Board Games. MIT Press, Cambridge (2023)
7. Huizinga, J.: Homo Ludens: A Study of the Play-Element in Culture. Beacon Press (1949). Originally published in 1938
8. Mignolo, W.D., Walsh, C.E.: On Decoloniality: Concepts, Analytics, Praxis. Duke University Press, Durham and London (2018)
9. Murray, S.: On video Games: The Visual Politics of Race, Gender and Space, vol. 27. Bloomsbury Publishing (2021)
10. Neris, V., Rosa, J., Maciel, C., Pereira, V., Galvão, V., Arruda, I.: GranDIHC-BR 2025-2035 - GC4: sociocultural aspects in human-computer interaction. In: Anais do XXIII Simpósio Brasileiro sobre Fatores Humanos em Sistemas Computacionais, pp. 988–1002. SBC (2024)
11. de Oliveira, L., et al.: GranDIHC-BR 2025-2035 – GC3: plurality and decoloniality in HCI. In: Anais do XXIII Simpósio Brasileiro sobre Fatores Humanos em Sistemas Computacionais, pp. 1067–1085. SBC (2024)
12. Quijano, A.: Cuestiones y horizontes: De la dependencia histórico-estructural a la colonialidad/descolonialidad del poder. CLACSO; Universidad Nacional Mayor de San Marcos, Fondo Editorial, Buenos Aires (2020)
13. Rankin, Y.A., Irish, I.: A seat at the table: black feminist thought as a critical framework for inclusive game design. Proc. ACM Hum.-Comput. Interact. **4**(CSCW2), 1–26 (2020)
14. Richard, G.T.: Intersectiong and diverging experiences across gender, identity, race and sexuality in game culture. In: Diversifying Barbie and Mortal Kombat: Intersectional Perspectives and Inclusive Designs in Gaming. Carnegie Mellon University: ETC Press (2017)
15. Salen, K., Zimmerman, E.: Rules of Play: Game Design Fundamentals. MIT Press (2004)
16. Sutton-Smith, B.: The Ambiguity of Play. Harvard University Press (1997)
17. Zambrano U, H.M.: Decolonial design in video games: subverting colonial narratives. In: 2023 IEEE Seventh Ecuador Technical Chapters Meeting (ECTM), pp. 1–6 (2023). https://doi.org/10.1109/ETCM58927.2023.10309000

Sounds in Game Design and Evaluation for Autistic People: A Literature Review

Bosco Borges$^{(\boxtimes)}$ and Ticianne Darin

Federal University of Ceará, Fortaleza, CE 60455-760, Brazil
boscoborges4@gmail.com, ticianne@virtual.ufc.br

Abstract. Serious games are recognized as a relevant tool for educational and therapeutic purposes, including those for individuals with Autism Spectrum Disorder (ASD), a neurodevelopmental condition characterized by difficulties in social communication and particularities in sensorial perceptions and stimuli, such as auditory. This difference in auditory processing affects the everyday behavior, social interactions, and daily life of individuals with autism. Hence, to inform the design of serious games that properly address sound aspects to provide a better gaming experience and contribute to the well-being of autistic players, it is essential to understand how auditory stimuli affect their gaming experience. As an initial step toward bridging this gap, the present study examines 49 papers in a Literature Review, aiming to identify how audio aspects have been considered in the design and evaluation of digital games for individuals with Autism Spectrum Disorder (ASD). Results show that, despite the diversity of purposes that sounds can assume in digital games, only few studies considered audio in the evaluation (whether from the user or from the game) and just as few games mentioned auditory feedback in their design. The results analysis corroborate that the effect of audio in games for autistic users still needs more attention. Furthermore, our findings bring discussions about the great predominance of autistic children as target users of game designs and evaluations, about the lack of evaluation of entertainment games with this audience, with a considerable prevalence of serious games and also about the heterogeneity of validations of therapeutic and educational games developed for autistic people.

Keywords: autism · ASD · audio · sound · auditory · games · evaluation · player experience

1 Introduction

Serious games represent an attractive and effective approach for interventions targeting individuals with special educational needs [33,34], including people with Autism Spectrum Disorder (ASD), particularly children. ASD is a neurodevelopmental condition defined by two general areas defined in the DSM-5 [52]. Social communication deficits include persistent social-emotional reciprocity

© The Author(s), under exclusive license to Springer Nature Switzerland AG 2026
T. Darin et al. (Eds.): WIPlay 2025, CCIS 2623, pp. 29–48, 2026.
https://doi.org/10.1007/978-3-032-01426-9_3

deficits, nonverbal communication, and relationship challenges [15]. Restricted, repetitive behavior requires at least two of the following characteristics: stereo-typed movements, insistence on sameness, circumscribed interests, and sensory abnormalities (e.g., hyper- or hypo-reactivity) [15], a core aspect that demands careful consideration in game design.

For this audience, serious games serve a dual purpose: to entertain and to fulfill a specific educational, therapeutic, or skill-development goal [5, 49]. Their design often incorporates narratives that invite players to overcome obstacles by applying their knowledge and skills, and their mechanics and dynamics such as feedback, rewards, and missions are key factors to motivate students [21].

Several characteristics make serious games suitable for individuals with ASD. They can offer a safe, anxiety-free environment for skill acquisition [49], their structure can be adjusted to the cognitive processes of individuals with ASD, and they often allow for adaptation to specific needs and individual casuistry ([20]. Furthermore, visual and multimodal interactions in these games can stimulate assimilation and learning, potentially reducing cognitive load [20, 49]. However, while such elements may enrich the experience of neurotypical players, they can pose a source of discomfort or overload for individuals with ASD, directly relat-ing to these inherent sensory processing differences. Indeed, systematic reviews of serious games for this population, while acknowledging sensory sensitivities, often lack a detailed synthesis of specific audio adaptation strategies imple-mented in games or a focus on how these distinct audio features are evaluated [5, 20, 49].

Among the affected sensory domains in people with ASD, auditory perception plays a central role, as they often exhibit atypical responses to auditory stimuli. These responses may include hypersensitivity to specific sounds or difficulties in processing complex auditory stimuli, resulting in sensory overload and, in more severe cases, reactions of discomfort or anxiety [32, 40]. These differences in auditory processing not only affect sensory well-being but also directly influence social interactions and everyday behavior. For instance, people with ASD may face challenges in unpredictable auditory environments, which can limit their participation in social interactions and contribute to feelings of isolation and loneliness [25].

Developing a nuanced understanding of how audio affects the experience of these players is essential not only to promote accessibility but also to guide the development of more inclusive and effective design practices, particularly given the variability in auditory processing within the ASD population. Given this context, and the limited focus within existing review literature on the specifics of auditory considerations, the objective of this study is to identify the nature and extent to which audio has been considered in the evaluation and design of digital games with autistic individuals. To achieve this, we conducted a systematic literature review, collecting articles that presented or reported evaluations of games with users with ASD, gathering and assessing aspects of audio, whether from the players themselves or from the sound effects of the evaluated games.

The results indicate that, although audio is considered in some game evaluations with this population. the specific evaluation of the impacts of game audio on player experience remains scarce. The structure of this work is organized into the following sections: (i) theoretical background on autism, auditory aspects, and digital games, (ii) related work, (iii) methodology adopted for the literature review, (iv) results, (v) discussion, and (vi) conclusion.

2   Autism, Video Games and Sound

Individuals on the Autism Spectrum may experience difficulties and special conditions in their daily interactions, such as social deficits, which can lead to low levels of social interaction and occupational activities, as well as high levels of anxiety and depression. For instance, autistic adults may experience anxiety and sensory overstimulation during social interactions, which can result in loneliness or a sense of isolation [25].

Despite these social and sensory challenges, autistic individuals may show a strong interest in digital games [26]. Besides several aspects that differentiate digital games from other types of software, games can provide opportunities for players to master skills, achieve accomplishments, and receive in-game rewards for their actions [31].

Moreover, digital games are usually designed to provide visual and auditory experiences, aiming to achieve immersion and engagement as crucial factors, typically regarded as good indicators in this field.

The study of auditory perception in individuals with ASD is a well-established topic in the health sciences, particularly in psychology and psychiatry. People with this condition, to varying degrees, tend to be more sensitive to sensory stimuli, including and especially auditory stimuli. Auditory perceptual capacity is heightened in individuals with autism, both children and adults. In many cases, this heightened capacity may be accompanied by sensations of "overexcitement" (a high level of sensory stimulation) or hyperacusis (in which common or harmless sounds can cause distress) [40].

Connor [32], in their study, conducted a literature review on auditory processing in individuals on the autism spectrum, analyzing how different types of sounds—ranging from speech tones to various frequencies and types of everyday sound waves—can affect different groups of people with this condition. His findings indicate that atypical auditory information processing is an inherent feature of autism spectrum disorder, with manifestations that may range from impaired or failed speech processing to hypersensitivity to various sounds, noises, and auditory stimuli [32].

These differences in the processing of auditory stimuli can significantly influence daily interactions for individuals with ASD, ranging from interactions with other people—affecting how they relate to family members and peers—to interactions with other sound sources such as videos, television, electronic devices, and computer systems.

3   Related Work

The use of serious games and gamified environments for individuals ASD has been a subject of increasing research, as evidenced by several literature reviews. For instance, Carvalho et al. [5] conducted a systematic literature review focusing on the evaluation methods applied to serious games for autistic children. They identified shared methodologies, quality dimensions evaluated, and participant profiles, mentioning the lack of a shared evaluation methodology and citing the employment of sensory evaluation assisted by instruments such as the Adolescent/Adult Sensory Profile questionnaire in some of the evaluations [5].

Azadboni et al. [49] conducted a systematic review of the effectiveness of serious games on social skills training for autistic adults. They determined that these types of games have a positive effect and said that these types of games can be created with "visual and auditory environments to meet the individual needs of these individuals," though they were less concerned with how the sensory, and more specifically sound, is assessed, and more concerned with treatment effectiveness [49].

Likewise, López-Bouzas & del Moral-Pérez [20] discussed studies on gamified settings and serious games, mentioning benefits, limitations, and typical design priorities, e.g., socio-emotional skills. They claimed that audiovisual environments favor learning and gave examples of sensory hypersensitivity games [20]. Yet, their review gives a general overview instead of a detailed examination of how the auditory aspect of games is taken into account in assessment procedures in people with ASD.

While these reviews offer valuable insights into evaluation methodologies, game effectiveness, and general design considerations, a more granular focus on how game audio specifically is considered and assessed during evaluations with autistic individuals, particularly in light of their diverse auditory processing characteristics, remains less synthesized. They do not analyze how specific game audio design features are adapted for varied auditory processing in ASD, nor does it present findings on the effectiveness of particular audio design choices or detailed methodologies for evaluating game audio itself (as distinct from general sensory profiles or using recordings as observational data). Their focus remained on the broader landscape of evaluation methods for serious games. This review thus seeks to fill this particular gap by particularly investigating primary research studies that have reported on game testing among this group, and how they consider sound both in game design and evaluation.

4   Methodology

The main goal of this research was to identify how audio have been considered in the design and evaluation of digital games for autistic individuals. In order to reach a clear comprehension on that, we also aimed to understand how games for people with Autism Spectrum Disorder (ASD) have been developed and designed, and how games have been evaluated with autistic users. To achieve this goal, we conducted a literature review based on the steps outlined in the review model proposed by Creswell and Creswell [7]. The review aimed to gather articles that addressed evaluations of any type of game involving autistic users, or articles that presented or developed an original game specifically created for autistic people.

To ensure a replicable process, the review presented in this article followed a protocol organised into several steps (Fig. 1). Two researchers with different backgrounds and expertise defined the research protocol and performed the research itself. The first researcher is a master's student in Computer Science with a research focus in Player Experience (PX). The second researcher has a PhD in Computer Science, with over 15 years of extensive experience in HCI and PX research.

First, both researchers identified keywords related to the research topic, which emerged from prior readings and preliminary searches for articles on the subject. These keywords were then defined and used to compose search strings, which were subsequently applied to online databases to gather relevant articles. The first researcher submitted the resulting articles to a duplicate removal step, followed by two filtering processes that considered a set of including and excluding criteria (Table 1), formulated by both researchers, to select articles that were both useful and relevant to the aims of this study. In this screening and filtering process, we included (1) papers that proposed (developing and/or designing) a game or a Multimodal Interaction Virtual Environment (MIVE) [8] for autistic users, (2) papers that evaluated any game or MIVE with autistic people, (3) papers written in English or Portuguese and (4) peer-reviewed papers. We excluded papers that (1) were not readily available online for reading, (2) papers that did not propose or evaluate a game or MIVE, (3) papers that proposed a game or MIVE, but not for autistic people, (4) papers that evaluated a game or MIVE, but not with autistic users and (5) papers shorter than six pages. Finally, a set of data was extracted from the selected articles, containing information relevant to the stated objective, and then this dataset was subsequently analysed.

The implementation of these steps supported the investigation of the following research questions (RQ): What games have been developed and evaluated for autistic people? (RQ1); How have games been evaluated with autistic people? (RQ2); How have auditory aspects been considered in game design and evaluation for autistic users? (RQ3).

Initially, the researchers tested a bunch of keywords, which emerged from previous reading or knowledge about the theme or from preliminary searches for articles about games for autistic people and its evaluations. The final resulting set of keywords was organized into a synonyms Table 2, with synonyms for three key terms: autism, video games, and evaluation, as well as specific audio-related keywords (e.g., "sound," "music," "auditory"). After that, we used the keywords to compose and test search strings. However, pilot searches indicated that incorporating specific audio-related keywords alongside the broader terms within the chosen databases did not significantly yield additional relevant papers that weren't already being captured by the focus on general game evaluation with autistic users.

We selected search databases that index relevant conferences and journals that could potentially gather themes like Human Computer Interaction (HCI), video games and autism, both in global and Brazilian scenario. Therefore, we chose three databases as source for this research: IEEE Xplore, ACM Digital Library and SOL OpenLib. After testing different search strings and making adjustments to it, we defined the final string as the following:

Table 1. Inclusion and Exclusion Criteria

Criterion Type	Description of Criteria
Inclusion Criteria	(I1) Papers that proposed (developing and/or designing) a game or a Multimodal Interaction Virtual Environment (MIVE) for autistic users (I2) Papers that evaluated any game or MIVE with autistic people (I3) Papers written in English or Portuguese (I4) Peer-reviewed papers
Exclusion Criteria	(E1) Papers not readily available online for reading (E2) Papers that did not propose or evaluate a game or MIVE (E3) Papers that proposed a game or MIVE, but not for autistic people (E4) Papers that evaluated a game or MIVE, but not with autistic users (E5) Papers shorter than six pages

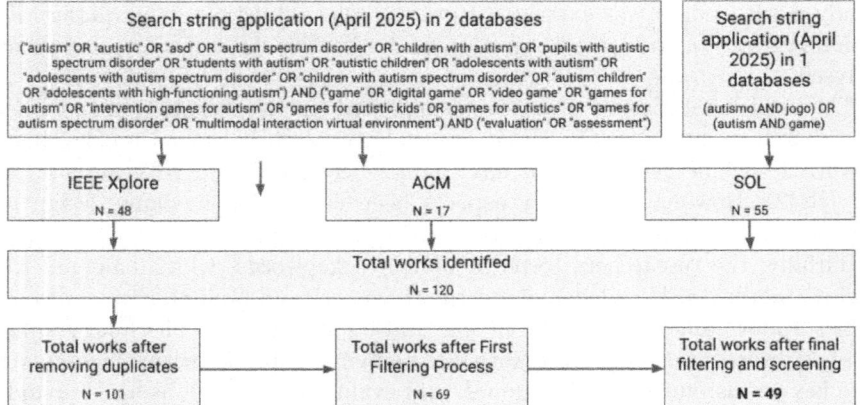

Fig. 1. Literature review process.

```
[("autism" OR "autistic" OR "asd" OR "autism spectrum
    disorder" OR "children with autism" OR "pupils with
    autistic spectrum disorder" OR "students with autism"
     OR "autistic children" OR "adolescents with autism"
    OR "adolescents with autism spectrum disorder" OR "
    children with autism spectrum disorder" OR "autism
    children" OR "adolescents with high-functioning
    autism') AND ("game" OR "digital game" OR "video game
    " OR "games for autism" OR "intervention games for
    autism' OR "games for autistic kids" OR "games for
    autistics" OR "games for autism spectrum disorder" OR
     "multimodal interaction virtual environment") AND ("
    evaluation" OR "assessment")]
```

We used this string to search for these terms in titles, abstracts and keywords of papers indexed in IEEE Xplore and in ACM Digital Library. Due to limitations within the search mechanisms in SOL OpenLib databases regarding the use of operators and synonyms, we adopted a simplified version specially

Table 2. Synonyms and Related Terms for Key Search Concepts

Key Concept	Synonyms / Search Terms Used
Autism	– Autism – Autistic – ASD – Autism Spectrum Disorder – Children with autism – Pupils with autistic spectrum disorder – Students with autism – Autistic children – Adolescents with autism – Adolescents with autism spectrum disorder – Children with autism spectrum disorder – Autism children – Adolescents with high-functioning autism
Video Games	– Game – Digital game – Video game – Games for autism intervention – Games for autism – Games for autistic kids – Games for autistics – Games for autism spectrum disorder – Multimodal interaction virtual environment
Evaluation	– Evaluation – Assessment

for this source. After some tests with the same set of keywords, we decided to use the following strings to look for these terms in any part of the papers: (autism AND game) e (autismo AND jogo). As a result of the search for papers in the three databases, using the selected strings, we initially found 120 articles, comprising 55 (%45,83) from SOL OpenLib, 17 (40%) from IEEE Xplore, and eight (14,17%) from ACM Digital Library. These references were exported from each database and organized using the Rayyan tool [39], where duplicates were removed, resulting in a set of 101 articles. After that, we conducted a filtering process based on the set of excluding and including criteria presented before (Table 1). These criteria helped us to ensure that the selected articles were relevant to cover our goals and to answer our research questions, focusing directly on papers that proposed or evaluated games with autistic users. Additionally, the length and peer-review criterion ensured that the final set of papers had sufficient information for our analysis and excluded white papers and editorials.

Using the Rayyan tool [39], we conducted the filtering process of the 101 papers in two stages, considering the presented inclusion and exclusion criteria. The first stage of filtering consisted of reading the title, abstract and keywords of the articles, looking for those that fit the themes we were looking for. As a result of this first filter, 69 articles were included. These 69 articles went through the second stage of the filtering process, which consisted of accessing the full articles, to confirm that they fit the exclusion criteria and to remove articles that were shorter than 6 pages and/or that were not readily available online for reading. After the filtering process, 49 papers remained, so these comprised our final set of articles selected in the literature review process. It is important to notice that some versions of the Rayyan tool disposes of an artificial intelligence (AI) that can support the screening process and the papers' analysis. In this research, we only used the free version, that do not have or use AI for these or any other purposes or tasks.

The final set of papers underwent a data extraction process, using a structured form to gather relevant information to address our research questions. In this data extraction, we aimed to gather characteristics of the games presented and/or evaluated in the articles (firstly if a game was designed, the purpose of the game, its main device or platform and the types of feedback it applied), as well as information about the evaluations performed (primarily if a evaluation was performed, the methods or techniques used, the participants, the constructs evaluated, the session's duration, the period of time that encomprised the evaluation process and if it compared typical and autistic users). Finally, we also sought to collect data on whether and how audio was considered in the evaluations presented in the articles, collecting information about the type of audio, the source of the audio, and the purpose of the audio evaluated. We used the data set that we sought to extract (Table 3) from the articles in an online form, using the Google Form tool [13], examining each paper in detail and submitting its informations to the online form, thus collecting the same informations from each of the 49 articles in the set resulting from the literature search.

Finally, we tabulated and analyzed the data extracted from the papers, categorizing the data for each type of information collected from the articles. We categorized the data in a way that its organization would help answer each research question, separating it into: data on the games evaluated, data on the evaluations carried out and data on the audio, when this was considered in some way in the evaluation. Regarding the data about how the evaluations considered audio features, we analyzed thematically the informations about the type of audio of the games the papers reported in the evaluations, categorizing them into the types described by Nunes & Darin (2024) [28]. Additionally, we made a quantitative count of the data collected regarding the other aspects of audio evaluation. The results of our analysis and the trends that it reveals are presented in the next session.

5   Results

The literature review resulted in 49 final articles that present games for autistic individuals or evaluate games with autistic participants. In this section, we present the analysis of the data collected from the articles. First, we provide an overview of the selected articles, including general information such as the databases from which they were retrieved, the language of publication, and the year of publication. Next, in the following subsections, we present the data relevant to answering each of the research questions (RQ) previously established and presented in earlier sections.

5.1   Overview

Among the 49 selected articles, 21 (42%) came from the IEEE Xplore database, 20 (40%) from the SOL database, and eight (16%) from the ACM Digital Library. Thirty-three (67%) of the 49 articles are written in English and only 16 (33%) in Portuguese.

Regarding the year of publication, the papers were distributed from 2009 to 2025. The highest concentration occurred in 2024, with 10 articles (20%), followed by 2020, 2021 and 2023, with seven articles each (12%). The least published years were 2009 and 2015, with only one (2%) paper each, follower by 2016 and 2019, with only two (4%) papers each one. Figure 2 shows the full distribution of articles by year.

We selected papers that developed a game for autistic people and/or that evaluated a game with autistic users. Among the 49 papers, 46 (94%) presented a game developed (e.g. [29,38]) and only three (6%) did not developed a game (e.g. [48]). Forty-one (83%) articles presented an evaluation of a game (e.g. [3,14]) and eight (17%) only presented a game, but did not evaluate it (e.g. [16]).

Table 3. Data Extraction Form for Literature Review

Category	Data Points to Extract
General Characteristics of Papers	– Title – Authors – Year – Language
Characteristics of the Game (Presented and/or Evaluated)	– Was a game designed/proposed? (Yes/No) – Purpose of the game – Main device or platform – Types of feedback applied
Information about Evaluations Performed	– Was an evaluation performed? (Yes/No) – Methods or techniques used – Participants involved – Constructs evaluated – Session's duration – Period of time encompassing the evaluation process – Comparison between typical and autistic users (Yes/No)
Data about Target Users / Autistic Participants	– Age range – Autism severity level
Data about Audio Consideration in Evaluations	– Was audio considered in the evaluation? (Yes/No) – If yes: • Type of audio evaluated • Source of the audio (User / Game) • Purpose of the audio evaluated

The games evaluated or presented in the articles could operate on multiple platforms or device types, so that one game could use or have a version for more than one type of platform. The most common were mobile devices, used by 20 games (40%, e.g., [19, 22, 43]), followed by desktop platforms with 12 (24%) games (e.g., [6, 10, 30]), web-based games with four (8%) (e.g. [27]), virtual or augmented reality with four (8%) (e.g. [18]), and robotics with two game (4%) (e.g. [53]).

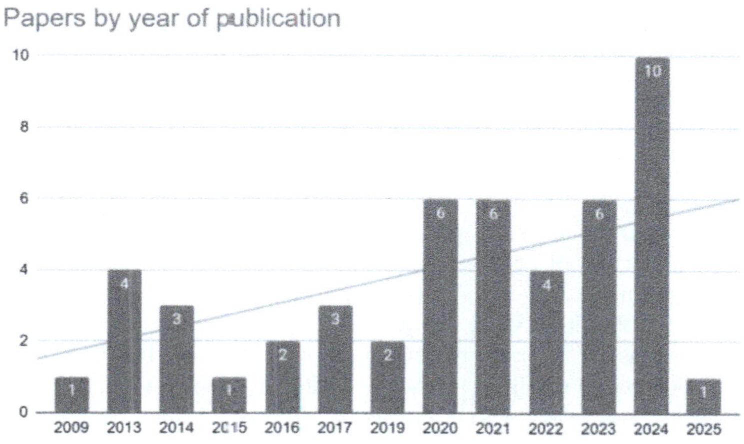

Papers by year of publication

Fig. 2. Papers by year of publication.

5.2 What Games Have Been Developed and Evaluated for Autistic People? (RQ1)

We collect information about the games developed and/or evaluated by the articles, such as the purpose of the game, the specific purposes for the autistic audience and the types of feedback used by the games. Concerning the purpose of the games presented by the papers, 30 games (61%) had therapeutic objectives related to autism characteristics (e.g. [4,35]), including improvement in social skills, emotion recognition, and cognitive aspects such as attention and memory. Ten games (20%) aimed to assess autism-related aspects or symptoms (e.g. [2,36]), such as the development of social skill and emotion recognition or cognitive evolution. Additionally, nine games (18%) had educational objectives (e.g. [16]), aiming to teach autistic individuals various subjects, such as computational thinking or basic school disciplines.

When an evaluated or developed game had its main purpose aimed at the autistic public, whether therapeutic or assessment, we looked for identify what specific purpose the game had for this public. Twelve (24%) games had the specific purpose of aid or assess the autistic users' emotion recognition (e.g. [12,35]), while seven (14%) focused on users' visual aspects (e.g. [43]) and also seven (14%) on motor skills (e.g. [44]). Six games (12%) focused its therapeutic or assessment purpose on cognitive aspects of the autistic users (e.g. [42]) and only one (2%) game focused on aspects related to users' touch [18]).

We collected information about the types of feedback used by the games. Forty-seven games (96%) included visual feedback (e.g. [30,37]), 23 (47%) included auditory feedback (e.g. [36,38]), one (2%) included tactile feedback [29], and two articles (4%) did not mention or show any feedback type in the presented or evaluated games. Note that many games may have used more than just visual feedback, but our analysis considered only what the authors explicitly reported in their descriptions.

5.3   How Games Have Been Evaluated with Autistic People? (RQ2)

We analyzed information about the game evaluations performed focusing autistic people, collecting data about the methods, types of instruments and technique used in the evaluations, the participants involved, the constructs evaluated or the purpose of the evaluation, the duration and length of time the evaluation took, the age range of the users involved, the autism severity level of the users and if the evaluation compared autistic and neurotypical people in any way.

Among the set of 49 articles, 41 (83%) performed an evaluation of game focusing autistic users. The evaluations could use more than one method or technique, so that 20 (40%) used the analysis of game logs and/or scores (e.g. [45, 53]), 19 evaluations (38%) used questionnaires (e.g. [9, 48]), 10 (20%) evaluations used observation based methods (either by video or in person) (e.g. [4, 47]), seven 14%) used interviews (e.g. [14, 41]) and six (12%) used physiological sensors (such as EEG) (e.g. [50]).

Regarding the period of time used for the evaluation, 30 (61%) papers reported an episodic evaluation, which occurred in only one moment (e.g. [14]), while 10 (20%) papers reported longitudinal evaluation and/or those that were carried out in more than one session (e.g. [48]). Regarding the duration of each evaluation session, 37 papers did not mention how much time it took, while seven (14%) papers reported evaluation above 30 min (e.g. [23]) and five (10%) reported evaluations under 30 min (e.g. [51]).

Although the evaluations focused on autistic people, the articles not necessarily performed it only with autistic users. Thirty (61%) did involved autistic users in the evaluation (e.g. [4, 35]), while 10 (20%) also involved teachers or preceptors (e.g. [2, 46]). Eight evaluations (16%) also involved neurotypical users (e.g. [45, 55], five (10%) had the participation of parents or tutors (e.g. [54]) and also five (10%) involved one or more researcher as an assistant or actively being part of the interaction with the autistic user, for example (e.g. [22]). Three papers (6%) reported that therapists also was part of the public involved in the evaluations (e.g. [41]).

We collected and analyzed some information about the autistic users that participated in the evaluations. Regarding the age range of the users, an evaluation could involve people with different ages. Twenty-eight papers (57%) presented an evaluation with children users (e.g. [11, 55]), while nine (18%) involved adolescents (e.g. [9, 50]) and only two (4%) mentioned involving adults [2, 24]. Four (8%) did not mentioned the age range of the users or didn't involved users in the evaluation process. Among the articles that presented an evaluation, four (8%) mentioned involving low-functioning autistic users (e.g. [4]) and two (4%) involved high-functioning autistic users (e.g. [35]). Thirty-five papers did not mentioned the autism severity level of the users or did not involved autistic users in the evaluation. Thirteen papers (26%) compared autistic users with neurotypical developed users in its evaluations (e.g. [36]), while twenty eight (57%) did not compared or didn't mentioned a comparison between them.

5.4   How Auditory Aspects Have Been Considered in Game Design and Evaluation for Autistic Users? (RQ3)

Aiming to answer our third research question, we collected and analyzed information about how audio was considered in the games developed and in the evaluations for autistic users. We looked for papers that considered audio in the evaluations, the source of the audio (if it was from the user or the game) and the methods and techniques used for evaluate the audio. If the audio was from the game, we looked for distinguish different types of audio, using a categorization presented by [28], that, in their literature review about audio in Player Experience evaluations, categorized audio in three types: Speech and Dialog, Sound-Effects and Music. For game sounds, we also collected information about the purpose of the audio.

Among the set of 49 papers, only seven (14%) considered audio in the evaluation process (Table 4). Four papers (8%) considered audio from the game evaluated (e.g. [36]) and three (6%) reported that analyzed audio from the users (e.g. [53]). Among the papers that considered audio in the evaluation, four used video and/or audio recording analysis (8%) (e.g. [4], two used interviews (with the users, parents or therapists) to assess audio related questions (e.g. [55]) and one (2%) used ethnography (e.g. [36]).

Regarding the purpose of the audio, for the four articles in which the source of the sounds was the game, they all reported different purposes, so that one of them worked as sound feedback [41], another had the purpose of being an audio narration [55], another one worked as background music [36] and the last one had the purpose of expressing the users' physical movements [38]. Examining the type of audio, these game-generated sounds were categorised according to [28], so that in two cases the audio was a Sound-Effect, in other game the audio was a Music in the background and in the last one it was a Speech-Dialog sound.

Table 4. Summary of analyzed papers regarding their use of audio.

Paper	Audio source	Methods, instruments or techniques	Purpose of the audio	Type of game audio
[17]	User	Recording	Non-specified	Not applicable
[38]	Game	Users' video/audio recording	Express users' movement	Sound-effects
[55]	Game	Interview	Audio narration	Speech and dialog
[36]	Game	Ethnography	Background music	Music
[41]	Game	Interview	Auditory feedback	Sound-effects
[4]	User	Recording	Non-specified	Not applicable
[53]	User	Video recording	Non-specified	Not applicable

6   Discussion

Our study results indicate that despite many games have been designed for autistic people and part of them have been evaluated with these users, there is still just very few that properly address the auditory aspects of games. Besides that, both development and evaluation of games with autistic people lack of variety in some aspects, such as the age range of the target users and the purposes of the games.

Based on the data we collected from the selected papers, its analysis and on the theoretical background about audio, autism and digital games, we highlighted relevant topics about how audio has been used in game design for autistic people and how it has been evaluated with these users.

Autism Spectrum Disorder is characterised, among other aspects, by atypical sensory processing experienced by autistic individuals. Autistic individuals are usually more sensitive to auditory stimuli. The capacity for auditory perception tends to be heightened in autistic people [40]. According to Connor [32], this atypical auditory processing may manifest in different ways, such as hypersensitivity to certain noises and sound frequencies.

In our study, we gathered information about which types of feedback the articles mentioned as present in the games. Most of the articles mentioned, in some way, having visual feedback for their interactions, but only 23 mentioned auditory feedback. Even though more games, among the articles collected, made use of auditory feedback, the lack of direct mention of this feedback in their design (or evaluation, when this was carried out), regardless of the purpose of the game, may indicate a lack of attention to the sensory stimuli that they can cause in the autistic audience or to how they can alter, positively or negatively, the experience. An inappropriate approach to sound features, such as the use of certain frequencies or types of sounds, can generate negative sensory experiences in autistic people. In addition, this atypical sensory processing may cause overexcitement, and even common sounds can cause distress [40].

Despite being considered in some evaluations, it is necessary that auditory stimuli be treated with more attention both in game evaluations with autistic people and in game design. Of the 41 articles that evaluated games, only 7 considered audio aspects, directly or indirectly (i.e., actively investigating these aspects or merely reporting on them in more general evaluations of the game). The approach to audio with autistic users can be especially useful to assess aspects of common objectives in evaluations, such as therapeutic assistance for the development of motor skills (e.g. [1], refinement of emotion recognition (e.g. [30], and improvement of social interactions (e.g. [53]), as well as monitoring the evolution of these aspects. The appropriate use of sounds can enhance the expected results of this type of game for autistic users, either by directing attention to the appropriate elements or by generating relevant associations for educational and therapeutic objectives.

Audio features can have a significant role in Player Experience, and this is even more critical for autistic players. Although there were few articles that mentioned addressing sound aspects in some way in the evaluations they conducted, all four cited different purposes for audio. One of them considered audio only as sound feedback [41], another collected data on an audio narration used in the game [55], while another considered background music in the evaluation process [36]. One article considered audio as a central element in the interaction of the developed game [38], with the audio being produced by the system to represent, in sound, the physical movements that users (autistic children) performed while interacting. Although small in number, these results provide a glimpse into the possibility of using audio as a powerful tool to impact the experience of autistic players and can be useful in stimulating and contributing to the therapy of other aspects of Autism Spectrum Disorder, such as social interactions, cognitive aspects such as attention and perception, recognition of emotions, and also in enriching the learning process.

It is therefore necessary that, in the design and development process of digital games for autistic people, special care be taken in how audio is used, what types of audio will be implemented, and how it will be perceived by the target users. This is important not only to prevent negative experiences for autistic players and unwanted reactions due to sensory overstimulation, but also to take advantage of the potential of audio to generate healthy engagement for the objectives of the games (whether therapeutic, educational, or for the entertainment of this audience). In addition, this special attention to audio is also important in the evaluation of games, of any nature, with autistic users, to clarify how different uses of sound are received and perceived by autistic users, highlighting more appropriate paths for a more adequate use of audio in game development and illuminating the understanding we have about the relationship between autistic people and digital games.

7   Limitations and Future Works

This study aims to highlight research gaps about audio in games' evaluation and design for autistic people. In order to achieve this goal, we conducted a literature review, looking for papers in three databases and collecting data about the studies. Nevertheless, it is important to notice that this very study has its limitations, such as using only three databases, which may have caused relevant articles on the topic to be left out of the final set of articles found. In addition, the scope and amount of data collected may limit the understanding of some important aspects of audio in this context - for example, the study could benefit from data that addressed theoretical bases considered for the design of games for autistic people, or from more in-depth information on the purpose of each game evaluated or developed and its relationship with sound aspects. A deeper look at the sound feedback used in the games studied and its relationships with the games themselves and with autistic users could also be beneficial for the research. Thus, by combining the contributions of this study and the potential limitations presented, future research work can benefit from the insights revealed in this article both to deepen the collection of data on audio in games, as well as to address research gaps revealed by the analyzed data, such as evaluating the direct and indirect impact of game audio (be it background music, sound feedback or narrated voice) on autistic users, seeking to understand how audio in games can affect users of different ages, the role of user sounds (such as speech and sound expressions) in game evaluations and in the experience of autistic players themselves.

8   Conclusion

Games can provide meaningful sensory experiences for autistic individuals, especially serious games, which can not only generate entertainment but also serve educational or therapeutic purposes. For autistic individuals, the visual and auditory stimuli that make up games can both enrich the experience and cause negative adverse reactions, due to hypersensitivity to sensory stimuli, which is common in autistic people. This study aimed to clarify, through a literature review, how audio has been considered both in game design for autistic people and in the evaluation of games with this audience. Our results indicate that, despite being considered in some cases, greater attention to audio, especially in game evaluation, is still needed. Although there are few studies directly considering game audio in their evaluations, the few that did so showed a variety of potential uses of sounds (from background music [36] to user movement expression [38]), for games with different purposes and purposes. In digital game design, although some authors report the use of sound feedback, there is little evidence about the impacts of this on the target audience on the autistic spectrum, in addition to many games that do not accurately mention the use of this type of feedback in their games, which may indicate a lack of due concern for this aspect that is so important for how autistic individuals experience digital games.

As next steps for this research, we consider deepening studies on how sound elements commonly used in games can have an impact on the autistic public, investigating the evaluated effects of different types of audio already used in digital games for autistic users, in order to understand and provide useful insights about how to design audio and evaluate it for and with ASD players.

Acknowledgments. This paper is a partial result of the project Digital Well-Being supported by CNPq (CNPq/MCTI N° 10/2023 - UNIVERSAL) under grant number 404559/2023-9.

Disclosure of Interests. The authors have no competing interests.

References

1. Azevedo, G., Gunsch, M.L., Lacerda, M.G., Borges, L.C.L., Nunes, E.P.D.S.: Serious game com técnicas de treinamento motor fino como tecnologia assistiva para encorajar a colaboração de crianças com tea. In: Escola Regional de Informática de Mato Grosso (ERI-MT), pp. 136–145. SBC (2023)

2. Barbosa, B., Ribeiro, M.W., Berretta, L., Carvalho S.: Diagnostea: a digital game as a tool for the diagnosis/therapy of autism spectrum disorder. In: Simpósio Brasileiro de Jogos e Entretenimento Digital (SBGames), pp. 1707–1718. SBC (2024)
3. Bei, R., et al.: StarRescue: the design and evaluation of a turn-taking collaborative game for facilitating autistic children's social skills. In: Proceedings of the 2024 CHI Conference on Human Factors in Computing Systems, pp. 1–19 (2024)
4. Calpa, G.F.M.S., Raposo, A.B.: Par (peço, ajudo, recebo): Um jogo colaborativo em mesa multi-toque para apoiar a interaçao socia. de usuários com autismo. In: Concurso de Teses e Dissertações (CTD), pp. 29–34. SBC (2013)
5. de Carvalho, A.P., Braz, C.S., Prates, R.O.: An analysis of the evaluation methods being applied to serious games for autistic children. J. Interact. Syst. **15**(1), 55–78 (2024)
6. Chien, Y.L., et al.: Game-based social interaction platform for cognitive assessment of autism using eye tracking. IEEE Trans. Neural Syst. Rehabil. Eng. **31**, 749–758 (2022)
7. Creswell, J.W., Creswell J.D.: Research Design: Qualitative, Quantitative, and Mixed Methods Approaches. Sage Publications (2017)
8. Darin, T., Andrade, R., Sánchez, J.: Usability evaluation of multimodal interactive virtual environments for learners who are blind: an empirical investigation. Int. J. Hum Comput Stud. **158**, 102732 (2022)
9. El-Gohary, M., Aborizka, M., El-Sheikh, M., El-Nagar, Z.: Shopping training to autistic children and adolescents for enhancing daily life shopping skills using virtual reality and leap motion. In: 2022 1st IEEE International Conference on Cognitive Aspects of Virtual Reality (CVR), pp. 000055–000060. IEEE (2022)
10. Finkelstein, S., Barnes, T., Wartell, Z., Suma, E.A.: Evaluation of the exertion and motivation factors of a virtual reality exercise game for children with autism. In: 2013 1st Workshop on Virtual and Augmented Assistive Technology (VAAT), pp. 11–16. IEEE (2013)
11. Garcia-Garcia, J.M., Cabañero, M.D.M., Penichet, V.M., Lozano, M.D.: EmoTEA: teaching children with autism spectrum disorder to identify and express emotions. In: Proceedings of the XX International Conference on Human Computer Interaction, pp. 1–8 (2019)
12. Gomes, V., Sarinho, V.: TEAPET: Desenvolvendo pets digitais voltados para indivíduos portadores do transtorno do espectro autista. In: Simpósio Brasileiro de Computação Aplicada à Saúde (SBCAS), pp. 482–487. SBC (2020)
13. Google LLC: Google Forms: Online Form Builder (2025). https://www.google.com/forms/about/. Acesso em: 19 maio 2025
14. Honorato, N., dos Santos A.J., Delabrida, S., de Freitas, A.R.R., Oliveira, W.: Strong: Desenvolvimento e avaliação de um jogo para auxiliar no tratamento do espectro do autismo. In: Simpósio Brasileiro de Jogos e Entretenimento Digital (SBGames), pp. 582–591. SBC (2021)
15. Huerta, M., Bishop, S.L., Duncan, A., Hus, V., Lord, C.: Application of DSM-5 criteria for autism spectrum disorder to three samples of children with DSM-IV diagnoses of pervasive developmental disorders. Am. J. Psychiatry **169**(10), 1056–1064 (2012)
16. Kamaruzaman, N.N., Jomhari, N.: Digital game-based learning for low functioning autism children in learning Al-Quran. In: 2013 Taibah University International Conference on Advances in Information Technology for the Holy Quran and Its Sciences, pp. 184–189. IEEE (2013)

17. Khabbaz, A.H., Pouyan, A.A., Fateh, M., Abolghasemi, V.: An adaptive RL based fuzzy game for autistic children. In: 2017 Artificial Intelligence and Signal Processing Conference (AISP), pp. 47–52. IEEE (2017)
18. Koirala, A., Yu, Z., Schiltz, H., Van Hecke, A., Armstrong, B., Zheng, Z.: A preliminary exploration of virtual reality-based visual and touch sensory processing assessment for adolescents with autism spectrum disorder. IEEE Trans. Neural Syst. Rehabil. Eng. **29**, 619–628 (2021)
19. Kołakowska, A., Landowska, A., Karpienko, K.: Gyroscope-based game revealing progress of children with autism. In: Proceedings of the 2017 International Conference on Machine Learning and Soft Computing, pp. 19–24 (2017)
20. Lopez, J.Y.A., Huaycho, R.N.N., Santos, F.I.Y., Talavera-Mendoza, F., Paucar, F.H.R.: The impact of serious games on learning in primary education: a systematic literature review. Int. J. Learn. Teach. Educ. Res. **22**(3), 379–395 (2023)
21. López-Bouzas, N., Del Moral-Pérez, M.E.: Gamified environments and serious games for students with autistic spectrum disorder: review of research. Rev. J. Autism Dev. Disord. **12**(1), 80–92 (2025)
22. Luongo, M., Simeoli, R., Marocco, D., Ponticorvo, M.: Exploring motor patterns in autism spectrum disorder using raw data and artificial intelligence: a pilot study. In: 2023 IEEE International Conference on Metrology for eXtended Reality, Artificial Intelligence and Neural Engineering (MetroXRAINE), pp. 1006–1011. IEEE (2023)
23. Malpartida, K.F.C., da Hora Rodrigues, K.R.: Building serious games to exercise computational thinking: initial evaluation with teachers of children on the autism spectrum. J. Interact. Syst. **16**(1), 148–162 (2025)
24. Martins, J.J., Castelo-Branco, M., Simões, M.: Immersive virtual reality serious game for facial expression training. In: 2024 IEEE 12th International Conference on Serious Games and Applications for Health (SeGAH), pp. 1–7. IEEE (2024)
25. Mazurek, M.O., Engelhardt, C.R., Clark, K.E.: Video games from the perspective of adults with autism spectrum disorder. Comput. Hum. Behav. **51**, 122–130 (2015). https://doi.org/10.1016/j.chb.2015.04.062. https://www.sciencedirect.com/science/article/pii/S0747563215003581
26. Mazurek, M.O., Shattuck, P.T., Wagner, M., Cooper, B.P.: Prevalence and correlates of screen-based media use among youths with autism spectrum disorders. J. Autism Dev. Disord. **42**, 1757–1767 (2012)
27. Morais, J.G., Maia, F., Calderon, I.: Jogando pela inclusao: Gamificaçao como ferramenta para ensinar os ods a crianças autistas. In: Simpósio Brasileiro de Sistemas de Informação (SBSI), pp. 386–392. SBC (2025)
28. Nunes, C., Darin, T.: Echoes of player experience: a literature review on audio assessment and player experience in games. Proc. ACM Hum.-Comput. Interact. **8**(CHI PLAY), 1–27 (2024)
29. de Oliveira, D.M., Parra, V.G., Borges, M.A.: Processo de desenvolvimento de um jogo educativo para crianças autistas. In: Workshop de Informática na Educação Inclusiva (WIEI), pp. 27–35. SBC (2024)
30. Oliveira, S.E.S., Arantes, A., Mota, V.F.: Meu jardim de emoções: jogo para compreensão de expressões faciais para crianças e adolescentes autistas. In: Simpósio Brasileiro de Jogos e Entretenimento Digital (SBGames), pp. 549–555. SBC (2021)
31. Olson, C.K.: Children's motivations for video game play in the context of normal development. Rev. Gen. Psychol. **14**(2), 180–187 (2010)
32. O'Connor, K.: Auditory processing in autism spectrum disorder: a review. Neurosci. Biobehav. Rev. **36**(2), 836–854 (2012). https://doi.org/10.1016/j.neubiorev.2011.11.008. https://www.sciencedirect.com/science/article/pii/S0149763411002065

33. Papanastasiou, G., Drigas, A., Skianis, C., Lytras, M.D.: Serious games in K-12 education: benefits and impacts on students with attention, memory and developmental disabilities. Program **51**(4), 424–440 (2017)
34. Papanastasiou, G., Drigas, A., Skianis, C.: Serious games: how do they impact special education needs children. Technium Educ. Eum. **2**(3), 41–58 (2022)
35. Piana, S., Malagoli, C., Usai, M.C., Camurri, A.: Effects of computerized emotional training on children with high functioning autism. IEEE Trans. Affect. Comput. **12**(4), 1045–1054 (2019)
36. Pires, S.V., et al.: Um jogo sério para triagem das funções executivas como subsídio pedagógico para crianças com tea na educação infantil. In: Simpósio Brasileiro de Informática na Educação (SBIE), pp. 2764–2778. SBC (2024)
37. Pontoh, S.H., Sholikah, R. W., Suryotrisongko, H., Alimboyong, C.R.: Mobile-based serious game for learning facial expression recognition in children with autism spectrum disorder using MobileNet model. In: 2024 International Conference on Computer Engineering, Network, and Intelligent Multimedia (CENIM), pp. 1–6. IEEE (2024)
38. Ragone, G., Good, J., Howland, K.: OSMoSIS: interactive sound generation system for children with autism. In: Proceedings of the 2020 ACM Interaction Design and Children Conference: Extended Abstracts, pp. 151–156 (2020)
39. Rayyan Systems Inc.: Rayyan: Intelligent Systematic Review Tool (2025). https://www.rayyan.ai. Acesso em: 19 maio 2025
40. Remington, A., Fairnie, J.: A sound advantage: Increased auditory capacity in autism. Cognition **166**, 459–465 (2017). https://doi.org/10.1016/j.cognition.2017.04.002. https://www.sciencedirect.com/science/article/pii/S0010027717300963
41. Ribeiro, P.C., Raposo, A.B.: ComFiM: a game for multitouch devices to encourage communication between people with autism. In: 2014 IEEE 3nd International Conference on Serious Games and Applications for Health (SeGAH), pp. 1–8. IEEE (2014)
42. Sampaio, L., Nascimento, E., Pereira, C.: Soldierontnebridge: um jogo aplicado à melhoria da memória e da atenção em crianças com autismo. In: Escola Regional de Computação Bahia, Alagoas e Sergipe (ERBASE), pp. 66–71. SBC (2019)
43. Sampaio, L.P., Pereira, C.P.: Jogo digital educativo para auxílio a crianças com autismo. In: Simpósio Brasileiro de Informática na Educação (SBIE), pp. 597–608. SBC (2022)
44. Sampaio, L.P., Pereira, C.P.: Autibots: Jogo digital educativo para desenvolvimento cognitivo e motor de crianças com autismo. Revista Brasileira de Informática na Educação **33**, 1–34 (2025)
45. Shahab, M., et al.: Social virtual reality robot (V2R): a novel concept for education and rehabilitation of children with autism. In 2017 5th RSI International Conference on Robotics and Mechatronics (ICRoM), pp. 82–87. IEEE (2017)
46. Silva, A.H., Santos, P.H., Cunha, M.X.: Letramundo: Um jogo sério para alfabetização de crianças com transtorno do espectro autista (tea) em ambiente escolar. In: Simpósio Brasileiro de Informática na Educação (SBIE), pp. 2747–2756. SBC (2024)
47. Silva, G.F.M., Raposo, A.B.: Identifying awareness requirements in face-to-face collaborative applications for users with autism spectrum disorders. In: Simpósio Brasileiro de Sistemas Colaborativos (SBSC), pp. 1305–1319. SBC (2016)
48. Souza, J., Oliveira, F., Silva, L., Toda, A., Isotani, S.: The impact of serious games on the learning of students with autism spectrum disorder. In: Workshop de Informática na Escola (WIE), pp. 459–468. SBC (2020)

49. Talebi Azadboni, T., Nasiri, S., Khenarinezhad, S., Sadoughi, F.: Effectiveness of serious games in social skills training to autistic individuals: a systematic review. Neurosci. Biobehav. Rev. **161**, 105634 (2024). https://doi.org/10.1016/j.neubiorev.2024.105634. https://www.sciencedirect.com/science/article/pii/S0149763424001039

50. Tseng, Y.L., et al.: Characterizing autism spectrum disorder through fusion of local cortical activation and global functional connectivity using game-based stimuli and a mobile EEG system. IEEE Trans. Neural Syst. Rehabil. Eng. (2024)

51. Tseng, Y.L., et al.: Electroencephalography connectivity assesses cognitive disorders of autistic children during game-based social interaction. IEEE Trans. Cogn. Dev. Syst. **16**(2), 782–793 (2023)

52. Turygin, N.C., Matson, J.L., Adams, H., Belva, B.: The effect of DSM-5 criteria on externalizing, internalizing, behavioral and adaptive symptoms in children diagnosed with autism. Dev. Neurorehabil. **16**(4), 277–282 (2013). https://doi.org/10.3109/17518423.2013.769281. pMID: 23617257

53. Wainer, J., Robins, B., Amirabdollahian, F., Dautenhahn, K.: Using the humanoid robot KASPAR to autonomously play triadic games and facilitate collaborative play among children with autism. IEEE Trans. Auton. Ment. Dev. **6**(3), 183–199 (2014)

54. Wasala, K.S., Dhanawansa, V., Velayuthan, M., Samarasinghe, P.: Automated child social attention evaluation. In: 2022 4th International Conference on Advancements in Computing (ICAC), pp. 375–380. IEEE (2022)

55. Yuan, X., Ye, H., Tang, Z., Zhu, X., Yao, Y., Tong, X.: RedCapes: the design and evaluation of a game towards improving autistic children's privacy awareness. In: Proceedings of the Eleventh International Symposium of Chinese CHI, pp. 110–126 (2023)

A Hybrid Board Game with Augmented Reality to Assist in Chemistry Teaching to Deaf or Hard of Hearing Students

Natalia Da Silva Fernandes[3], Felipe Henrique Araújo[1],
Jose Nunes da Silva Junior[2], Antônio José Melo Leite Júnior[1],
and Windson Viana[1(✉)]

[1] UFC Virtual, Universidade Federal do Ceará, Fortaleza, CE 60440-454, Brazil
{melojr,windson}@virtual.ufc.br
[2] Departamento de Química Orgânica e Inorgânica, Universidade Federal do Ceará,
Fortaleza, CE 60451-970, Brazil
[3] Centro Interdisciplinar de Investigação Marinha e Ambiental (CIIMAR), Faculdade
de Ciências da Universidade do Porto (FCUP), Porto, Portugal
up202300994@edu.fc.up.pt

Abstract. Teaching chemistry poses significant challenges, as most students perceive it as complex and abstract, which hinders learning. For deaf or hard of hearing students, these challenges intensify due to the predominance of educational approaches designed for hearing learners. This article presents the development and evaluation of an inclusive hybrid game that uses Augmented Reality to support chemistry education. We conducted an experimental study with 21 third-year high school students from a Brazilian Professional Education Center, including six deaf students. Using a controlled pre-test and post-test design, we analyzed learning outcomes. The results showed no significant performance differences between deaf and hearing students, and overall, the game enhanced conceptual understanding. Additionally, responses to the MEEGA+ questionnaire indicated that students enjoyed the game. Despite some inconclusive results regarding learning, the general findings suggest the game is a promising complementary tool for teaching chemistry alongside traditional problem-solving activities promoting student engagement and inclusion.

Keywords: Deaf · Learning · Games · Augmented Reality · Chemistry

1 Introduction

Since ancient times, games have played an important role in cultural expression and human social interaction [17]. With technological advancements, digital games have contributed significantly to the widespread popularity of this phenomenon, which extends beyond just entertainment. Today, both analog and digital games are embedded in various sectors of society and are increasingly

© The Author(s), under exclusive license to Springer Nature Switzerland AG 2026
T. Darin et al. (Eds.): WIPlay 2025 CCIS 2623, pp. 49–66, 2026.
https://doi.org/10.1007/978-3-032-01426-9_4

used in fields such as education [46, 48] and healthcare [9, 36], for example, showcasing their versatility and potential for positive impact. The global expansion of the gaming market has also driven interest in exploring new formats. One such development is the emergence of hybrid games, which combine digital and non-digital components to create novel aesthetic experiences and modes of interaction [20]. Research has already demonstrated positive outcomes from adopting hybrid games, particularly in education. For example, studies in language learning have reported increased participation and enjoyment among students [7], while others have observed improvements in learning and comprehension [1].

Chemistry is an area of science that studies matter, its transformations, and the energies involved in these processes, playing a fundamental role in the technological advancement of society [8]. Chemistry is present in many aspects of our daily lives, from producing food and medicines to creating new materials and energy sources [5].

According to the Brazilian guidelines of the National Common Curricular Base (BNCC), the central purpose of teaching chemistry in High School is to address students' everyday issues, to awaken in each of them an awareness of their role in society, and foster the development of their critical capacity to understand, analyze and transform real situations[1].

Unfortunately, several studies have shown that students generally need help with chemistry. The complexity of abstract concepts, technical language, and the need to understand mathematical relationships are some challenges reported [39]. Additionally, chemistry requires critical thinking, problem-solving, and logical reasoning skills, which can be an obstacle for some students [37].

When we turn specifically to Brazilian deaf students, these difficulties can be even more accentuated [28]. Lack of familiarity with the Portuguese language, which is commonly used in teaching methodologies in Brazil, can make it difficult to understand concepts in chemistry. People who are deaf or hard of hearing (DHH) have a different linguistic relationship, as they mainly use the Brazilian Sign Language (Libras) as a means of communication, which is the mother tongue of this community [14].

In this context, it is essential to recognize these difficulties and adopt different teaching strategies to improve the learning experience for both hearing and especially deaf students. Since the deaf person is considered a visual subject, that is, who uses vision to access information about the world, inclusive and adapted educational approaches based on visual resources, it is necessary to offer visual resources, such as images, graphs, and diagrams, relevant for the construction of knowledge as a whole [16].

Currently, new teaching methodologies have been used to satisfactorily meet the specific needs of deaf students, such as the use of mobile devices and accessible virtual learning environments, among others [2, 32].

Regarding chemistry learning, one approach that has shown particular promise is integrating games into pedagogical practices [40]. Incorporating games into chemistry classes is an approach that can improve the learning experience.

---

[1] https://basenacionalcomum.mec.gov.br/.

Games encourage socialization, the development of creativity, and critical thinking [27]. But they must balance the playful aspect with the construction of knowledge to be effective as teaching tools [47].

A particular game modality that has gained a lot of prominence in school spaces and has shown itself to be very promising is hybrid games, which combine elements of analog games, such as boards and cards, with electronic and digital ones, such as smartphones or Augmented Reality (AR) [33]. In particular, AR can be integrated into hybrid games to bring virtual elements into the user's real world, stimulating kinesthetic learning and facilitating the visualization of abstract concepts, thus making it possible to establish new alternatives in teaching people with deafness [31].

Studies have demonstrated the effectiveness of hybrid games with AR as teaching tools in several areas, including chemistry [40]. These approaches have shown positive results in increasing student motivation and improving communication and the quality of learning. However, the availability of accessible products for deaf people in the educational field, especially in AR, is still limited [13].

Given this scenario, we decided to develop, implement, and evaluate an adapted version of the game Interactions 500 [41] to promote the teaching and learning of organic chemistry for deaf and hearing students who are in the third year of High School. Another research group developed the original game in four different languages, and our adaptation uses hybridization techniques and augmented reality to provide adequate support for the educational process of Brazilian deaf students while also considering the hearing ones. The activities developed and their results, presented in the following, contribute to more inclusive teaching and promote greater autonomy in the learning process.

2   Theory Foundation

2.1   Hybrid Games

"Game" is a term with many and broad definitions. To contribute to this idea, Tekinbas and Zimmerman (2003) [44] presented in their book eight different definitions in addition to the one they adopted: a game is a system in which players engage in artificial conflict, defined by rules, resulting in a quantifiable outcome. This term has evolved with new adaptations in its definition. For instance, Zubek (2020) [49] adds current concepts, such as experience, where he defines games as syntheses of various disciplines whose combination is capable of generating a great experience for users.

Hybrid games embody this definition. They can be defined as games that use physical and virtual components, such as smartphones or tablets, to enrich the user's gaming experience [24]. However, under this definition, any digital game with a physical controller could be considered a hybrid. Arjoranta et al. (2016) [3] propose a more comprehensive and philosophical definition in which hybrid games are those games that combine two cognitive domains that are not usually associated.

In this paper, we adopted an intermediate definition in which hybrid games have distinct levels of hybridization, ranging from games closer to entirely physical (or analog) to digital [34]. Hybrid games use analog elements such as cards, dice, and boards and extend the gaming experience with digital technologies such as smartphones, interactive tables, projections, sensors, and haptic devices. Thus, hybrid games can be viewed as a subset of Pervasive Games [21].

Hybrid game design becomes increasingly complex, as it requires the careful harmonization of physical and digital components to optimize the user experience. For example, Ali *et al.* (2022) [1] identified several disadvantages associated with the use of augmented reality in hybrid educational games, such as increased costs, development challenges, unstable electronic performance, and insufficient physical space for the application of technology.

Therefore, it is essential to adhere to established guidelines for hybrid game design, such as those proposed in Kasapakis and Gavalas (2017) [20]. The authors formulated 17 design principles that assist developers in mitigating common pitfalls and making informed trade-offs. Notable principles include: *integration* (ensuring seamless incorporation of digital elements to avoid disrupting player immersion), *tangibility* (preserving the physical manipulation of game components), *rule modification* (providing flexibility to amend rules in response to design limitations or player preferences), *availability* (leveraging ubiquitous devices such as smartphones to facilitate gameplay), and *added value* (substituting analog components with digital enhancements to enrich the gaming experience).

In the present study, we adhered to these design principles.

2.2 Games and Chemistry Teaching

The first records of using games to teach chemistry date back to 1925, when crossword puzzles were used to reinforce basic chemical concepts [6,45]. These initial proposals were playful and aimed to increase student engagement in a context still dominated by traditional methods. During the following decades, scientific production on the subject was sparse, with isolated initiatives focusing, for example, on games to review nomenclatures [19] and basic properties of chemical elements [11].

Despite the problems in teaching chemistry, games remained occasional resources with limited scientific output for several decades. However, this did not hinder, for example, the creation in the 1970s of the first computer games specifically developed to support the understanding of electronic structures and organic synthesis [43].

But from the 1990s onward, a new phase emerged with a growing interest in learning theories focused on active, student-centered education, advances in digital technologies, and the consequent expansion of academic interest.

Then, chemistry teaching could explore new possibilities, and various games emerged, providing dynamic visualizations and simulations that go beyond the limitations of traditional textbooks and physical models, offering students opportunities for self-paced, interactive, and exploratory learning [40].

Many of these studies have evolved, and now games cover the most different subjects in chemistry, adopting diverse formats, ranging from 3D immersion [10] and online systems [42] to multiplayer environments [22] and cooperative learning in laboratories [26].

Regarding Chemistry education for DHH students, the construction of chemical knowledge by deaf learners may require more time compared to hearing students who can listen to the teacher's explanations. To mitigate these challenges, it is necessary to adopt redirected pedagogical practices, ensuring that deaf students have the same learning opportunities as their hearing peers. According to Gomes *et al.* (2015) [15], teaching Chemistry to deaf students demands a pedagogy based on visual strategies, employing multimodal, images, and concrete resources that facilitate associations with the content being taught.

But, although there are already a good number of publications about games aimed at teaching chemistry, there are still a few initiatives involving inclusive chemistry games, such as in Kucukkal and Kahveci (2019) [25] and Escudeiro *et al.* (2022) [12]. The distinctive aspect of our research lies in the development of a hybrid game specifically designed to engage a diverse audience, including both DHH and hearing students, using AR.

2.3   Augmented Reality and DHH Students

As part of this study, we conducted a systematic review on the use of Augmented Reality (AR) in education for deaf or hard of hearing individuals. From an initial pool of 1,582 documents, 26 studies published between 2006 and 2020 in journals and conferences were selected. The review aimed to synthesize the main AR applications, methodological approaches, evaluation procedures, and to highlight the key benefits and limitations of AR for DHH education.

Findings revealed that the most frequent application domain was language education (12 studies), followed by mathematics (4 studies). Notably, only one study addressed science education, indicating a gap and the need for further research employing AR for DHH learners in this field. Additionally, marker-based AR solutions predominated (60%), due to their accessibility (e.g., printed markers using images, text, or QR codes) and ease of implementation in classroom settings. In terms of technology, Vuforia and Unity 3D were the most commonly used platforms, appearing in 20% and 23% of studies, respectively.

A representative example is the work by Atanar *et al.* (2017) [4], who developed a technology-enriched classroom for deaf students. The environment was equipped with smartphones and multiple QR code markers distributed across the space. When scanned, these markers displayed text and images on topics such as plant structure, reproduction, growth, and natural resources, embedded in books and posters. Students used AR-enabled smartphones to interact with these markers and complete an investigative task assigned by the teacher. The content was supplemented with sign language (SL) to enhance comprehension. The post-test scores demonstrated an 84.62% improvement, underscoring the effectiveness of the approach. The Chemistry game proposed in this paper draws inspiration from such solutions.

The review also identified several benefits of AR in educational activities for DHH students, including improvements in writing, reading, communication, social interaction, and personal motivation. However, limitations were also reported in 10 out of the 25 analyzed studies. Common drawbacks included discomfort with head-mounted displays (40%), initial difficulties in interpreting AR visuals (20%), software usability issues (20%), and the requirement for advanced hardware (20%). For instance, Ioannou and Constantinou (2017) [18] reported participant discomfort due to ill-fitting AR glasses, while Salomia *et al.* (2018) [38] noted smartphone detection issues with AR markers during traffic sign learning sessions.

In our study, we opted for a smartphone-based AR approach that is minimally intrusive, strategically integrated at two points in the game: for displaying animated molecular models and for guiding navigation on the physical game board.

3   Methodology

This work's methodology involved a review of secondary studies and an iterative process based on User-Centered Design (UCD). Defined by Lowdermilk (2013) [30], it is a software development methodology for developers and designers. Its main goal is to create software that meets the needs of users. UCD aims to bring the users into the creation process, integrating them into intermediate testing cycles.

The present study was divided into five stages. In the first stage, we conducted a Systematic Literature Review (SLR), which, according to Kitchenham et *al.* (2009) [23], is a research approach that follows rigorous protocols and seeks to bring coherence and structure to a large documentary corpus. Our SLR aimed to identify the main applications of Augmented Reality (AR), the methods employed, and the evaluation processes conducted by the authors, as well as to analyze the main benefits and limitations of using AR in the education of deaf students. A summary of the findings from this review was presented in the previous section and is detailed at Fernande *et al.* (2024) [13].

From the second stage onward, the methodology followed an iterative approach based on UCD. Initially, a first **analogical** adaptation of the original game Interactions 500 was created and tested with both deaf and hearing participants to learn organic chemistry. We held two game sessions, one with and one without the presence of an interpreter, to understand how the game worked in practice and to identify possible adjustments. The game did not use any digital resources yet.

In the third stage, a second game version was developed and presented to a new group of deaf and hearing high school students, with the primary goal of familiarizing them with the game rules. In the fourth stage, this second version was reapplied to the same group, with observations and evaluations conducted to refine gameplay. Finally, in the fifth stage, a hybrid version was developed, implemented, and evaluated, incorporating a mobile app, inclusive videos in Libras for DHH participants, and interactive AR features.

The results from the fifth stage are the ones detailed in this article. This research evaluation project was approved by the ethics committee of the Universidade Federal do Ceará, in Brazil, under the process 5.461.328. All students or their direct guardians signed informed consent forms to participate in the tests.

4   An Inclusive Hybrid Game

In this work, we present a hybrid game, which is aimed at teaching organic chemistry while promoting interaction between high school students, including DHH ones. The idea is to apply the game during chemistry classes. It is a free and easy-to-play bilingual hybrid game (Portuguese and Libras) that can be played simultaneously by two to ten participants. It consists of a physical board and a mobile application, developed using the Unity 3D platform[2] together with Vuforia[3].

This dynamic and fun game uses rules and cards to guide players' actions. It provides challenges that require applying knowledge in organic chemistry to advance from a lower point on the board, which simulates a war field, to the trench in the upper part. All game material is available at https://shorturl.at/UZA2s, and the respective app is free for download for smartphones and tablets with the Android operating system. A video showing the gameplay is available at https://shorturl.at/Azxd7.

The game is composed of the mobile application (Fig. 3) and physical elements: a board (Fig. 1); 10 pawns, and 35 cards containing QR codes (Fig. 2).

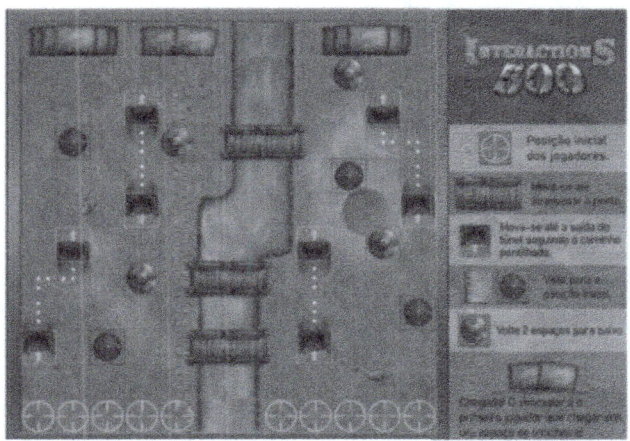

Fig. 1. The physical game board, which can be attached to the classroom board, contains paths, challenges, and shortcuts leading to the finish.

---

[2] https://unity.com/.

[3] https://developer.vuforia.com/home.

Fig. 2. Game card featuring a 2D pattern that the app can recognize and map to both a question and a corresponding 3D object in augmented reality.

4.1 Playing the Game

At the beginning of the game, players must determine, through a draw, their starting points in the positions marked as "Posição inicial dos jogadores" on the board (Fig. 1). They must also establish the order in which the pieces move. Each player will then use a mobile device to access the app.

Players can choose some options from the main screen (Fig. 3). To start the game, they must draw a card from the 35 available (the same card will be used by all players in the round) and click on "Jogar", which is the play button. The application will then use the mobile device's camera to scan the card's 2D pattern. Depending on the card, the app may display a 3D model of an organic molecule using AR, linked to the question's context. Finally, players should click the "Question" button to view the corresponding question (Fig. 4).

The text of the statement can be viewed in Portuguese or Libras, with the player choosing to select the language by clicking on the helmets that appear in the upper right part of the screen (Fig. 4). The player must classify the statement as true ("Verdadeiro" in Portuguese) or false ("Falso" in Portuguese) by pressing the corresponding "V" or "F" buttons.

Then, the student must click the confirm button to check if the answer is correct (Fig. 4). Those who answer correctly must point their mobile device's camera at the physical board and move their pieces one space in the direction indicated by the app. The player will not move on the board if the answer is incorrect. After the move, if the player lands on a space with an obstacle (e.g., bombs in Fig. 1), they must move back two spaces on the board or return to the starting position, depending on the type of trap that affected them. And if they land on a tunnel entrance, they must move to the other end, progressing in the game map.

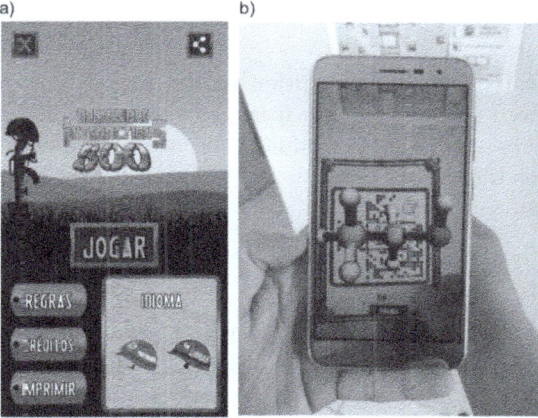

Fig. 3. The figure shows two screens from the game. On the left, we see the start screen with the options to play ("Jogar"), access to the game rules ("Regras"), access the PDF containing the game cards to be printed ("Imprimir"), and view the game creators' credits ("Créditos"). The second screen shows the Augmented Reality feature displaying a 3D animation of a molecule that will be the subject of the game's question.

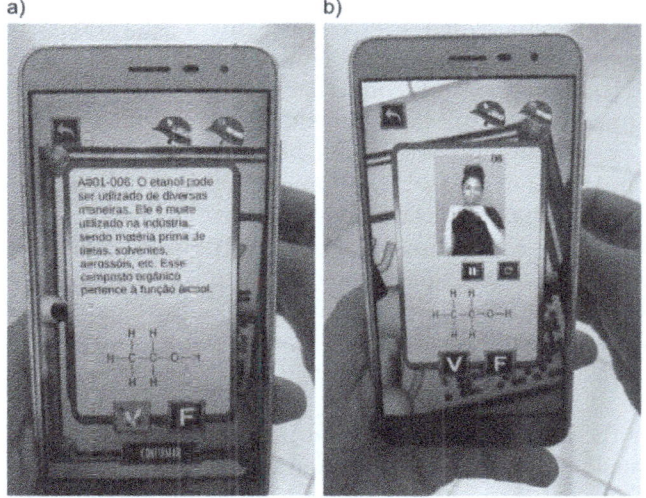

Fig. 4. An example of a chemistry question associated with a card, along with the corresponding Libras video in case the student wants a translation.

The player must click the "Next" button to move on to the next round. The game's winner will be the first player to reach the top of the board. An example of a gameplay video is available at the link below[4].

---

[4] https://shorturl.at/Azxd7.

5 Evaluation

To assess the effectiveness and reception of the proposed game, a study was conducted with high school students from a Professional Education Center in Brazil. The primary goal was to evaluate the usability/player experience and learning impact of the game, particularly focusing on its inclusivity for DHH and hearing students.

5.1 Subjects

The study involved 21 third-year high school students, comprising six deaf and 15 hearing participants. 6 deaf students were all over 18 years old, with one male. The other 15 students, with only eight over 18 years old, included 10 women and five men. All hearing and deaf students were fluent in Libras, attending the same educational level in the same classroom. They had previously received formal instruction on organic chemistry, which served as the foundation for the game content.

5.2 Procedure

To evaluate whether the game is a complementary educational tool that can assist students in their learning, we conducted an experimental study using a controlled pre-test and post-test, consisting of 13 questions, later comparing the number of correct answers for each student.

The pre-test was administered to all 21 students, and one week before its administration, the students had a 110-min lecture on organic chemistry. This test aimed to verify students' learning on the topic.

The post-test was also administered to all 21 students after administering the game and the MEEGA+ questionnaire. The objective of the post-test was to verify whether there was a significant difference in the students' learning of organic chemistry when using the game as an alternative method of reviewing content compared to the teaching they had constructed during the traditional lecture class.

Soon after the post-test, usability and user experience were evaluated using the printed version of the MEEGA+ questionnaire [35], containing nine statements with answers based on a Likert scale [29] to evaluate usability (regarding aesthetics, learnability, operability, and accessibility), and 22 statements to assess the player's experience (regarding confidence, challenge, satisfaction, social interaction, fun, focused attention, relevance, and Perceived Learning).

Figure 5 summarizes the methodology used to evaluate learning.

Fig. 5. Methodology used to assess the instructional role of the game.

6 Results and Discussion

6.1 Learning Impact

When we compared the results of the pretest with the posttest, we observed that five deaf students improved, and 1 had a much worse grade, which may have disturbed the results of the analysis (Fig. 6-a). Regarding hearing students, six of them improved their grades, six worsened, and three maintained similar grades (Fig. 6-b).

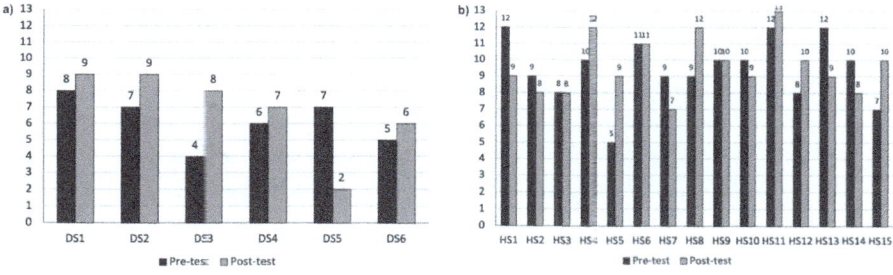

Fig. 6. Post-test results: a) deaf students and b) hearing students.

Despite the small sample, a paired t-test was performed to check whether there was a significant difference between the pretest and posttest results, with a significance level of $p < 0.05$ ($p < 0.05$ indicates a statistically significant difference between the groups; $p > 0.05$ suggests that there is no statistically significant difference between the groups). For both hearing and deaf students, the results showed no significant differences.

However, not all students improved their scores on the post-test; it is clear that the average grade has improved. Therefore, new studies are needed to understand the impact of long-term use of the game on learning.

6.2 Perception and Acceptance

All 21 students answered the MEEGA+ questionnaire (Figs. 7 and 8). Of the nine items related to usability, 7 (78%) received exclusively positive and indifferent expectations. An example of this was item 2, which concerns the colors of texts

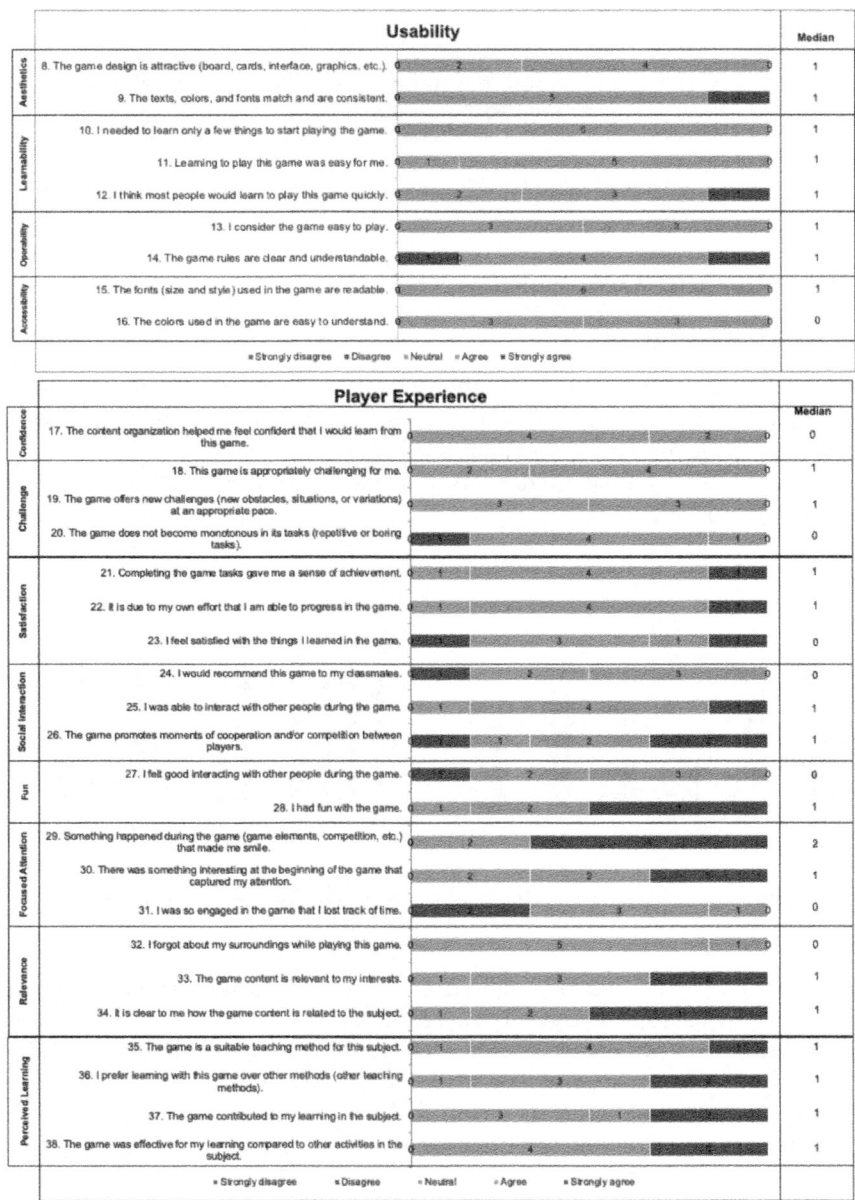

Fig. 7. MEEGA+ questionnaire results - deaf participants.

and fonts, which received approval from 100% of deaf people and 93% of hearing people. Likewise, item 8, related to font size and style, was approved by 83% of deaf and 100% of hearing people.

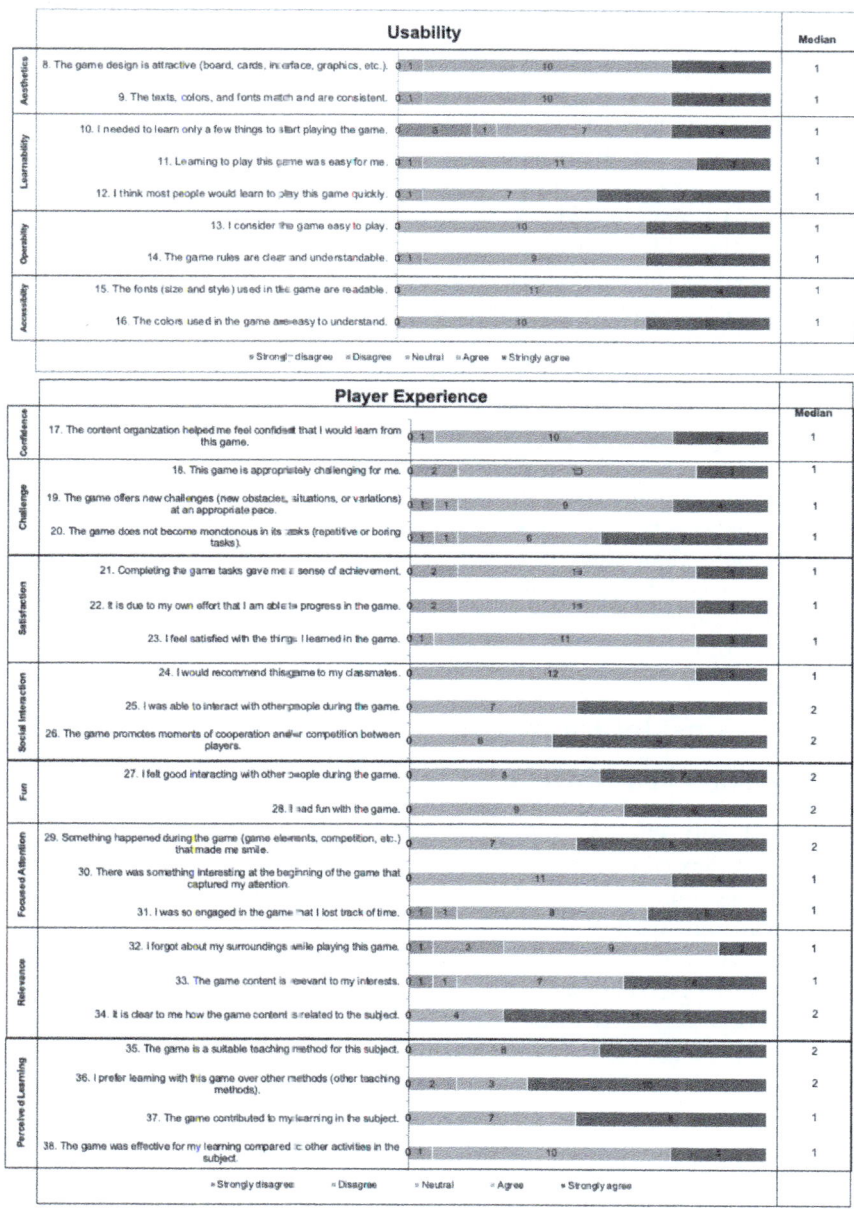

Fig. 8. MEEGA+ questionnaire results - hearing participants.

Regarding the player experience comprising 22 items, 13 (59%) received only positive and indifferent reviews. An example is item 22, which is related to smiling during the game and received 100% approval from deaf and hearing people. Likewise, item 27, which refers to the relationship between the game and the discipline, received approval from 83% of deaf people and 100% of hearing people.

In general, responses to item 31 demonstrated high levels of agreement, with many participants agreeing or agreeing strongly with the statements. Considering the other answers still, results indicate that the game is perceived as dynamic, fun, and easy to play, in addition to having an attractive design that captures players' attention. The game questions are clear and well-designed, covering the content studied in class. Furthermore, students agree that the game represents an innovative teaching tool capable of helping them review organic chemistry.

It is worth noting that the differences in acceptance of some items in the MEEGA+ questionnaire between deaf and non-deaf individuals may be related to greater difficulty in collecting the data; deaf individuals marked the indifferent option more often and may have misinterpreted the pictograms associated with the items.

Despite the inconclusive results regarding the learning impact, the acceptance of students suggests that the game was well-received in terms of user experience. But, much more than that, it is clear that the engagement promoted by the game, allowing collaboration between deaf and hearing students, has a much stronger effect than the act of "teaching", contributing to greater motivation for everyone to "study".

7   Final Considerations

7.1   Takeaways and Insights

Games are highly effective educational tools, allowing students to playfully assimilate complex content while encouraging discussion, resulting in deeper collective learning. Our game has been very well received as an educational tool by both deaf and hearing students. Although the learning outcomes between participants did not show statistically significant differences, with an outlier result among the DHH students and mixed results among the hearing ones, the proposal of this work is relevant. Creating an inclusive hybrid game with Augmented Reality elements represents a significant advance in developing accessible educational tools, promoting engagement and active participation of all.

7.2   Threats to Validity and Limitations

This study presents some factors that may have compromised the results obtained. One of them is the fact that the subjects selected for the evaluations were not chosen randomly. The evaluations were also not carried out with a control group to compare the effects of the game with other traditional teaching methodologies. Therefore, the context in which the results were applied still prevents the generalization of the results.

However, this does not invalidate the results since it is easy to note that the game promoted the participation of deaf students, actively collaborating with those hearing ones. It only indicates a clear need to carry out more studies to evaluate how to promote the inclusion of deaf people seeking to ensure learning gains for them, and also hearing ones.

7.3 Future Works

Using games to promote the inclusion of deaf people is a latent demand that increasingly requires studies and applied research. Thus, even with inconclusive results, the pedagogical and inclusive potential of the solution presented in this paper justifies its continuation and deepening in future studies. So, it is interesting to conduct more evaluations of the proposed game, focusing on other metrics and with a broader target audience. These efforts should minimize the limitations and threats to the validity of the results achieved, ultimately leading to a deeper understanding of the game's educational and inclusive impact. In the medium term, inserting more cards and AR elements is desirable, providing a greater variety of content to be explored during gameplay.

Acknowledgments. This research was partially supported by the Brazilian National Council for Scientific and Technological Development (Conselho Nacional de Desenvolvimento Científico e Tecnológico [CNPq]), under grant numbers 314425/2021-7 and 406318/2023-9, and the Strategic Funding (ref. 2024.00475.BD) through the Portuguese National Funding Agency for Science, Research, and Technology (Fundação para a Ciência e a Tecnologia [FCT]).

References

1. Ali, N.A., Sadiq, M.H., Albabawat, A.A., Salah, R.M.: Methods and applications of augmented reality in education: a review. In: 2022 International Conference on Computer Science and Software Engineering (CSASE), pp. 175–181 (2022). https://doi.org/10.1109/CSASE51777.2022.9759807
2. Alshawabkeh, A.A., Woolsey, M.L., Kharbat, F.F.: Using online information technology for deaf students during covid-19: a closer look from experience. Heliyon **7**(5) (2021)
3. Arjoranta, J., Kankainen, V., Nummenmaa, T.: Blending in hybrid games: understanding hybrid games through experience. In: Proceedings of the 13th International Conference on Advances in Computer Entertainment Technology, pp. 1–6 (2016)
4. Atanan, Y., Sombunsukho, S., Boonlue, S.: E-future classroom: a study mixed reality learning environment for deaf learners in Thailand. Int. J. Environ. Sci. Educ. **12**(10), 2291–2315 (2017)
5. Balaban, A.T., Klein, D.J.: Is chemistry 'the central science'? How are different sciences related? Co-citations, reductionism, emergence, and posets. Scientometrics **69**(3), 615–637 (2006)
6. Beardsley, K.D.: Chemistry cross-word puzzle. J. Chem. Educ. **2**(1), 90 (1925). https://doi.org/10.1021/ed002p90

7. Berns, A., Isla-Montes, J.L., Palomo-Duarte, M., Dodero, J.M.: Motivation, students' needs and learning outcomes: a hybrid game-based app for enhanced language learning. Springerplus **5**, 1–23 (2016)
8. Brown, T.L.: Chemistry: the Central Science. Pearson Education (2009)
9. Chao, F.L., Feng, C.S., Fanjiang, B., Sun, C.L.: Design jigsaw puzzle and app for nostalgia-based support on elderly with dementia. In: 2017 IEEE 8th International Conference on Awareness Science and Technology (iCAST), pp. 284–289. IEEE (2017)
10. Chen, M.P., Wong, Y.T., Wang, L.C.: Effects of type of exploratory strategy and prior knowledge on middle school students' learning of chemical formulas from a 3D role-playing game. Educ. Tech. Res. Dev. **62**, 163–185 (2014)
11. Demuth, H.: Chemastery. J. Chem. Educ. **25**(8), 459 (1948)
12. Escudeiro, P., Escudeiro, N., Gouveia, M.C.: A chemistry inclusive and educational serious game. In: 2022 31st Annual Conference of the European Association for Education in Electrical and Information Engineering (EAEEIE), pp. 1–6. IEEE (2022)
13. Fernandes, N., Leite Junior, A.J.M., Marçal, E., Viana, W.: Augmented reality in education for people who are deaf or hard of hearing: a systematic literature review. Universal Access Inf. Soc. **23**(3), 1483–1502 (2024)
14. Gesser, A.: Libras, que língua é essa? Parábola Editorial (2009)
15. Gomes, E.A., Catão, V., Soares, C.P.: Articulação do conhecimento em museus de ciências na busca por incluir estudantes surdos: analisando as possibilidades para se contemplar a diversidade em espaços não formais de educação. Experiências em Ensino de Ciências **10**(1), 81–97 (2015)
16. da Hora Correia, P.C., Neves, B.C.: A escuta visual: a educação de surdos e a utilização de recurso visual imagético na prática pedagógica. Revista Educação Especial **32**, 1–19 (2019)
17. Huizinga, J.: Homo Ludens ILS 86. Routledge (2014)
18. Ioannou, A., Constantinou, V.: Augmented reality supporting deaf students in mainstream schools: two case studies of practical utility of the technology. In: Auer, M.E., Tsiatsos, T. (eds.) IMCL 2017. AISC, vol. 725, pp. 387–396. Springer, Cham (2018). https://doi.org/10.1007/978-3-319-75175-7_39
19. James, H.: Chemical bank. J. Chem. Educ. **6**(10), 1790 (1929)
20. Kankainen, V., Paavilainen, J.: Hybrid board game design guidelines. In: Digra Conference (2019)
21. Kasapakis, V., Gavalas, D.: Revisiting design guidelines for pervasive games. Int. J. Pervasive Comput. Commun. **13**(4), 386–407 (2017)
22. Kavak, N., Yamak, H.: Picture Chem: playing a game to identify laboratory equipment items and describe their use. J. Chem. Educ. **93**(7), 1253–1255 (2016)
23. Kitchenham, B., Brereton, O.P., Budgen, D., Turner, M., Bailey, J., Linkman, S.: Systematic literature reviews in software engineering-a systematic literature review. Inf. Softw. Technol. **51**(1), 7–15 (2009)
24. Kosa, M., Spronck, P.: What tabletop players think about augmented tabletop games: a content analysis. In: Proceedings of the 13th International Conference on the Foundations of Digital Games, pp. 1–8 (2018)
25. Kucukkal, T.G., Kahveci, A.: PChem challenge game: reinforcing learning in physical chemistry. J. Chem. Educ. **96**(6), 1187–1193 (2019)
26. Li, L., He, T.: Card lab: an educational game to support chemistry laboratory learning. J. Chem. Educ. **100**(1), 192–198 (2022)
27. Li, M.C., Tsai, C.C.: Game-based learning in science education: a review of relevant research. J. Sci. Educ. Technol. **22**, 877–898 (2013)

28. Lianda, R.L.P., et al.: O aprendiz surdo e a química/deaf students and learning of chemistry. Holos **5**, 1–19 (2020)
29. Likert, R.: A technique for the measurement of attitudes. Arch. Psychol. (1932)
30. Lowdermilk, T.: User-Centered Design: A Developer's Guide to Building User-Friendly Applications. O'Reilly Media, Inc. (2013)
31. Luna, S.M., et al.: Communication, collaboration, and coordination in a co-located shared augmented reality game: perspectives from deaf and hard of hearing people. In: Proceedings of the 2024 CHI Conference on Human Factors in Computing Systems, pp. 1–14 (2024)
32. Martins, P., Rodrigues, H., Rocha, T., Francisco, M., Morgado, L.: Accessible options for deaf people in e-learning platforms: technology solutions for sign language translation. Procedia Comput. Sci. **67**, 263–272 (2015)
33. Oh, S., So, H.J., Gaydos, M.: Hybrid augmented reality for participatory learning: the hidden efficacy of multi-user game-based simulation. IEEE Trans. Learn. Technol. **11**(1), 115–127 (2017)
34. Paiva, F., Mendonça, G., Viana, W.: A systematic mapping of hybrid games in the academy. In: Extended Proceedings of the XXI Brazilian Symposium on Games and Digital Entertainment, pp. 128–137. SBC (2022)
35. Petri, G., Gresse von Wangenheim, C., Borgatto, A.F.: MEEGA+, systematic model to evaluate educational games. In: Lee, N. (ed.) Encyclopedia of Computer Graphics and Games, pp. 1112–1119. Springer, Cham (2024). https://doi.org/10.1007/978-3-319-08234-9_214-1
36. Raminhos, C., Cláudio, A.P., Carmo, M.B., Carvalhosa, S., de Jesus Candeias, M., Gaspar, A.: A serious game-based solution to prevent bullying. In: Proceedings of the 13th International Conference on Advances in Mobile Computing and Multimedia, pp. 63–72 (2015)
37. Reyes-Cárdenas, F.D.M., Cafaggi Lemus, C.E., Llano Lomas, M.G.: Evaluación y aprendizaje basado en habilidades de pensamiento en un curso de laboratorio de química general. Educación química **30**(3), 79–91 (2019)
38. Salomia, A., Ciupe, A., Meza, S., Orza, B., Trifan, G.: Assistive AR technology for hearing impairments in driving lessons. In: 2018 IEEE International Conference on Automation, Quality and Testing, Robotics (AQTR), pp. 1–6. IEEE (2018)
39. da Silva, A.M.: Proposta para tornar o ensino de química mais atraente. Rev. Quim. Ind. **711**(7) (2011)
40. da Silva, J.N., Teotonio, M.D.S.C., Silveira Juca, R.C., Castro, G.D.L., Melo Leite, A.J.: 1925–2024: one century of educational games in chemistry. J. Chem. Educ. **102**(4), 1492–1510 (2025)
41. da Silva Júnior, J.N., et al.: Interactions 500: design, implementation, and evaluation of a hybrid board game for aiding students in the review of intermolecular forces during the covid-19 pandemic. J. Chem. Educ. **97**(11), 4049–4054 (2020)
42. da Silva Junior, J.N., et al.: Nomenclature bets: an innovative computer-based game to aid students in the study of nomenclature of organic compounds (2018)
43. Smith, S.G., Chabay, R.: Computer games in chemistry. J. Chem. Educ. **54**(11), 688 (1977)
44. Tekinbas, K., Zimmerman, E.: Rules of Play: Game Design Fundamentals. ITPro Collection. MIT Press (2003). https://books.google.com.br/books?id=UMxyczrZuQC
45. Van Vleet, R.C.: Crossword puzzles in Hollywood high school. J. Chem. Educ. **2**(4), 292 (1925). https://doi.org/10.1021/ed002p292

46. Vanbecelaere, S., Van den Berghe, K., Cornillie, F., Sasanguie, D., Reynvoet, B., Depaepe, F.: The effects of two digital educational games on cognitive and non-cognitive math and reading outcomes. Comput. Educ. **143**, 103680 (2020)
47. Vargas, J.A., García-Mundo, L., Genero, M., Piattini, M.: A systematic mapping study on serious game quality. In: Proceedings of the 18th International Conference on Evaluation and Assessment in Software Engineering, pp. 1–10 (2014)
48. Zarraonandia, T., Montero, A., Diaz, P., Aedo, I.: "Magic Flowerpot": an AR game for learning about plants. In: Extended Abstracts of the Annual Symposium on Computer-Human Interaction in Play Companion Extended Abstracts, pp. 813–819 (2019)
49. Zubek, R.: Elements of Game Design. MIT Press (2020)

Mnema: Bridging Research and Art to Combat Gender Inequity in the Gaming Sector

Luciana Lima[1,2]([✉]) [iD], Inês Costa[3] [iD], Carolina Bonzinho[3] [iD], Sheila Correia[3] [iD], and Carolina Martins[4] [iD]

[1] Interactive Technologies Institute (ITI/LARSyS), Lisbon, Portugal
luciana.lima@tecnico.ulisboa.pt
[2] University of Lisbon, Lisbon, Portugal
[3] Porto, Portugal
[4] Infinity Games, Lisbon, Portugal
https://iti.larsys.pt/member/luciana-lima/

Abstract. This paper describes the collaborative work of women artists and researchers in Human-Computer Interaction and gender studies who were involved in the creation of the animated short film entitled Mnema. Drawing from interviews with eight Portuguese women in the video game industry and an analysis of archives documenting the rise of gaming culture in Portugal, the film incorporates elements of video game language and aesthetics to highlight the experiences of cisgender women in this male-dominated field. Mnema is an audiovisual creative endeavour that establishes a link between the testimonies of real women and fictional storytelling, aiming to raise awareness about the cycle of exclusion of women in the digital games industry and envision a change in this sector, while translating academic research into a docufiction video artwork.

Keywords: Collaborative research · Gender equity · Animated film

1 Introduction

"I think we have passed the stage of saying it is a problem. While it is undeniable that the problem still exists. I think we are now at a point where we need to focus on solutions, and that is often the hardest part." This statement from a Portuguese professional in the gaming industry refers to the ongoing cycle of exclusion faced by women (or rather, anyone who does not identify as a cisgender man) in this industry.

Over the last decades, many voices have complained about the micro-processes that exclude women and other people who do not fit into the standards of gender, race/ethnicity, age and sexual orientation established in this sector. In the late 20th century, for example, Cassel and Jenkins [6] pointed out how the

---

I. Costa, C. Bonzinho and S. Correia—Independent Researcher.

T. Darin et al. (Eds.): WIPlay 2025, CCIS 2623, pp. 67–83, 2026.
https://doi.org/10.1007/978-3-032-01426-9_5

design and advertising of children's games in the 1980s and 1990s meant designing computer games for a male audience, with the result that game companies denied the existence of female gamers. Kafai and colleagues [11] highlighted how gender stereotypes reinforced the assumption that girls and women were not interested in games and/or did not play. Studies by Carr [5], Cote [7], Shaw [19], and Kowert, Breuer and Quandt [12] have also contributed to the understanding that the differences between male and female gamers reflect patterns of access to and consumption of games according to the cultural and social practices in which they are embedded, as well as power structures and the hegemonic nature of the industry that exclude people who are not aligned with the hegemonic masculinity embedded in Western gaming culture. In addition, other research suggests that exclusion and sexism in gaming culture are socialized from an early age, with different expectations and interests encouraged for boys and girls [20].

Lima and colleagues [16] concluded that even though girls are exposed to the toxicity of gamer culture from the moment they start playing games, they maintain an interest in digital games and become fans of gaming culture. However, they do not intend to pursue a profession in the field of digital games or work in the gaming industry, which reveals how gender stereotypes and the microprocesses of exclusion of women in this sector have repercussions on their career aspirations in the gaming industry.

Thus, addressing and combating this cycle of exclusion is a priority for many researchers, activists, journalists, and professionals within the gaming sector. We are adding our voices to this effort. In this paper, we will explore how a group of women artists and researchers based in Portugal are fostering discussion and raising awareness about the challenges faced by women in the Portuguese digital games industry through various research outcomes, including an animated short film.

At the outset, we considered how best to disseminate the results of our academic research to non-specialist audiences, including younger people and Portuguese-speaking communities. We chose animation as our primary visual language to interpret and communicate the complexity of our findings. This decision was especially fitting, given that many of the women we interviewed had been hired by digital games companies to create 2D and 3D animations, as well as character and environment illustrations. This animated film, therefore, emerged as both a creative and socially engaged response. In other words, an arts-based approach aimed at raising awareness and making our research more accessible and engaging for a wider audience.

To that end, we developed Mnema, an animated film that blends fiction and non-fiction storytelling. The testimonies of the participants were foregrounded, providing them the visibility and narrative weight they deserve. The film specifically focuses on the lived experiences and challenges of eight Portuguese women in the gaming industry, selected from a larger group interviewed by the first author as part of a funded academic research project. This artistic project began in March 2023 and had a first screening for the film's sponsor and colleagues at our research center in May 2024.

This paper makes a threefold contribution. First, by detailing the creation process of the animated film Mnema, we explore how interdisciplinary and arts-based academic research can follow the logic of horizontality, participatory research, and, above all, collaboration. In this artwork project, the process of film creation was fully shared among all participants, encouraging "the building [of] environments where all kinds of people are welcome, are treated fairly, and have an equal opportunity for participation and agency" [9, p. 481]. Second, this project may inspire other researchers and artists to develop works that incorporate new uses of animation as a social tool, opening pathways for creatively engaging with game-inspired animated films. Our visual project draws heavily on the aesthetics and culture of video games.

Finally, the interdisciplinary and collaborative approach used in this project is particularly relevant to the HCI research community, especially to humanistic HCI researchers [3,4], who engage with critical, creative, and socially transformative research practices [2,8]. By leveraging arts-based research, this work contributes to a growing recognition of artistic practices as rigorous modes of knowledge production within HCI and beyond.

Besides the introduction, this paper is organized into three key sections. First, we provide an overview of the Portuguese digital games industry and offer a brief contextualization of the research that informed the creation of Mnema. This background is essential to understanding the socio-professional landscape in which the women's testimonies are situated. Next, we detail the process of creating the animated film, describing each phase, from pre-production to post-production, as a collaborative, interdisciplinary, and arts-based research practice. Here, we emphasize the methodological decisions, aesthetic influences, and collective dynamics that shaped the final work. Lastly, we conclude with reflections on the outcomes of the project and discuss potential directions for future work, both in terms of Mnema's dissemination and the broader conversation around this theme.

Throughout the paper, the testimonies of the women interviewed will serve as a narrative thread, illustrating and deepening the themes explored in each section. Their voices are central to the film and to this paper, not only as sources of data but as active agents in the co-creation of meaning through visual storytelling.

2 Portugal's Game Development Scene: An Overview and the Research Behind the Film Mnema

In recent years, the Portuguese digital games industry has experienced notable growth, supported by an increasing number of small to mid-sized studios, government funding opportunities, and international collaborations. While still developing in comparison to larger European markets, Portugal's gaming sector has demonstrated a growing interest in narrative innovation, artistic expression, and cross-disciplinary experimentation. Despite this progress, the industry remains characterized by significant gender disparities, both in terms of representation and workplace experience. When, in 2021, one of the women we interviewed said, *"the Portuguese video game industry is small and, because there aren't many job positions, many Portuguese qualified professionals go abroad,"* she was referring to what she (and other participants) described as a homebrew and leisure industry. According to these accounts, the sector was composed largely of small indie studios that struggled to attract investment and was not recognized by the Portuguese government as a profitable or strategically important creative industry. This perception was echoed by multiple interviewees, who expressed frustration over limited local opportunities and the lack of institutional support.

Although frequently described as "fragmented and small," the Portuguese gaming industry is not insignificant in scale. As of 2023, it included 51 active studios (see Fig. 1) and generated a revenue of 48.6 million euros, according to the National Statistics Institute. Between 2016 and 2020, the Portuguese Society of Video Game Sciences published two major reports mapping and characterizing the industry and its workforce. These reports documented steady growth

Fig. 1. Map of Portugal, including mainland and the Azores and Madeira islands, providing an overview of the distribution of active game development studios. Source: Spotlight Magazine, Issue 02, 2024, published by *Game Dev Lisbon* (For a detailed view and further information, refer to the original publication available at https://gamedevlisbon.com.).

in the number of qualified professionals while also revealing persistent gender imbalance. The latest figures suggest that between 986 and 1,270 individuals were employed in the sector, with approximately 97% of companies reporting an overwhelmingly male workforce [18].

To the best of our knowledge, there is currently no updated or official data on the demographic profile of workers in the sector, largely due to a lack of continuity in data collection through industry-wide surveys. However, academic research by Pinto [17] and Lima [15] further characterizes the industry as young, male-dominated, and highly educated. Pinto [17] also points to structural limitations, such as low wages and a relatively underdeveloped support ecosystem, that compel many professionals to seek better opportunities abroad or to diversify their income sources.

Despite these limitations, the sector benefits from a growing number of higher education programs in games and multimedia, which are steadily expanding the talent pool. In 2021, the same year the Association of Portuguese Video Game Producers was founded, approximately 7,100 students were enrolled in academic programs related to game development or digital media, according to *Portugalglobal* magazine [1]. This educational infrastructure suggests a strong foundation for future growth, although concerns remain regarding the retention of talent and the inclusivity of the industry.

It was within this context that our research project emerged, seeking to center the voices of women working in Portuguese game development, particularly in creative and visual roles often marginalized in industry discourse. The qualitative interviews conducted during the study revealed a shared experience of precariousness, resilience, and creative innovation.

Freelancing is a widespread practice in Portugal's game development sector, with many professionals working as independent contractors, part-time collaborators, or project-based contributors [17]. This model of employment reflects both the flexibility and the precarity of the industry, especially for those in creative roles such as artists, animators, and designers. The rise of remote work, accelerated by the COVID-19 pandemic, has reshaped the professional landscape, enabling Portuguese game developers to collaborate with international teams and studios. Remote work has, in many cases, allowed professionals to circumvent the limitations of the domestic job market, offering access to a wider range of opportunities, creative projects, and income sources [16].

Despite these adaptive strategies, the local industry's structural challenges continue to affect long-term professional stability and visibility, particularly for underrepresented groups. Women working in animation and game art often navigate a landscape where freelance arrangements and remote contracts may limit opportunities for career advancement, visibility, or leadership roles within companies. This highlights the need not only for economic investment but also for inclusive policies and institutional accountability that prioritize equity within the sector.

One recent development aiming to address some of these systemic gaps is the launch of the *eGames Lab* in 2022. Backed by approximately 30 million euros from the Recovery and Resilience Plan[1], the *eGames Lab* is a national consortium that brings together technology companies, universities, and game development studios. Its mission is *"to position Portugal as a competitive player in the global digital games market."*[2] its objectives are the internationalization of the Portuguese games sector by 2025, the promotion of locally developed games, and the attraction of international investment and talent.

While these ambitions mark an important step toward professionalizing and globalizing the national industry, the concrete impacts of the *eGames Lab* remain to be fully understood. At the time of writing, its contributions to reshaping employment practices, gender equity, and creative autonomy in the sector have not been systematically assessed. Further research will be necessary to evaluate how inclusive and effective this initiative is, particularly in relation to freelance professionals, emerging women developers, and other underrepresented voices within the Portuguese gaming ecosystem.

2.1   The Research Insights that Shaped Mnema

Between 2019 and 2022, the first author conducted empirical research involving both students and professionals in Portugal's digital gaming sector [13]. This included four focus groups with students enrolled in game development programs, as well as twenty-three semi-structured interviews with industry professionals (13 women and 10 men). Alongside this fieldwork, the research team also explored how information technology media narratives from the 1980s contributed to the historical marginalization and invisibility of women in electronic gaming and microcomputing in Portugal.

The findings reveal that issues of equity and diversity remain largely overlooked within the Portuguese gaming industry, where the primary focus is on fostering economic growth and international competitiveness. Among students in specialized training programs, there is limited engagement with gender-related issues or awareness of the structural barriers faced by women in the field. Efforts to address these gaps are largely driven by women already active within the game development community, underscoring a lack of institutional initiative.

The research also identified three widespread misconceptions about the gaming profession in Portugal: that game development inherently requires programming expertise; that it is an unprofitable or unstable career path; and that it is a field naturally suited to men. These misconceptions are deeply intertwined with gendered cultural narratives surrounding gaming. As one female participant reflected, *"Actually, being a geek, being a gamer, being all that was something to be ashamed of. You were ashamed of being a gamer, liking anime, ashamed*

---

[1] The Recovery and Resilience Plan (RRP) is an investment program funded by the European Union through the *NextGenerationEU* mechanism. It is intended to promote economic recovery following the COVID-19 pandemic. In Portugal, the RRP aims to foster sustainable growth through structural investments in areas such as digital transformation, climate transition, and social and economic resilience.

[2] Further information is available at https://egameslab.pt/.

of liking video games to the point where, in my case, I didn't want to work in it." Such narratives contribute to gendered socialization processes that alienate women from participating in the industry. Additionally, the tendency to frame game development as a purely technological domain reinforces the perception that it aligns more closely with boys' career aspirations, further discouraging girls from pursuing related paths.

The outcomes of this research were initially disseminated through conventional academic channels, including peer-reviewed journals, edited volumes, and conference presentations. However, the research team recognized the need to reach broader audiences and foster public dialogue around gender representation in the gaming industry. In addition to maintaining a project website and active social media presence, the team pursued innovative forms of outreach aimed at non-specialist publics. In 2023, with support from Atlantic Culture Promotion Agency (APCA Madeira) funding, the team launched the production of Mnema, an animated short film designed to translate key research findings into an accessible, emotionally resonant format. Thus, this arts-based initiative sought to challenge persistent gender stereotypes, raise awareness about the underrepresentation of those who do not identify as cisgender men, and advocate for a more inclusive and equitable future for the gaming sector.

3   Crafting Mnema: A Behind-the-Scenes Journey from Pre-production to Post

This section provides detailed insights into our collaborative work and the effort involved in bringing Mnema to fruition, including activities, processes, and actions that occurred in producing this animated short film.

3.1   Mind Map and Storyboard

As mentioned before, this artwork project took shape after APCA Madeira funded the film in March 2023. At that point, one of the filmmakers (the second author) was already a collaborator in the Game Art and Gender Equity (GAGE)[3] research project. Subsequently, Inês Costa assumed responsibility for assembling the film production team, inviting two of this paper's co-authors (Carolina Bonzinho and Sheila Correia) and an additional audio designer (João Beleza) to join what would become the Mnema film team.

Guided by a culture of collaborative and interdisciplinary research [10], which emphasizes the convergence of diverse forms of knowledge and creative practice [14], all stages of the film's production were shared among the team members, reflecting a commitment to non-hierarchical collaboration. The creative process behind Mnema was structured around a virtual, collaborative workspace and centered on the decoupage of pre-existing research interviews.

It is important to note that the original interviews, conducted via Zoom by the first author, were not initially intended for cinematic purposes; thus,

---

[3] More information about GAGE Project at https://gage1.webflow.io/.

the technical quality of the audio was not prioritized during data collection. These interviews, ranging in duration from 36 to 110 min, were carried out with Portuguese women working in the video game industry, both within Portugal and abroad.

The interview recordings were shared with the filmmakers to allow them to engage deeply with the research material and inform their creative decisions. In line with the project's objective to foreground female perspectives, eight interviews were selected, all involving women who were professionally active in the games industry at the time. Prior to incorporating excerpts into the film, participants were contacted to inform them of the project's new direction. The team ensured that ethical considerations, including participants' anonymity and the confidentiality of their testimonies, were rigorously upheld throughout the creative process.

Following the decoupage of the interview material, we organized the content using a mind map within the digital collaboration platform Miro. This process facilitated the development of an organizational framework, in which the interview excerpts were systematically categorized and subsequently distilled into a set of key thematic areas. It is important to emphasize the central role played by the Miro digital whiteboard throughout the production of Mnema. As an accessible and flexible collaborative tool, Miro functioned as a shared creative space, enabling team members to contribute ideas, structure and refine thematic categories, and document the evolving trajectory of the film. This platform supported both analytical and creative processes, fostering a dynamic environment for interdisciplinary co-creation.

The development of Mnema's storyboard emerged through regular collaborative exchanges among team members, during which notes, reflections, and creative suggestions were openly shared. This iterative process enabled the identification and refinement of the central themes to be addressed in the 10-minute animated short film. As thematic clarity increased, the team collectively decided to adopt a visual and narrative style inspired by the aesthetics and language of video games. This led to a creative brainstorming process in which we drew upon a wide range of gaming influences—from 1980s arcade classics to more recent independent titles. Notable references included the platforming dynamics of Super Mario (1985), the maze-like architecture of Pac-Man (1980), the linear storytelling of Mystery House (1980), the immersive atmosphere of Limbo (2010), and the exploratory mechanics of Journey (2012).

A particularly significant influence was Roberta Williams, creator of Mystery House and a pioneering figure in the use of computer graphics in game design. Her innovative approach informed both the narrative structure and visual composition of the storyboard. Our intention was to integrate recognizable video game aesthetics into the film's visual language in order to construct a fictional yet informative atmosphere—one that would be both accessible and engaging to a broad audience, including gaming enthusiasts. In doing so, we sought to deepen viewers' emotional connection to the narrative while addressing broader issues of representation in the gaming industry.

Through this game-inspired lens, the protagonist Mnema, confronts a series of challenges that metaphorically represent the structural and cultural barriers faced by people who do not identify as cisgender men within the gaming world. Her journey is populated by enigmatic creatures, labyrinths, obstacles, and mysterious doors that impede her progress. Each encounter functions as a metaphor for lived experiences of exclusion, while also offering opportunities for reflection and transformation. The narrative is guided by off-screen voices, which serve both as narrators and mentors, directing Mnema's actions and reinforcing the film's dialogic and pedagogical intentions.

The name Mnema is derived from Mnemosyne, a figure from Greek mythology, often known as the goddess of memory. Mnemosyne is particularly important because she personifies memory and the act of remembering, which is a crucial aspect of human experience and knowledge. She is also renowned for giving birth to the nine Muses (deities who inspire art, ideas, and creativity). The qualities associated with memory, artistic inspiration, and creativity align seamlessly with our protagonist. Moreover, this name encompasses the entire creative process, from the conception of an idea to the artistic work required to bring a story to life. Ultimately, Mnema also highlights the significance of memory, a vital element in understanding the present and shaping the future.

3.2   Mnema's Phases

The film unfolds in four phases. In the first phase, we introduce the character's oppression and fear, conveying her emotions without fully revealing the source of her distress. This phase symbolically aligns with the theme of deconstruction. The male gaze is subtly explored in a world of dark backgrounds and neon colors, where the character feels watched and judged, questioning everything around her. During this phase, Mnema enters a maze, marking the beginning of her journey and the obstacles she must overcome to progress. Driven by a blend of fear and curiosity, she finds the courage to move forward, determined to understand what's happening, even though she has not yet directly confronted the challenges before her.

In the second phase, we emphasize the social conditioning that dictates toy choices and entertainment based on gender. A giant doll appears, representing another villain from the character's fictional world (see Fig. 2). To move forward, she must face this challenge. The voices surrounding her influence her actions, helping her conquer the fear of being crushed by the towering doll. The video game console controller takes on a symbolic role here, representing the character's longing to engage with gaming culture without limitations or societal restrictions.

In the third phase of the film, we incorporate archival footage to confront Mnema with the lack of representation of people like her in the gaming world. She embarks on a path lined with doors that initially suggest opportunities, only to realize that these chances are not as accessible as they seem. The archival images reference stereotypical female characters, resembling the opening screens of video games where players select their avatars. These images depict hypersexualized women and helpless princesses, highlighting how these stereotypes permeate our imagination and create idealized bodies that we are expected to conform to.

Fig. 2. Art Study of the Mnema's phases. From left to right, top to bottom: (1) Mnema stares at a giant seated green doll; (2) Mnema walks along a path marked by green horizontal and vertical lines, with multiple doors; (3) Mnema encounters purple stone blocks with eyes and noses; (4) Mnema lies on the ground, looking sad; (5) Mnema walks in a gray meadow as small rocks fall from the sky; (6) Endless path with numerous green-shaded doors. (Color figure online)

The fourth phase focuses on collectivity and is marked by vibrant colors that evoke a sense of calm and security. Mnema discovers that she has control over her environment and is actively contributing to the creation of this world. It is a moment of creation and growth, where she explores the world, she is helping to build. The theme of collectivity is emphasized, with the world becoming more colorful as the character recognizes her involvement in a process of transformation and creation alongside others who share similar journeys.

3.3   Character Development

Mnema's appearance is minimalist yet expressive, characterized by soft, rounded shapes and smooth lines that give her an ethereal, graceful quality (see Fig. 3). This simplicity allows her emotions and actions to be conveyed through her body language, movements, and interactions with the world, making her feel like a non-binary figure who resonates with the emotional journey of all viewers. Her attire is simple, resembling a flowing gown or cover. In essence, Mnema's appearance is meant to evoke a sense of vulnerability, strength, and emotional transformation.

A key aspect of character development is the absence of dialogue. Her transformation is conveyed through the world around her and the voices that guide her, allowing viewers to connect with her journey by interpreting her actions and emotions through the film's art style, music, and progression.

Fig. 3. Mnema's appearance development, showing her whole body from front, back and side views, along with her face, hair, and different facial expressions.

At the start of the film, Mnema is physically fragile, struggling to move through the bleak, colorless world. Her movements are slow, and she lacks the abilities needed to navigate her surroundings. As the film progresses, the physical changes in her world, such as flowers blooming, rocks shifting, and structures rising from the ground, mirror her own growth, suggesting that she is not only evolving internally but is also actively shaping the world around her as she gains strength. Mnema's development is mirrored in the changing landscapes of her world. The initially barren, monochrome environment gradually blooms into vibrant color, symbolizing her empowerment. This shift in the environment parallels the protagonist's internal transformation, emphasizing that her growth is as much about her external world as it is about her internal one.

3.4 Compositing Strategies in Mnema: Stop-Motion Animation, Women's Voices, and Sound Design

The Mnema's scriptwriting and storyboard were subsequently transformed into an animatic (a digital version of the storyboard in which the timing of each keyframe is defined). During the pre-production phase, preliminary sketches of characters and sets were produced, alongside final art tests that helped establish the film's visual style and technical approach. Production constraints, however, significantly shaped the creative process. The project operated under a limited budget and a small team consisting of four members. While the initial plan was to employ digital frame-by-frame animation using the open-source software Krita, the intensive labor demands of this technique quickly proved unfeasible given the team size and time restrictions. Consequently, the animation method was revised to stop-motion, which offered a more manageable alternative through the use of articulated paper cut-outs. This approach not only simplified the animation process but also accelerated production without compromising the film's creative intent.

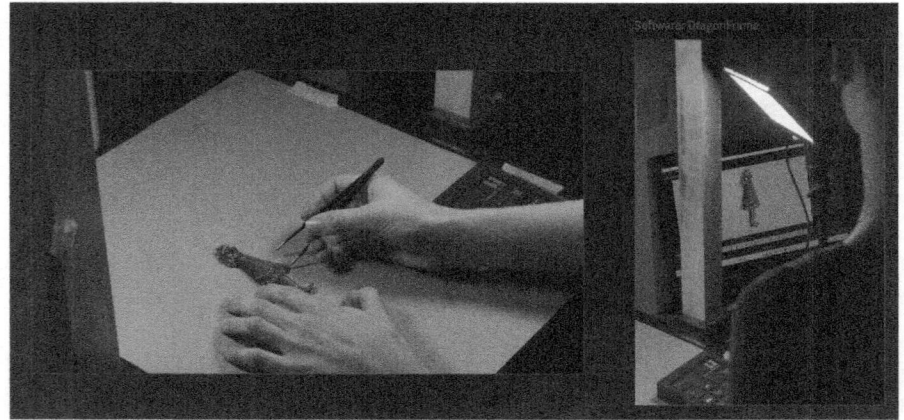

Fig. 4. Stop-Motion Animation. The image shows the hands of one of the film's directors using tweezers to gently move the cardboard model of Mnema.

The stop-motion technique required the manual construction of all sets and characters, primarily using cardboard and acetate. These elements were then arranged on a down-shooter multiplane animation stand and photographed using a camera connected to a computer running Dragonframe software (see Fig. 4). The animation itself was executed manually, with each cut-out incrementally repositioned and photographed at a frame rate of 12 frames per second[4]. This hands-on process lent a tactile quality to the final aesthetic, aligning with the project's commitment to artisanal production methods and interdisciplinary collaboration.

The shift from digital animation to stop-motion not only addressed practical constraints but also introduced new aesthetic and narrative dimensions to the

---

[4] The creation of an animated short film is an inherently intricate and time-intensive endeavor, requiring a sequence of images, typically ranging from 12 to 24 frames per second, to generate the illusion of motion.

film. The tactile quality of handcrafted elements, visible in the textures of cardboard, the transparency of acetate, and the physical layering of the multiplane setup, contributed to a unique visual identity that reinforces the themes of fragmentation, vulnerability, and resilience explored in the narrative. This analog approach contrasts with the digital worlds often associated with video games, prompting viewers to reflect on the materiality and labor behind creative production, particularly in contexts where resources are limited.

Moreover, the slower, more deliberate pacing inherent to stop-motion animation complemented the film's metaphorical journey, allowing viewers to engage more deeply with each symbolic obstacle encountered by the protagonist. The imperfections and slight variations between frames, characteristic of stop-motion, subtly echoed the emotional and experiential nuances of the testimonies on which the narrative is based. Thus, the shift in technique not only resolved logistical challenges but also enriched the film's expressive capacity, aligning its form with its content in a way that underscores the embodied and situated experiences of those marginalized within the gaming sector.

As Mnema navigates metaphorical challenges that represent real-world structural and cultural barriers, the viewer witnesses her transformation from uncertainty to empowerment. These narrative developments are further amplified by the original soundtrack[5], composed to reflect the protagonist's emotional states throughout her journey. The music accompanies each moment of tension, introspection, and triumph, underscoring the psychological depth of her experience. Notably, the soundtrack also incorporates audio elements reminiscent of classic video game sound effects, which serve as both aesthetic and symbolic bridges between the protagonist's story and the gaming culture she must navigate. Together, the stop motion animation and richly layered score form a cohesive audiovisual language that reinforces the central theme of overcoming marginalization through self-discovery and resilience. By integrating these elements, the film seeks not only to communicate its message but to evoke affective responses that invite reflection and identification, particularly among those who have faced (and are facing) exclusion in the gaming sector.

Finally, due to technical limitations in the original recordings of the interviews, many of which were conducted remotely over Zoom without professional audio equipment, the sound quality did not meet the standards required for integration into an animated film. As mentioned before, these recordings were never intended for audiovisual production, and as such, background noise, uneven audio levels, and poor clarity posed significant challenges during postproduction. In response, we invited some colleagues to reinterpret and give voice to the interview excerpts selected for the film. This choice, while initially pragmatic, became a creative and ethical strategy that honored the spirit of the original narratives while ensuring their intelligibility and emotional resonance

---

[5] João Beleza composed the soundtrack for Mnema. He holds a Master's in Electrical Engineering from the University of Porto (Portugal), specializing in programming, control systems, and analog/digital circuits. He blends engineering with music, developing audio circuits and performing award-winning harp solos and orchestral pieces.

within the animated medium. The use of reinterpretation also introduced a layer of collective voice, underscoring that the experiences shared by our interviewees are not isolated but reflective of broader structural issues faced by women in the gaming industry.

4 A Call for Change in the Gaming Sector: Work-in-Progress

The video game industry, once considered a niche form of entertainment, has evolved into a globally influential sector with a profound impact on billions of individuals worldwide. Despite significant advancements in technology, storytelling, and design, the industry continues to grapple with systemic challenges, particularly concerning equity, diversity, and inclusion. As highlighted by the women interviewed in our study, the sector remains marked by narrow representations of gender and race, both within game narratives and among those involved in their production. A growing body of literature has underscored how such limitations can marginalize players who seek characters and stories that resonate with their lived experiences. Enhancing representational diversity in games is not merely a matter of social justice, but also a critical step toward expanding the creative and cultural potential of the medium.

The Mnema project was conceived as a response to these concerns, aiming to inspire broader reflections on inclusion within the gaming landscape. As part of our outreach efforts, we have undertaken a series of dissemination and engagement activities that extend the film's impact beyond academic circles. Notable initiatives include:

- The release of the film's teaser on March 8, 2024 (International Women's Day) during a public event in Lisbon attended by stakeholders from the gaming industry and gender equity activists[6].
- Participation in a panel discussion in May 2024 in Funchal, Madeira, alongside the representative of the funding agency (APCA Madeira). The session brought together graduate students and game developers from Portuguese game companies, fostering dialogue between academia and industry.
- Presentation at a secondary school in Porto (North of Portugal) in January 2025, where the filmmakers shared the production process and thematic concerns of Mnema with younger audiences.

Looking ahead, we plan to further disseminate the Mnema project through a series of public-facing academic events intended to foster critical dialogue around the film's creative development. These events will adopt a conversational format and include curated displays of archival materials, stop-motion animation sequences, production photographs, and behind-the-scenes content. By foregrounding the process of collaborative, arts-based research, these sessions aim to enhance transparency and promote interdisciplinary reflection. In parallel, we

---

[6] https://iti.larsys.pt/game-art-and-gender-equity-closing-session/.

intend to offer participatory workshops inspired by the film's narrative and aesthetic. These workshops will encourage creative expression while supporting the acquisition of foundational digital media skills, particularly among younger and non-specialist audiences. The animated short is also currently under submission to national and international film festivals, with the goal of reaching diverse audiences and amplifying the project's impact beyond conventional academic channels.

These initiatives are part of a broader strategy to extend the social and educational reach of Mnema, using the film as a platform to initiate inclusive conversations around gender equity and representation in the gaming industry. Through community engagement, public programming, and pedagogical activities, we seek to promote socially engaged scholarship and to challenge prevailing narratives that marginalize underrepresented voices within digital game cultures.

5   Conclusion

Mnema emerges as both a creative and political gesture, combining empirical research, artistic experimentation, and interdisciplinary collaboration to address gender asymmetries in the Portuguese video game industry. By translating empirical research into a game-inspired animated short film, the project bridges academic inquiry and public engagement, offering a narrative that is at once accessible and critically grounded. The adoption of stop-motion animation, originally a response to limited resources, ultimately enriched the film's expressive capacity, lending it a distinct aesthetic that aligns with its themes of vulnerability, resilience, and transformation. The integration of gaming sound motifs into the original soundtrack further reinforces the dialogic relationship between the protagonist's fictional journey and the real-world experiences of those who face systemic exclusion in the gaming field.

Through its tactile visual language, evocative sound design, and metaphorical structure, Mnema invites audiences to reflect on how gendered socialization, professional stereotypes, and cultural norms shape women''s access to and participation in game development. More broadly, the film exemplifies how art-based research can function as a critical tool for social change, fostering dialogue beyond academic circles and challenging hegemonic narratives within the gaming industry. As such, Mnema is not only a product of research, but a visual poetic for reimagining who gets to play, create, and belong in the world of games.

The Mnema film's creation process involved full collaboration between us (authors of this paper). The digital collaborative platform Miro allowed the team to work in a flexible, non-linear way. While one or two members focused on decoupaging the interview, others were simultaneously researching animated documentaries, animations, and collecting aesthetic and sound references. Each phase of Mnema's development, from structuring the narrative to integrating game-inspired aesthetics, reflected practices commonly found in game design and interactive media production. These tools enabled team to collaborate across multiple layers, such as storylines, stages, and scenarios, all being developed in parallel.

Finally, this paper contributes to the HCI community by demonstrating how arts-based research methodologies, when combined with empirical data and interdisciplinary collaboration (see also [14]), can serve as powerful tools for exploring and addressing gender inequality in digital game development. Mnema exemplifies how alternative forms of knowledge production, such as animated storytelling and game aesthetics, can expand the ways in which HCI engages with issues of inclusion, representation, and cultural critique. By centering marginalized voices and translating their experiences into an accessible and affective medium, this work offers new pathways for participatory design, critical reflection, and public engagement within HCI scholarship and practice, particularly for those who focus on critical, creative, and socially transformative research methodologies.

Acknowledgments. We thank all the women who kindly shared their stories for the creation of the film Mnema, and Casa da Animação, Associação Cultural (Porto), for their support and equipment. We are also grateful to the Atlantic Agency for the Promotion of Culture (Madeira) for funding the film. This research was funded by the Portuguese Recovery and Resilience Program (PRR), through IAPMEI/ANI/FCT, under Agenda C645022399-00000057 (*eGames Lab*).

Disclosure of Interests. The authors have no competing interests to declare that are relevant to the content of this article.

References

1. Agência para o Investimento e Comércio Externo de Portugal: Indústria de video-jogos sobe de nível em portugal. Revista Portugalglobal (177) (2024)
2. Almeida, T., Balaam, M., Comber, R.: Woman-centered design through humanity, activism, and inclusion. ACM Trans. Comput.-Hum. Interact. **27**(4), 1–30 (2020). https://doi.org/10.1145/3397176
3. Bardzell, J., Bardzell, S.: Humanistic HCI and methods. In: Humanistic HCI. Synthesis Lectures on Human-Centered Informatics, pp. 33–64. Springer, Cham (2015). https://doi.org/10.1007/978-3-031-02214-2_3
4. Bardzell, J., Bardzell, S.: Humanistic HCI. Interactions **23**(2), 20–29 (2016). https://doi.org/10.1145/2888576
5. Carr, D.: Contexts, pleasures, and preferences: girls playing computer games. In: Weber, S., Dixon, S. (eds.) Growing Up Online, pp. 151–160. Palgrave Macmillan US, New York (2007). https://doi.org/10.1057/9780230607019_10
6. Cassell, J., Jenkins, H.: From Barbie® to Mortal Kombat: Gender and Computer Games. MIT Press (2000)
7. Cote, A.C.: Gaming Sexism: Gender and Identity in the Era of Casual Video Games. In: Gaming Sexism. New York University Press (2020). https://doi.org/10.18574/nyu/9781479838523.001.0001
8. Danilovic, S., Chee, K., Skop, M.: Playful resilience: empowering recovery through autobiographical game-based storytelling in the opioid epidemic. Proc. ACM Hum.-Comput. Interact. **8**(CHI PLAY), 1–35 (2024). https://doi.org/10.1145/3677095
9. Friman, U., Ruotsalainen, M., Ståhl, M.: Diversity, equity, and inclusion in esports. In: Routledge Handbook of Esports, pp. 540–550. Routledge (2024)

10. Gouveia, P., Lima, L., Unterholzner, A.: Interactive multimedia experiences in higher education: gaming, augment and virtual reality, and research. In: Handbook of Research on Acquiring 21st Century Literacy Skills through Game-Based Learning, pp. 180–193. IGI Global Scientific Publishing (2022). https://doi.org/10.4018/978-1-7998-7271-9.ch010

11. Kafai, Y.B., Heeter, C., Denner, J., Sun, J.Y.: Preface: Pink, purple, casual, or mainstream games: Moving. Beyond Barbie and Mortal Kombat: New Perspectives on Gender and Gaming (2011). https://doi.org/10.7551/mitpress/7477.003.0002

12. Kowert, R., Breuer, J., Quandt, T.: Women are from FarmVille, men are from ViceCity: the cycle of exclusion and sexism in video game content and culture. In: New Perspectives on the Social Aspects of Digital Gaming, pp. 136–150. Routledge (2017). https://doi.org/10.4324/9781315629308-9

13. Lima, L.: Pensar o Género a Partir dos Jogos Digitais: Uma Análise Sobre as Assimetrias de Género na Indústria Portuguesa de Jogos Digitais. Editora BAND, Porto (2023)

14. Lima, L., et al.: (in)visible women: multidisciplinary creation and collaborative research in transmedia art and gaming in Portugal In: Proceedings of the 29th International Symposium on Electronic Arts, vol. 1, pp. 451–458 (2024). https://doi.org/10.5204/book.eprints.256296

15. Lima, L., Gouveia, P.: Gender asymmetries in the digital games sector in Portugal. In: Abstract Proceedings of DiGRA 2020 Conference: Play Everywhere (2020). https://doi.org/10.26503/dl.v2020i1.1178

16. Lima, L., Gouveia, P., Cardoso, P., Pinto, C.: Never imagined I would work in the digital game industry. In: 2021 IEEE Conference on Games (CoG), pp. 1–7. IEEE (2021). https://doi.org/10.1109/CoG52621.2021.961913

17. Pinto, C.S.N.: Identidade profissional: o caso dos produtores de videojogos em Portugal. Master's thesis Faculdade de Letras, Universidade do Porto, Portugal (2019). https://hdl.handle.net/10216/124167

18. Romeiro, P., Nunes, F., Santos, P.A., Pinto, C.: Atlas do Setor dos Videojogos em Portugal (2). Sociedade Portuguesa de Ciências dos Videojogos, Lisboa (2020)

19. Shaw, A.: Gaming at the Edge: Sexuality and Gender at the Margins of Gamer Culture. University of Minnesota Press (2015)

20. Vermeulen, L., Bauwel, S.V., Looy, J.V.: Tracing female gamer identity. An empirical study into gender and stereotype threat perceptions. Comput. Hum. Behav. 71, 90–98 (2017). https://doi.org/10.1016/j.chb.2017 01.054

Ethical Game Design and Responsible Gaming

From Understanding to Intervention: Towards an Agenda for Countering Dark Patterns in Games

Ticianne Darin[✉] and Nayana Carneiro

Federal University of Ceará, Fortaleza, CE 60455-760, Brazil
ticianne@virtual.ufc.br, nayanatcl@alu.ufc.br

Abstract. Human-Computer Interaction (HCI) research has significantly advanced our understanding of Deceptive or Dark Patterns (DPs) in digital games through identification, ethical analysis, and awareness initiatives. However, a critical gap persists in developing robust, empirically validated methods to counteract these manipulative designs effectively. Prevailing business models and financial incentives often lead to the perception that proposing countermeasures is unrealistic despite widespread concerns about fairness and exploitation. This position paper directly challenges this assumption, arguing that moving beyond foundational understanding towards applied, interventionist research is crucial to bridge the 'implementation gap' between ethical insight and design practice. We call for expanding HCI games research and outline an agenda that prioritizes developing player-centric interventions informed by rigorous evidence and creating actionable design strategies for practitioners. Such initiatives are essential not only for mitigating DPs harms but also for demonstrating the feasibility of designing for genuine player well-being alongside sustainable developer goals, thereby paving a path toward ethical game design.

Keywords: Digital Games · Video Games · Games · Game Design · Games Research · Dark Patterns · Deceptive Design · Deceptive Patterns · Deceptive Design Patterns · Manipulative Patterns · Manipulative Design · Deceptive Design Practices · Malicious Design · Manipulation · Ethical Game Design · Ethical Design · Design Ethics · Ethics · Responsible Design · Awareness

1 Introduction

The pervasive use of Deceptive or Dark Patterns (DPs) in online gaming—i.e., design approaches crafted to shape player behavior, frequently for commercial reasons—has drawn considerable critical attention in the Human-Computer Interaction (HCI) field [13,15,35]. HCI researchers have made significant contributions in uncovering and classifying these trends [13], exploring their consequences to players [9,18,32], drawing their implications for ethics [16], and bring-

T. Darin et al. (Eds.): WIPlay 2025, CCIS 2623, pp. 87–101, 2026.
https://doi.org/10.1007/978-3-032-01426-9_6

ing attention to them through pedagogical efforts [7,38]. Even with advancements toward understanding DPs in games, we still lack tested, empirically supported ways to counteract them effectively. Little HCI-focused, empirically tested interventions or design alternatives exist that are as easy to implement or can be simply integrated into workflows as DPs currently are.

Indeed, some have argued that critically examining and proposing countermeasures to these patterns is an impractical and futile effort, given their perceived alignment with prevailing business models and financial incentives within the games industry [1,29]. This perspective emphasizes the documented conflicts: video game developers express the strain of economic pressures, specifically in games-as-a-service models, while simultaneously recognizing the ethical issues surrounding game elements they commonly use (for example, loot boxes) [1,5]. Furthermore, attempts at top-down regulation face significant hurdles; for instance, Belgium's 'ban' on paid loot boxes has been reported as largely ineffective due to poor industry compliance, enforcement challenges linked to funding and scale, and the ease with which players can circumvent technical blocks [40,41]. This contrasts with player attitudes, where strong concerns about fairness, transparency, exploitation, and manipulation are prevalent [9,31], alongside broad consensus on the need for mitigation policies [31].

This complex and somewhat contradictory scenario is echoed in conferences, workshops, and collaborative projects, where many fellow games and HCI researchers and practitioners applaud the attempts at actively countering deceptive design practices for their moral value but deem them ultimately unrealistic. Although anecdotic evidence, this type of perception reflects (and is possibly reinforced by) the real-world regulatory struggles [40,41], the documented tension between developer constraints and perceived market demands [1], and the only moderate feasibility for several proposed mitigation strategies, such as consumer protection regulations or industry self-regulation [5,6].

This position paper directly challenges that pragmatic (or perhaps resigned) perspective. We consider that this oftentimes underlying assumption prematurely closes off opportunities for necessary and actionable design innovations in this field. The critical question then becomes not *if* we can counter dark patterns in games, but *how* HCI and game researchers can effectively lead this task in such a way that practitioners can readily incorporate their findings and proposals in their game development workflow.

While acknowledging the economic realities, we believe that a sustained emphasis on identification and awareness, as important as these are, is not enough to effect real change. The pursuit of ethical game design, rather than a utopian exercise in conflict with industry sustainability, can enhance player engagement, build deeper trust, and ultimately support a more sustainable gaming environment. However, to realize this potential, there is an actual "implementation gap" [23] between ethical insight and design practice that must be bridged. It is precisely this gap – the need for robust, tested, and game-specific countermeasures – that HCI and games research should spearhead.

Therefore, we call not for a shift but a systematic expansion of HCI games research to dedicate significant effort towards more interventionist and practical methodologies, complementing the necessary ongoing work in identifying and analyzing DPs in games. This paper shares reflections on current practices and visions for the community's future, as well as research on games' DPs. We highlight the need to prioritize the systematic evaluation of targeted countermeasures, the empirically guided design of player-centered intervention instruments, and the development of further implementable design strategies that practitioners can directly apply. Such efforts are needed to reduce the harms of DPs in games and demonstrate the feasibility and validity of designing for actual player well-being as a primary ethical consideration while also exploring its conjunction with sustainable developer goals.

2 How HCI Has Been Approaching Dark Patterns in Games

HCI researchers have increasingly addressed DPs in the last few years. Almost since the coining of the term "Dark Pattern" in 2010, HCI scholars and practitioners have been central to this discourse, and the prominence and volume of research on this topic have only risen, especially since 2021 [13,15]. HCI research has significantly advanced our understanding of DPs in digital games by focusing on understanding and detecting these patterns and their effects on users and developing ethical frameworks to protect players from manipulative design strategies.

2.1 Identification and Classification Work

Research on DPs has mainly focused on their classification and detection [28]. Zagal, Björk, and Lewis presented in 2013 one of the earliest and most influential works to define DPs in games and categorize different types [42]. Since then, HCI researchers have spent considerable efforts detecting and classifying more DPs or supporting existing taxonomies and typologies. For instance, Niknejad et al. [29] conducted a large-scale study on nearly 1,500 mobile games, using Zagal and colleagues' taxonomy as a basis for this analysis. Their study highlighted how these DPs exploit players through temporal, monetary, social, and psychological means.

Another example is the Dark Pattern Analysis Framework (DPAF) [28], which categorizes 68 types of DPs and provides game-specific examples, adding 20 DPs types in comparison to a recent taxonomy by Gray et al. [14]. Other HCI studies classify DPs in games in both traditional and emerging forms, such as augmented and virtual reality, focusing on how game features can intensify their impact on players [1,19]. Researchers also examine the interplay between cognitive biases and DPs, identifying when users are most susceptible to manipulation and suggesting ethical interventions [26].

The classification field has advanced significantly over the past decade, shifting from simple taxonomies to more detailed categories considering digital platforms and cognitive biases. However, efforts to create a universally accepted taxonomy for DPs continue. Detection methods have also progressed from manual to semi-automated or fully automated approaches [24]; nonetheless, studies reveal that current tools only detect 45% of known patterns [29], highlighting the need for more robust detection models.

2.2 Awareness and Education Initiatives

HCI research has proposed mitigation strategies, such as regulatory support, ethical design guidelines, and user protection mechanisms, to reduce the harm caused by DPs in games [12,19,26]. There are also educational initiatives aimed at expanding awareness of DPs among designers, developers, and users and integrating these topics into design and computing curricula to foster more responsible and ethically informed design practices.

For example, Iantorno and McKee [17] argue for embedding critical discussions of deceptive design into HCI and design education, proposing pedagogical frameworks that make space for ethical reflection and resistance strategies. Similarly, Gray et al. [12] call for including dark pattern literacy in UX education, suggesting that formal training can prepare future designers to identify and avoid manipulative design practices. Efforts like these aim not only to inform but also to instill professional responsibility and critical engagement with the ethical dimensions of interface design.

Researchers have also explored serious and persuasive games as educational countermeasures for users [1,20]. Such games aim to inform and foster behavioral change through immersive, interactive experiences. Unlike static awareness tools, these games strive to engage players in a way that mirrors real-world manipulation, making them a promising HCI-based approach for educating users about deceptive design in games.

However, research has increasingly highlighted the limitations of simply raising user awareness to combat the effects of deceptive patterns in interfaces. While initial studies focused on informing users about the existence of manipulative designs, emerging evidence shows that awareness by itself often falls short [4,20]. For instance, Bongard-Blanchy and colleagues [4] observed that even users who are aware of manipulative strategies often feel incapable of opposing them, signaling the need for more diverse and effective interventions that go beyond just placing responsibility on users.

2.3 Ethical, Legal, and Health Considerations

HCI research has critically examined how DPs can distort player experience, undermining autonomy, trust, and long-term satisfaction. Scholars have advocated for user-first game design principles that foreground transparency, informed consent, and user agency [1,26]. These critiques highlight the ethical concerns surrounding manipulative mechanics – such as exploiting cognitive biases or guilt-tripping players – to drive engagement or monetization at the expense of player well-being [11].

Additionally, legal and policy-oriented research within HCI has begun shaping public discourse by framing DPs as unfair commercial practices. This type of work contributes to regulatory efforts that seek to align design with consumer protection laws [15,25]. Interdisciplinary workshops and position papers have further advanced this agenda, calling for collaborative action across ethics, law, health, and design domains to address the broader societal harms posed by deceptive game mechanics [35,37].

While ethical, legal, and health-focused research has been essential in exposing the harms of DPs in games, it is not sufficient on its own to counter them effectively. Ethical critiques often remain theoretical and lack mechanisms for enforcement, while regulatory approaches are slow to adapt and challenging to apply consistently across jurisdictions [15,25]. Health-oriented research has noted adverse psychological effects, such as compulsive play and diminished well-being [3], but these findings rarely lead to enforceable standards. Besides, industry pressures and monetization often undermine ethical intentions, making it hard for designers to resist manipulative mechanics [1]. Without integrated strategies that include education, design accountability, and better policy coordination, these efforts struggle to challenge the commercial logic sustaining DPs in games.

Taken together, this body of work suggests that HCI research is moving toward increasingly multidisciplinary approaches, drawing on design, law, psychology, and ethics to tackle the challenges posed by deceptive patterns in games. While taxonomies and critical analyses have provided valuable conceptual foundations, concrete and efficacious countermeasures remain scarce. Addressing this gap requires an expanded, more interventionist, and practice-oriented approach – e.g., one that incorporates player advocacy into design processes, fosters cross-sector collaboration among HCI researchers, policymakers, and industry stakeholders, and advances the development of real-time detection mechanisms and transparency tools for players.

3   A Call To Action: Why (and How) We Can (and Should) Go Beyond Our Current Efforts

HCI, by definition, sits at the crossroads of human psychology, design, and technology. This position affords a particular advantage in addressing DPs in games, not by imposing ethical dictates or making policy alone, but by analyzing how interactive systems can better serve both players and developers. HCI researchers are specialists in finding out about users—in this case, players. We find out about players' needs, contexts, motivations, cognitive processes, and psychological needs, such as autonomy, competence, and relatedness, through methods like ethnographic research, playtesting, experiments, and player experience studies, to name a few perspectives of our work. The empirical understanding that this type of research produces is the foundation. Ethicists can tell us what harm is, and legislators can legislate against it, but HCI researchers and practitioners can look at how to counteract it in practice. HCI can investigate **not only the nature and impact of DPs but also the intrinsic nature of particular design choices** on fundamental human needs like autonomy and informed consent, viewing these as rights to be upheld within the interactive experience.

Hence, we as a community can focus on **how to fight DPs practically in games**. While it is valuable to discuss ethical game design principles [16] or game design patterns [27], HCI can take these concepts further. We can make, build, and test physical interfaces and interaction techniques that **actively promote** player autonomy and well-being. And this should not have to be at the expense of the game industry's business goals. For instance, HCI researchers are equipped to investigate *in what way* a game's progression system may be portrayed to communicate effort vs. reward without exploitative grinding, or in-game purchase offers may be presented to honor informed choice rather than exploiting urgency. HCI provides the tools to both formulate and empirically test such alternatives.

The task is not so much to eliminate monetization or engagement mechanics but to design them sustainably and ethically. HCI can take the lead with novel interfaces and interaction techniques that aim for genuine player engagement through enjoyment and intrinsic motivation rather than compulsion. For example, if a game is highly compelling and treats player agency with respect, it has a greater likelihood of developing long-term loyalty and favorable community attitudes that are also business assets. HCI can examine and demonstrate *how* designs rooted in respect for player well-being can foster genuine engagement, which in turn may supplement or even redefine sustainable business objectives rather than simply optimizing for pre-existing ones. For example, systems that provide players with explicit control of their playtime and data or interfaces that overtly disclose monetization mechanics could be a space for HCI-led innovation.

Therefore, our task is not to replace the fundamental work of ethicists, lawyers, psychologists, or teachers. Instead, we call for HCI research to *produce* concrete strategies and tools informed by empirical evidence upon which those other disciplines can rely. We can show *what* is effective at the interface level to avert harm and strengthen positive player experience. This evidence-based, pragmatic, design-centered approach, with a focus on the design of the interaction itself, is HCI's distinctive and core contribution to addressing DPs in games. We must aim to truly equip developers with well-informed tools that allow them to create compelling games people enjoy without resorting to behaviors undermining their autonomy and well-being. Building on this view, the following subsections indicate practical alternatives and tangible outputs we envision to foster a game development ecosystem that prioritizes player autonomy through empirically validated ethical design practices.

3.1   Collaboration to Document Positive Patterns and Share Working Examples of Ethical Game Design Elements

Recent studies, such as those by Miranda and coauthors [27], propose alternative design patterns called "radiant game design patterns" to mitigate DPs and satisfy player psychological needs. Lewis [22] similarly suggests "motivational design patterns" while also warning against DPs that cause long-term motivational harm. Aagaard and colleagues [1] delineate the origins of DPs in mobile game development, use, and commercialization and advocate for game experiences that prioritize player and industry professionals' well-being. However, as valuable as they are, these concepts and guidelines are not often incorporated by the game industry for various reasons, one being that conceptualizations like these remain primarily descriptive, lacking readily actionable translations.

To bridge this gap and to advance initiatives like these, **a collaborative effort** in designing, prototyping, and empirically evaluating is necessary. This effort would involve demonstrating *how* ethical, "radiant" or "motivational" and other positive design ideals translate into concrete, context-specific practices that incorporate player dignity and informed choice. For instance, Frommel & Mandryk [10] found that daily quest rewards, while engaging, can negatively impact players through fear of missing out or feeling like a chore. Based on their insights, the community could develop, test, and document alternative reward systems. And then, sharing these vetted examples *grounded in empirical findings and clear design rationales* to easily accessible channels, including but not limited to formal repositories. The idea is to ease the bridge between academic knowledge and general industry use.

Before establishing cooperative collections or databases, a common ground for documenting and sharing these ethical game design elements requires fostering a shared understanding and robust methodologies. A key element is the collaborative creation of a rich lexicon for describing problematic patterns (based on well-founded taxonomies) and their ethical counterparts—designs that respect player agency as a primary concern. This requires ongoing dialogue within the HCI and games research community, facilitated through diverse collaborative platforms such as workshops, dedicated tracks at conferences, special interest groups, and open online forums for discussion and co-creation of documentation.

Standardized yet flexible ways to validate "working examples" are also necessary to fulfill this vision. As research groups worldwide will pursue various research questions, they would benefit from shared principles for empirical verification, possibly including metrics related to both player well-being and engagement. For instance, the "System Darkness Scale" [30] represents an interest in quantifiable evaluations, offering a potential starting point, which could be adapted and combined with mixed-method approaches to capture the positive dimensions of ethical designs. The emphasis here is on demonstrating respect for the player, not solely optimizing engagement metrics.

While a dynamic, web-based repository – perhaps inspired by collaborative platforms or open-source documentation projects rather than just static sites owned by a particular researcher – remains a valuable long-term goal for structured sharing, the immediate focus should be on *diverse modes of collaboration and dissemination*. That would ideally allow researchers to contribute comprehensive documentation of design patterns. This documentation should go beyond visual layouts and interaction sequences. It should also explicitly articulate the ethical principles and psychological constructs addressed alongside robust empirical validation. Peer review, community-led curation including developers, and versioning would be essential for maintaining this shared knowledge's quality, integrity, and evolving nature.

To encourage broad participation in these collaborative documentation and sharing efforts, the processes must be inclusive and offer clear value to contributors, such as opportunities for co-authorship, peer recognition, and fostering a community of practice around ethical game design. These shared resources can also serve as powerful educational tools, complementing efforts to raise awareness on the impact of DPs, like serious games developed with this aim [7,36,38], by providing concrete examples of ethical design in action.

Funding and sustaining such collaborative endeavors will probably represent significant challenges. Support could come from research consortia, university partnerships, or grants from foundations promoting ethical technology and open knowledge. Most importantly, sustained community engagement and shared ownership are essential for these shared resources' ongoing and long-term development, relevance, and ethical stewardship.

The decentralized nature of research can be valuable here. Various groups can contribute expertise on specific game genres, diverse player populations (e.g., children or those with particular vulnerabilities), or nuanced ethical issues (e.g., data privacy, fair monetization). Well-orchestrated collaborative efforts and thoughtfully designed sharing platforms can consolidate these diverse insights, **making specialized knowledge and practical examples of ethical design accessible** to the broader game development community, thereby promoting a design ethos grounded in respect for the player.

Despite the ambitious scope, fostering collaboration for documenting and sharing ethical design knowledge aligns with the core tenets of scholarly research. It directly addresses the demand for actionable solutions to ethical challenges in game design, as highlighted by Aagaard et al. [1]. Such collaborative efforts, focused on creating and disseminating practical, ethically grounded knowledge, can significantly accelerate the adoption of design principles that genuinely prioritize player well-being within the game industry.

3.2   Development of Software Artifacts to Foster Real-Time Awareness on Users and Developers

Good gains have been achieved in enhancing player sensitivity and insight into manipulative practices by developing and piloting serious games [7,21,36,38,39] and developing tools that enable users to spot manipulative design elements [2,7]. To provide but one illustration, Fiedler and colleagues [7] showed that their serious game significantly improves the ability of participants to identify DPs, and Kronhardt and coauthors [21] showed how game-adapted DPs integrated into a serious game can raise awareness through immediate consequences.

While raising awareness is necessary because it provides the cognitive tools for detection, HCI research can augment this impact by designing interactive software artifacts with real-time support and intervention. Extending the learning possibilities of such projects, we propose a focused research effort on two types of software artifacts. First, *player-assisting tools*, such as browser extensions or in-game overlays. Their main goal would be to help transfer the pattern recognition skills games into immediate, contextual guidance. Such tools might highlight potential DPs as they appear, explain their manipulative mechanisms (drawing on the typologies and user reactions), and perhaps even suggest alternative actions derived from a validated repository.

The advantage provided herein is the immediate empowerment of players within their interaction, upholding their right to informed choice, and alleviating the sense of being "deceived" [38]. That could potentially enable players to bypass choices that could harm their autonomy. However, these tools are not supposed to trick the user into 'making a better choice.' That would also hurt their autonomy. Moreover, as Xiao and Denoo discussed, advanced players or game platforms might devise methods to circumvent or compromise the efficacy of such tools [40]. Instead, these mechanisms should aim to enhance player agency by fostering real-time awareness, not to diminish it by dictating choices. The core intention is to transform potentially deceptive or manipulative encounters into opportunities for informed decision-making.

There are specific concerns to consider. These tools must avoid alert fatigue from excessive notifications and monitor subtle DFs across gaming interfaces without generating high false positives. Additionally, they need to minimize being seen as intrusive to maintain a positive gaming experience.

The second type would be **developer-supported tools** for major game engines, which might proactively integrate ethical considerations into the development process. The goal here is to support developer objectives that align with player well-being. Plugging in the research on the root of DPs in design development and the issues designers encounter, such tools could help identify potentially problematic design decisions at development time and help designers brainstorm healthier alternatives. They could check against predefined DPs definitions derived from the vast literature that describes them and suggest ethically informed alternatives from the proposed repertoire of different proposals of positive design patterns.

The primary benefit is proactive, encouraging inherently ethical practices and support for designers working towards creating healthier experiences, particularly when they might not have clear guidance or face strict time limits [23]. This approach may help developers better consider, negotiate, and make informed design decisions on how to be more ethically engaged in their workflows. Of course, there are potential challenges to be considered. They include the difficulty of developing intelligent and context-aware tools that make practical proposals to players instead of just giving trivial notifications. Also, developers risk working around or dismissing such tools if they are perceived as creativity limitations, too limiting in design choices, or conflict with perceived financial objectives.

Of course, these tools' successful adoption and efficacy would be influenced by the industry's willingness to embrace ethical design standards and integrate such support. However, this integration is a necessary embodiment of ethical principles rather than a strategy to enhance tool efficacy. It requires a broader shift towards embedding these standards deeply within development cultures. Besides, developing such software products demands an insightful grasp of player psychology founded on research surrounding cognitive bias and DPs and the pragmatics of game development. Rigorous empirical testing will also be essential to guarantee that such tools are effective and easy to use, balance the empowerment of both end-users and developers' sustainable goals, and foster a healthy interactive experience.

It is important to note that while designing developer-support tools is crucial for fostering ethical game design practices, it is equally essential to recognize the structural constraints within the game industry that may limit their adoption and impact. Many monetization-related decisions are typically made not by designers or developers but by higher-level stakeholders such as shareholders, executives, and product or monetization teams. These decision-makers often have limited or no background in game development and primarily rely on key performance indicators (KPIs) like player retention, session length, active user base, and revenue metrics to drive design directives. As a result, developers and designers may have little autonomy to reject manipulative practices, even when they are aware of the ethical concerns surrounding DPs. Given this context, we advocate for further empirical research – such as large-scale surveys or interviews with industry professionals, especially within the mobile and live-ops sectors – to better understand developers' awareness of DPs, their perceived agency in decision-making processes, and the organizational pressures they face. This line of inquiry could help clarify how deeply knowledge and decision power regarding DPs are distributed across different roles in game companies, potentially guiding more targeted and feasible counter-strategies in the future.

3.3 Advancing Methods and Measures for Assessing Dark Pattern Prevalence and Player Experience, Including Well-Being

Current HCI research excels at identifying and categorizing DPs, although not as much within games, and provides critical explorations of their ethical and psychological impacts [16]. Significant steps have been made toward evaluation tools, such as the System Darkness Scale [30] that assess a system's perceived "darkness," and frameworks like the ADD framework [8] for critically considering DPs in children's applications. While these analytical insights and identification methods are foundational, we advocate for expanding efforts to develop and validate robust methods and measures that can more **directly and quantifiably assess the impact of specific game design elements** on player autonomy, perceived manipulation, and holistic psychological well-being.

The aim is not merely to identify whether well-being is affected but to understand and quantify this relationship with greater nuance, particularly when evaluating the efficacy of proposed countermeasures. It involves developing or adapting specific player experience instruments, such as validated questionnaires or carefully designed behavioral metrics, that explicitly capture core tenets of ethical interaction. These instruments should focus on perceived autonomy, fairness, transparency, the sense of being respected (or manipulated), and critical aspects of psychological well-being, drawing inspiration from well-established theories like the Self-Determination Theory [33,34]. Such measures would allow researchers to move beyond general assessments of "darkness" to indicate how specific patterns or their alternatives influence these fundamental human needs, a necessary point of departure to investigate how to counteract them.

Building upon existing frameworks, we call for creating standardized yet adaptable methodologies for evaluating both the presence and, crucially, the impact of DPs across diverse game genres and monetization models. It includes refining our approaches to measure the actual effect of interventions designed to mitigate DPs or enhance player awareness. For example, understanding why some educational interventions show limited impact on knowledge about DPs matters [39] requires more sensitive evaluation protocols to determine true efficacy and identify areas for improvement.

Addressing these challenges involves **not only identifying the absence of DPs but also evaluating the effectiveness of ethical design choices** in creating a positive, engaging game experience driven by genuine enjoyment, not coercion. We can enhance our use of gameplay data by developing telemetry and behavioral analytics to uncover patterns that indicate compromised player autonomy or manipulative mechanics. Integrating this data with qualitative insights and refined player experience tools can lead to a more comprehensive assessment. Additionally, we could improve methodologies for assessing the prevalence of DPs in new games by combining expert evaluations tailored to specific game types and monetization strategies, along with emerging automated detection approaches where ethically appropriate.

Developing and adapting methods and validated measures is not an end in itself. Instead, it is a step toward generating highly specific, empirically grounded guidelines that practitioners can trust and readily apply. These methods will allow us to move from general advice to concrete, evidence-backed recommendations (e.g., "*To uphold player autonomy in reward systems, design X which demonstrably leads to Y outcome in perceived fairness, as measured by Z*"). By focusing on quantifiable impacts on core aspects of ethical player experience, we can make assessments more systematic, comparable across studies, and ultimately more impactful in driving real change in game design practices.

4   Forging Ahead: A Research Agenda

This position paper argued for systematically expanding the focus of HCI games research regarding game DPs. It means moving from identifying what is problematic to demonstrating what is possible. We urge a dedicated focus on interventionist and practical methodologies that enrich and are enriched by our existing foundational understanding of DPs, creating a robust cycle of theory and application. The aim is not to offer definitive, one-size-fits-all solutions, as the landscape of game design and player experience is far too diverse and dynamic for such prescriptions. Instead, we have intended to outline a call to action, highlighting specific areas where research efforts can make a tangible difference in fostering more ethical and player-respecting game environments.

From our discussion, a research agenda emerges, embracing the complexities and committing to developing empirically grounded, actionable knowledge by:

- **Developing and Validating Ethical Solutions:** How can the HCI community collaboratively document, prototype, and rigorously evaluate specific positive patterns or ethical design alternatives for familiar game mechanics prone to exploitation? What methodologies best capture their impact on player autonomy, well-being, and potential alignment with sustainable developer goals?
- **Creating and Assessing Intervention Tools:** What types of player-assisting software artifacts (e.g., real-time awareness tools, contextual guides) can effectively empower players against DPs without being overly intrusive or easily avoided? Conversely, how can we design developer-support tools to seamlessly integrate ethical considerations into existing game development workflows, offering practical guidance rather than mere warnings? What are the most effective ways to empirically test the real-world impact of such tools?
- **Refining Methods for Impact Assessment:** How can we develop more nuanced and validated metrics and methodologies to assess the prevalence of DPs and their tangible impact on player well-being and perceived fairness? Can we create standardized yet flexible protocols for evaluating the effectiveness of countermeasures across diverse game genres and player populations?
- **Translating Research into Actionable Guidance for Practitioners:** What are the most effective formats and channels for translating empirical findings into practical, context-specific design guidelines and heuristics that game developers can readily understand and apply? How can we better bridge the implementation gap between academic research and industry practice?

Addressing these questions requires a multi-faceted approach, integrating qualitative depth with quantitative rigor and fostering stronger collaborations between researchers, designers, developers, and players. More importantly, it should come from people from different backgrounds and countries, including the Global South perspective. This endeavor is not about dictating what games should be but expanding their palette – engaging, entertaining, and fundamentally respectful of the individuals who play them. This call to action is an invitation to the HCI and games research community. By focusing our collective expertise on these interventionist and practical trajectories rooted in theory, we can move beyond critique to creation, spearheading the development of knowledge and tools that genuinely support designing a more ethical future for digital games.

Acknowledgments. This work is a partial result of the project Digital Well-Being, supported by CNPq (CNPq/MCTI Call No. 10/2023 – UNIVERSAL), under grant number 404559/2023-9. We would like to thank the anonymous reviewers for their insightful comments and valuable suggestions, which helped strengthen the discussions presented in this paper.

Disclosure of Interests. The authors have no competing interests.

References

1. Aagaard, J., Knudsen, M.E.C., Bækgaard, P., Doherty, K.: A game of dark patterns: designing healthy highly-engaging mobile games. In: CHI Conference on Human Factors in Computing Systems Extended Abstracts, pp. 1–8 (2022)
2. Baroni, L.A., Pereira, R.: Deceptive patterns under a sociotechnical view. In: Proceedings of the XXIII Brazilian Symposium on Human Factors in Computing Systems, IHC 2024. Association for Computing Machinery, New York (2024). https://doi.org/10.1145/3702038.3702081
3. Birk, M.V., Van Der Hof, S., Hodent, C., Gerling, K. Van Rooij, A.J.: Behavioural design in video games: ethical, legal, and health impact on players. In: Extended Abstracts of the 2023 CHI Conference on Human Factors in Computing Systems, pp. 1–4 (2023)
4. Bongard-Blanchy, K., Rossi, A., Rivas, S., Doublet S., Koenig, V., Lenzini, G.: "I am definitely manipulated, even when i am aware of it. It's ridiculous!" - dark patterns from the end-user perspective. In: Proceedings of the 2021 ACM Designing Interactive Systems Conference, DIS 2021, pp. 763–776. Association for Computing Machinery, New York (2021). https://doi.org/10.1145/3461778.3462086
5. Brock, T., Johnson, M.: The gamblification of digital games (2021)
6. Colder Carras, M., Carras, M., Labrique, A.B.: Stakeholders' consensus on strategies for self-and other-regulation of video game play: a mixed methods study. Int. J. Environ. Res. Public Health **17**(11), 3846 (2020)
7. Fiedler, K., Schäfer, R., Borchers, J., Röpke, R.: "Deception Detected!"—a serious game about detecting dark patterns. In: Schönbohm, A., et al. (eds.) GALA 2024. LNCS, vol. 15348, pp. 191–200. Springer, Cham (2024). https://doi.org/10.1007/978-3-031-78269-5_18. Chapter 18. The LNCS volume is formally part of the 2025 series, though published in late 2024
8. Fitton, D., Read, J.C.: Creating a framework to support the critical consideration of dark design aspects in free-to-play apps. In: Proceedings of the 18th ACM International Conference on Interaction Design and Children, pp. 407–418 (2019)
9. Freeman, G., Wu, K., Nower, N., Wohn, D.Y.: Pay to win or pay to cheat: how players of competitive online games perceive fairness of in-game purchases. Proc. ACM Hum.-Comput. Interact. **6**(CHI PLAY), 1–24 (2022)
10. Frommel, J., Mandryk, R.L.: Daily quests or daily pests? The benefits and pitfalls of engagement rewards in games. Proc. ACM Hum.-Comput. Interact. **6**(CHI PLAY), 1–23 (2022)
11. Gray, C.M., et al.: Mobilizing research and regulatory action on dark patterns and deceptive design practices. In: Extended Abstracts of the CHI Conference on Human Factors in Computing Systems, pp. 1–6 (2024)
12. Gray, C.M., Kou, Y., Battles, B., Hoggatt, J., Toombs, A.L.: The dark (patterns) side of UX design. In: Proceedings of the 2018 CHI Conference on Human Factors in Computing Systems, pp. 1–14 (2018)

13. Gray, C.M., Sanchez Chamorro, L., Obi, I., Duane, J.N.: Mapping the landscape of dark patterns scholarship: a systematic literature review. In: Companion Publication of the 2023 ACM Designing Interactive Systems Conference, DIS 2023, pp. 188–193. Companion, Association for Computing Machinery, New York (2023).https://doi.org/10.1145/3563703.3596635

14. Gray, C.M., Santos, C., Bielova, N.: Towards a preliminary ontology of dark patterns knowledge. In: Extended abstracts of the 2023 CHI Conference on Human Factors in Computing Systems, pp. 1–9 (2023)

15. Gray, C.M., Santos, C.T., Bielova, N., Mildner, T.: An ontology of dark patterns knowledge: foundations, definitions, and a pathway for shared knowledge-building. In: Proceedings of the 2024 CHI Conference on Human Factors in Computing Systems, CHI 2024. Association for Computing Machinery, New York (2024). https://doi.org/10.1145/3613904.3642436

16. Hodent, C., Blumberg, F., Deterding, S.: Ethical games: toward evidence-based guidance for safeguarding players and developers (2024)

17. Iantorno, M., Guadagnolo, D., Petterson, A.: Dark patterns and pedagogy: expanding scholarship and curriculum on manipulative marketing practices. AoIR Selected Papers of Internet Research (2023)

18. King, J., Fitton, D., Cassidy, B.: Investigating players' perceptions of deceptive design practices within a 3d gameplay context. Proc. ACM Hum.-Comput. Interact. **7**(CHI PLAY) (2023). https://doi.org/10.1145/3611053

19. Krauss, V., et al.: What makes XR dark? Examining emerging dark patterns in augmented and virtual reality through expert co-design. ACM Trans. Comput.-Hum. Interact. **31**(3), 1–39 (2024)

20. Kronhardt, K., Rolfes, K., Gerken, J.: Trickery: exploring a serious game approach to raise awareness of deceptive patterns. In: Proceedings of the International Conference on Mobile and Ubiquitous Multimedia, pp. 133–147 (2024)

21. Kronhardt, K., Rolfes, K., Gerken, J.: Trickery: exploring a serious game approach to raise awareness of deceptive patterns. In: Proceedings of the International Conference on Mobile and Ubiquitous Multimedia, MUM 2024, pp. 133–147. Association for Computing Machinery, New York (2024). https://doi.org/10.1145/3701571.3701588

22. Lewis, C.: Motivational design patterns. Ph.D. thesis, UC Santa Cruz (2013)

23. Lindberg, S., Karlström, P., Männikkö Barbutiu, S.: Cultivating ethics–a perspective from practice. In: Proceedings of the 11th Nordic Conference on Human-Computer Interaction: Shaping Experiences, Shaping Society, pp. 1–11 (2020)

24. Mathur, A., et al.: Dark patterns at scale: findings from a crawl of 11k shopping websites. Proc. ACM Hum.-Comput. Interact. **3**(CSCW) (2019). https://doi.org/10.1145/3359183

25. Mathur, A., Kshirsagar, M., Mayer, J.: What makes a dark pattern... dark? Design attributes, normative considerations, and measurement methods. In: Proceedings of the 2021 CHI Conference on Human Factors in Computing Systems, CHI 2021. Association for Computing Machinery, New York (2021). https://doi.org/10.1145/3411764.3445610

26. Mildner, T., Inkoom, A., Malaka, R., Niess, J.: Hell is paved with good intentions: the intricate relationship between cognitive biases and dark patterns. arXiv preprint arXiv:2405.07378 (2024)

27. Miranda, D.M., Pontes, R.M., de Gois Ribeiro Darin, T.: It's dark but just a game: towards an ethical and healthy game design practice. In: Proceedings of the 21st Brazilian Symposium on Human Factors in Computing Systems, pp. 1–7 (2022)

28. Nie, L., Zhao, Y., Li, C., Luo, X., Liu, Y.: Shadows in the interface: a comprehensive study on dark patterns. Proc. ACM Softw. Eng. **1**(FSE), 204–225 (2024)
29. Niknejad, S., Mildner, T., Zargham, N., Putze, S., Malaka, R.: Level up or game over: exploring how dark patterns shape mobile games. In: Proceedings of the International Conference on Mobile and Ubiquitous Multimedia, pp. 148–156 (2024)
30. van Nimwegen, C., Bergman, K., Akdag, A.: Shedding light on assessing dark patterns: Introducing the system darkness scale (SDS). In: 35th International BCS Human-Computer Interaction Conference, pp. 1–10. BCS Learning & Development (2022)
31. Petrovskaya, E., Zendle, D.: Predatory monetisation? A categorisation of unfair, misleading and aggressive monetisation techniques in digital games from the player perspective. J. Bus. Ethics, 1065–1081 (2022). https://doi.org/10.1007/s10551-021-04970-6
32. Petrovskaya, E., Zendle, D.: "These people had taken advantage of me": A grounded theory of problematic consequences of player interaction with mobile games perceived as "designed to drive spending". Hum. Behav. Emerg. Technol. **2022**(1), 1260174 (2022)
33. Ryan, R.M., Deci, E.L.: Self-determination theory and the facilitation of intrinsic motivation, social development, and well-being. Am. Psychol. **55**(1), 68 (2000)
34. Ryan, R.M., Deci, E.L.: Self-determination Theory: Basic Psychological Needs in Motivation, Development, and Wellness. Guilford publications (2017)
35. Sánchez Chamorro, L., Bongard-Blanchy, K., Koenig, V.: Ethical tensions in UX design practice: exploring the fine line between persuasion and manipulation in online interfaces. In: Proceedings of the 2023 ACM Designing Interactive Systems Conference, DIS 2023, pp. 2408–2422. Association for Computing Machinery, New York (2023). https://doi.org/10.1145/3563657.3596013
36. Santos Filho, L., Sousa Junior, A., Ribeiro, G., Darin, T.: They say that the world was built for two but deceptive patterns say otherwise: a critical game for player empowerment. In: Proceedings of the XXIII Brazilian Symposium on Human Factors in Computing Systems, IHC 2024. Association for Computing Machinery, New York (2024). https://doi.org/10.1145/3702038.3702076
37. Sas, M., Denoo, M., Mühlberg, J.T.: Informing children about privacy: a review and assessment of age-appropriate information designs in kids-oriented F2P video games. Proc. ACM Hum.-Comput. Interact. **7**(CHI PLAY) (2023). https://doi.org/10.1145/3611036
38. Tjostheim, I.: A serious game about apps, data-sharing and deceptive design. In: Guarda, T., Portela, F., Diaz-Nafria, J.M. (eds.) Advanced Research in Technologies, Information, Innovation and Sustainability, vol. 1936, pp. 332–343. Springer, Cham (2024). https://doi.org/10.1007/978-3-031-48855-9_25
39. Tjostheim, I., Ayres-Pereira, V., Wales, C., Manna, A., Egenfeldt-Nielsen, S.: Dark pattern: a serious game for learning about the dangers of sharing data. In: Proceedings of the 16th European Conference on Games Based Learning, vol. 16. Academic Conferences International Limited, Reading (2022). https://doi.org/10.34190/ecgbl.16.1.872. Section: Late Submissions
40. Xiao, L.Y.: Breaking ban: Belgium's ineffective gambling law regulation of video game loot boxes. Collabra Psychol. **9**(1), 57641 (2023)
41. Xiao, L.Y., Denoo, M.: What did players think about Belgium's 'ban'on loot boxes? In: Abstract Proceedings of DiGRA 2023 Conference: Limits and Margins of Games (2023)
42. Zagal, J.P., Björk, S., Lewis, C.: Dark patterns in the design of games. In: Foundations of Digital Games 2013 (2013)

What Risks and Opportunities Games Bring to Children? A Consultation on Platform Regulation

George Valença^(✉)

Computing Department, Federal Rural University of Pernambuco (UFRPE), Recife, Brazil
george.valenca@ufrpe.br

Abstract. The gaming industry, through its successful platforms, fosters the development of cognitive and social skills in children, such as increased socialization and even programming abilities. However, it also brings a range of challenges, including addiction, exposure to inappropriate content, and threats to privacy. This research aimed to identify the main risks and opportunities associated with gaming platforms to explore best practices and regulatory pathways. To achieve this, we analyzed data from the public consultation on platform regulation conducted by CGI.br in 2023, supplemented by a review of recent news articles. The study revealed six main risks, including harassment and the encouragement of purchases, as well as three opportunities, such as the development of technical and behavioral skills. Our analysis highlights the need for stronger regulation and safer business practices in models like Roblox's, particularly regarding child protection. Moreover, it is essential to adopt approaches that promote educational benefits and ensure inclusive digital environments, with regulations that balance innovation and the well-being of younger users.

Keywords: Games · Children · Regulation

1 Introduction

Electronic games have become increasingly popular among digital services, attracting a growing number of children around the world. In its 2024 edition, the TIC Kids Online survey conducted by NIC.BR reveals that 78% of children aged 9 to 17 list gaming as one of their main online activities—a figure that rises to 88% among those aged 11 to 12 [11]. This phenomenon reflects a significant shift in forms of children's entertainment. In just a few decades, children's leisure activities, which once primarily involved outdoor play and the use of physical toys (i.e., more offline time and fewer digital gadgets like Hello Barbie and Alexa), have come to be dominated by immersion in virtual platforms.

The visual appeal of electronic games has become a key factor in transforming how children have fun and interact - a phenomenon also identified as a manipulative design pattern called "Cuteness" [5]. Over 90% of American children spend

T. Darin et al. (Eds.): WIPlay 2025, CCIS 2623, pp. 102–111, 2026.
https://doi.org/10.1007/978-3-032-01426-9_7

an average of two hours per day in front of video game screens [1], and 25% of them report wanting to reduce this time but being unable to do so, according to the 2024 TIC Kids survey.

Although this screen time may seem excessive electronic games can offer significant benefits, such as cognitive development and improved skills in attention, memory, and problem-solving. Puzzle and strategy games, for example, can stimulate critical thinking and creativity [1]. However, the intense attention retention promoted by these games can also lead to several issues. Excessive focus can trigger a state of normative dissociation causing a reduced perception of time and decreased awareness of external stimuli [2]. While such states are common in various activities, their frequent occurrence can have negative impacts when linked to unethical design strategies.

This context involves widespread platforms such as Roblox, with millions of daily users, offering a world of creativity and interaction, especially for children and teenagers. However, this digital environment also presents challenges to the safety, privacy, and mental health of its younger users.

This article investigates the risks and opportunities that electronic gaming platforms present to children and adolescents. To this end, we gathered evidence from the 2023 public consultation on platform regulation conducted by CGI.br, a multistakeholder institution in Brazilian internet governance with high significance and credibility in the national context. This mapping revealed a total of six main risks, ranging from threats to privacy and distorted body image to harassment and online violence. In parallel, we identified regulatory opportunities for these software solutions, which also have the potential to foster the development of users' skills. Hence, the study provides input for the regulatory debate, aiming to foster a safer and healthier environment for young digital game users.

2   Conceptual Background

Once dominated by outdoor play and physical toys, children's leisure time is now largely characterized by immersion in virtual worlds. Digital gaming platforms have become one of the main sources of entertainment for children, significantly transforming the leisure landscape over the past decades. For example, over 90% of American children spend up to two hours daily playing video games, reflecting the strong visual and interactive appeal of these platforms [1].

Although this amount of screen time dedicated to gaming may seem concerning, part of it brings important benefits, such as cognitive development. Platforms like Roblox and Minecraft can enhance essential skills such as attention, memory, and problem-solving, while puzzle and strategy games show potential to stimulate critical thinking and creativity in children by providing challenges that require planning and logical reasoning [1]. Additionally, multiplayer games and platforms can foster greater socialization, allowing teenagers to develop communication and teamwork skills, for example. According to a report by the Entertainment Software Association, 60% of players believe that gaming helps them maintain connections with friends and family, demonstrating that virtual environments can play a positive role in social relationships.

However, this positive impact must be analyzed in light of the various risks associated with digital gaming access. The high capacity of digital games to retain attention can cause negative effects such as normative dissociation. In this situation, children deeply immersed in games may lose track of time and fail to notice external stimuli, affecting daily activities such as schoolwork or family interactions [2].

The phenomenon of gaming addiction can also compromise self-regulation, leading to compulsive behaviors and symptoms related to gaming disorder, a condition recognized by the World Health Organization since 2018. A review on the prevalence of gaming disorder and online gaming addiction estimates that the proportion of children and adolescents exhibiting behaviors consistent with gaming addiction varies widely, with rates ranging from 0.26% to 38% [4]. These variations reflect differences in diagnostic methods, definitions of addiction, and study populations. Prevalence is particularly variable among adolescents (ages 12 to 18), highlighting the challenges of measuring the disorder across different cultural and social contexts. These differences must be interpreted with caution, as the assessment of the disorder involves complex and diverse factors, including socioeconomic, psychological, and cultural aspects [4]

Another significant risk is exposure to inappropriate content. Open platforms like Roblox increase the chances of children interacting with strangers and accessing virtual environments containing violence or inappropriate language. Even with moderation tools in place, constant parental supervision remains essential to ensure a safe environment [10].

3   Research Method

The research reported in this article was guided by the following research question (RQ): *what risks and opportunities do electronic gaming platforms present for children and adolescents?* To answer it, we relied on the database from the consultation conducted by CGI.br regarding the regulation of digital platforms. Based on the findings, we then developed an analysis of Roblox as a paradigmatic case within this context.

In the initial phase, we considered the consultation data, which received nearly 1,400 contributions from Brazilian individuals and organizations across the governmental, nonprofit, and corporate sectors, along with participation from the scientific community. The results of this survey were published by CGI.br in the form of a report, available in different formats: website, CSV, and PDF[1] We conducted a mapping of the terms *game, jogo(s)* (game/games in Portuguese), and *Roblox* within the PDF data to collect all contributions addressing this context. In total, 24 text excerpts were gathered. No relevant results were found for *game*, and occurrences for *jogos* were identified in other contexts. Hence, such occurrences were considered out of scope or irrelevant for this research. For example, (i) live streaming of games on YouTube, (ii) expressions such as "the

---

[1] The data can be accessed here https://dialogos.cgi.br/documentos/debate/consulta-plataformas/.

game of capital" or "the game of radicalism" and (iii) games mentioned merely as examples in lists of other internet services.

In the next phase, the selected data were migrated to a text file, where we conducted a classification using the Thematic Synthesis approach [3], a systematic and flexible process for identifying and developing themes (categories) in qualitative data. This activity was carried out by one researcher, with findings discussed and validated with a second researcher. In the end, several themes were identified and grouped into two main categories: *risks* and *opportunities*. Each category included a set of subthemes. For example, under *Risks*, we identified *Threats to Privacy*, *Image Distortion*, and *Incentives to Purchase*, among others. The classified dataset can be accessed at https://tinyurl.com/5duhkkcw.

Finally, the dataset was synthesized. We derived explanations for each identified theme and subtheme, building a narrative that answers the RQ on risks and opportunities. We believe that the formulation and interpretation of this body of evidence may lead to recommendations and the identification of good practices that should be incorporated into the regulation of gaming platforms, ultimately fostering children's well-being online.

4 Results

The thematic analysis of the data from the public consultation on platform regulation conducted by CGI.br revealed a set of 6 risks and 3 opportunities or solutions, as illustrated in Fig. 1. They are described as follows.

4.1 Risks

Risks in online games, as highlighted in one of the contributions, are crosscutting and may vary in intensity depending on the specific characteristics of each game (e.g., operational model, existence of virtual communities, promotion by streamers, or the organization of tournaments). The most frequently reported risk in the consultation data (mentioned in four contributions) was access to **inappropriate content**, such as material of a violent, sexual, or exploitative nature. This, for example, can lead to *"the glorification of mass shooters"*, as one participant noted. These are games unsuitable for minors under 18 years of age, lacking effective age verification mechanisms, and in need of regulation *"to prevent or hinder access by children and adolescents, aiming to ensure their safety"*, according to the data. In this way, the fundamental rights of children and adolescents are upheld in the development of digital games.

Still within the context of safety, another risk identified was **harassment and online violence**. The presence of forums or chat features associated with games that encourage violence, hate speech, and bullying in digital environments is frequent and remains poorly controlled, especially given the *"simultaneous and live interactions"*, as one contribution pointed out. In other words, content moderation is even more complex in the context of online games.

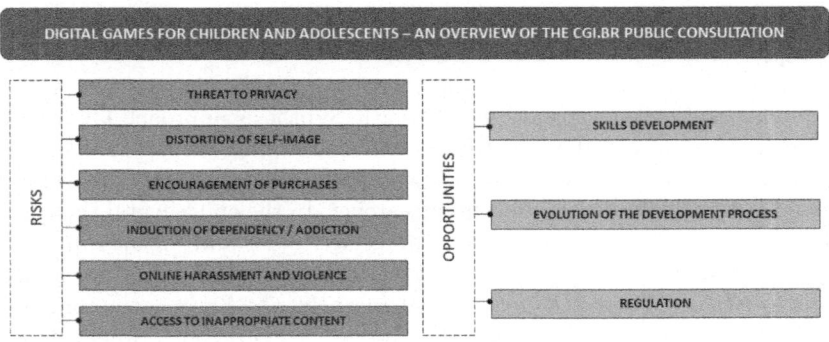

Fig. 1. Overview of risks and opportunities that digital games pose for young users.

From the perspective of data protection, the analysis also revealed the risk of **threats to privacy**. According to the Brazilian General Data Protection Law (LGPD), children's personal data must not be collected by controllers as a prerequisite for participation in games. However, given the vast set of online gaming apps, there is no effective guarantee that only the data strictly necessary for the activity is being collected when users install or regularly use these apps.

Certain types of games have a greater potential to promote the manipulative design strategy known as *Attention Capture* [6] - a set of design techniques aimed at increasing user retention, especially among children, who have less discernment regarding issues such as screen time or excessive device use. Gambling-style games, therefore, reinforce the risk of **addiction or real dependency** on the application, given their logical structure (in terms of algorithms and functionalities) oriented toward gambling mechanisms. The recent addition of loot boxes - *"surprise boxes that can be purchased in electronic games and provide rewards or advantages to the user in a random manner"*, as described in one of the consultation's contributions—introduces controversial rewards for children (deceptive, frustrating, and addiction-based).

The severity of emotional dependence has led to legal and institutional responses, including a public civil action by the National Association of Child and Adolescent Defense Centers, demanding the suspension of loot box sales and compensation for the children affected[2] Similarly, the Federal Council of Psychology issued a statement advocating for state action to protect children from loot boxes, as indicated in the consultation data[3] It is important to note that this risk feeds into another: the **encouragement of purchases**. Consumerism is embedded in digital game culture, where children perceive themselves within a dynamic of economic inequality in virtual environments and may even make purchases without parental consent.

---

[2] Tecnoblog - "Lawsuit to Ban Loot Boxes in Brazil Receives Support from the Public Prosecutor's Office" - 2021 - https://tinyurl.com/2p9mf5pe.

[3] Federal Senate – Opinion (SF) No. 50, 2023. GTEC report on electronic games and childhood. Available at: https://tinyurl.com/yc4zv2w9.

Finally, within the emotional sphere, one last risk was identified. The **distortion of self-image** due to the regular use of new skins by platforms and the construction of virtual personas fosters a change in self-perception, driven by a process of "avatarization" of the self. This issue requires an intersectional lens: *"children and adolescents avoid using Black avatars to avoid suffering racism in immersive environments"*, according to one contribution.

4.2   Opportunities

Despite the challenges identified in the contributions, the data also reveal a set of complementary opportunities and potential solutions. First, it is important to highlight that digital games can serve as vectors for the **development of both technical and behavioral skills** in children and adolescents. Beyond mere entertainment, engagement with this universe can foster greater autonomy and serve as *"an excellent opportunity for socialization, learning, and play"*, as summarized in one of the contributions to the public consultation on platform regulation. In particular, much like the pedagogical and supervised use of smartphones in classrooms, digital games can coexist with the school curriculum and enhance the learning process of elementary school students. When articulated with didactic-pedagogical, cultural, motivational, and multiliteracy practices, they can promote cognitive and holistic development in children.

A second point, now focused on the software industry, concerns rethinking the **business model and development process** of such applications. Game development teams could become even more diverse—not limited to roles in programming, design, storytelling, and UX/UI, but also incorporating educators, sociologists, and psychologists—bringing a *"multiplicity of knowledge that goes beyond mere technical expertise"*, as expressed in one of the contributions. Additionally, within the broader context of platforms and emerging technologies, there is a need to explore alternative business models for the software sector that

- (i) do not rely on an ecosystem centered on advertising and partners that demand user profiling and data extraction, and
- (ii) do not offer a "freemium" model, with a limited free version and a premium paid version with additional features, as highlighted in the consultation. This latter model enacts the manipulative design pattern known as *Forced Action*, which prevents users from fully accessing a solution unless they subscribe[4] Shifting away from such models is essential to fulfill the duty of care and uphold the rights of children online.

Finally, the data also emphasized aspects related to the **regulation of digital games**. On one hand, progress was noted in age verification and content rating. As digital platforms and applications accessed by minors under 18, online games in Brazil are already required to display age ratings, with *"oversight and criteria defined by the Ministry of Justice"*, according to one contribution. This initiative helps protect children from violent or sexual content and serves as a

---

[4] Deceptive Patterns. *Forced Action*: www.deceptive.design/types/forced-action.

means of communicating with families about the appropriate age group for each solution, *"in a way that respects the developmental stages of individuals"*.

In this regard, it was suggested that the State's role should go beyond regulation to include providing guidance to professionals, parents, and caregivers, as well as collaborating with digital platforms and game development companies to ensure that these technologies—accessed by or explicitly designed for children, whether for entertainment or educational purposes—are developed in ways that enhance cultural and recreational opportunities. From this perspective, laws such as the Legal Framework for Electronic Games[5] enacted in May 2024, should, according to the contributions, reinforce a child-centered approach based on the "notion of children's rights by design", while also encouraging innovation in game development aimed at fostering children's autonomy, personal growth, and enjoyment. The European Digital Services Act (DSA) also reinforces the need to reduce deceptive design and conduct annual risk assessments around the rights of the child, for example [7].

Finally, in legal terms, it was stressed that accountability and reparation for harm suffered by children and adolescents must go beyond simple content moderation and platform-based reporting mechanisms. It is necessary to improve access to justice (e.g., through awareness campaigns and dedicated reporting channels) and to avoid increasing the complexity of evidentiary requirements for the judicial recognition of crimes committed in digital environments—as illustrated by this excerpt from a contribution: "for example, email metadata or even requirements for notarial records".

5   Final Considerations

This paper presented an analysis of data from the public consultation on platform regulation, focusing on digital games. This section interprets our evidence and concludes the work by reinforcing its impact, limitations and future work.

5.1   Discussion

In terms of opportunities, our analysis revealed that digital games may promote the development of new skills on children. Here, we consider Roblox as an example. This platform has stood out as an innovative online gaming platform, combining elements of gaming and creation within a single virtual environment. Unlike other gaming platforms, where users primarily consume content, Roblox enables production, allowing players to develop and share their own experiences through the Roblox Studio tool. Its appeal lies in the combination of gaming and creation, providing an engaging and educational experience for children and adolescents. In other words, many users are not only consumers but also developers of environments, which fosters creativity and the acquisition of technological skills such as programming.

---

[5] Legal Framework for Electronic Games (Law No. 14,852). May 2024. Available at: https://tinyurl.com/mr4xtkfw.

Moreover, the open and collaborative environment enables real-time socialization among children of different ages and cultural backgrounds, forming a vibrant global community. This excerpt from the CGI.br consultation illustrates this benefit: *"digital platforms, beyond serving as a means of entertainment, also enable learning and the development of new skills, including for children and adolescents. Roblox, for example, is a virtual platform where users can both play and create games for others, interacting with each other"*.

At the same time, the critical view we aim to foster on caregivers and children themselves reveals the threats to privacy and security in this platform. Unlike social media platforms, which set 13 years as the minimum age for an online presence and profile creation, Roblox does not prevent users under this age from creating an account, as highlighted by a contribution to the consultation: *"unsurprisingly, about half of the players are under twelve years old"*. The presence of even younger children on the platform increases the need for user safety, particularly for children, which is one of the primary concerns. Aspects such as safety, age-appropriate design and privacy are pillars of Child's Rights by Design framework developed by 5Rights Foundation and the Digital Futures Commission, led by Professor Sonia Livingstone OBE (UK) [8].

Despite the company's efforts to implement moderation systems and content filters, the open nature of the platform makes it difficult to fully control interactions. There are reports of exposure to inappropriate content, such as violence, inappropriate language, and predatory behaviors. A recent investigation revealed alarming cases of abuse, including pedophilia and even kidnappings involving minors within the platform. These incidents underscore Roblox's vulnerabilities in ensuring the protection of its youngest users, placing the platform under increasing scrutiny from authorities and security experts [10]. The company, known for providing a space for virtual creation and interaction, faces pressure to improve its safety policies to protect minors from abuse.

Therefore, various legal initiatives have been proposed to enhance the safety of children on digital platforms. An example is the New York Children's Online Safety Act, which suggests implementing stricter measures such as making minors' profiles private by default, restricting messaging from strangers, and offering parents greater control over their children's accounts. However, Roblox has opposed being classified as a social media platform, fearing that such categorisation could lead to stricter regulations potentially affecting its business model - something that neglects the pillar "age-appropriate design", which is prioritising business models that are compatible with children's evolving capacities and agency [8]. The company's resistance to adopting these regulations reflects the complexity of the issues involved, particularly concerning privacy and age verification methods [9]. Thus, the definition of platforms and the responsibility of companies to protect more vulnerable users remain critical points of debate.

5.2 Impact

We believe that this analysis serves as an invitation for further reflection by academic researchers, offering a rich overview of risks and opportunities in this domain. In particular, the findings highlight challenges that call for a multidisciplinary approach to investigation, covering topics such as business models, child exploitation, and even the promotion of technical skills. Above all, our study benefits practitioners and institutions engaged in regulatory contexts. With the goal of strengthening online safety for children, we hope this analysis inspires the development of new norms to ensure privacy and protection for this group in games. These insights contribute to the broader movement pressuring platforms to assume greater responsibility for safeguarding young users. The recent approval of the Kids Online Safety and Privacy Act by the U.S. Senate exemplifies ongoing efforts to enforce stricter regulations on digital platforms.

5.3   Limitations and Future Work

One limitation of this study lies in its reliance on a narrow set of sources from the so-called gray literature, consisting of non-academic yet relevant texts such as government reports and news articles—used here as a supplementary data source. In addition, although the consultation adopted a multisectoral perspective (e.g., academia, NGOs), all participants were based in Brazil. While this still provides valuable insights for the intended context, a broader consultation that includes international perspectives could yield additional or different insights.

In future research, we intend to expand this dataset by combining the findings of the CGI.br consultation with

- a systematic review of news media regarding the risks posed by games;
- interviews with professionals from industry, government, and civil society organizations specialized in this area (from a more global perspective; not restricted to the Brazilian scenario). This multi-stakeholder perspective will allow us to explore the topic in greater depth and to derive concrete recommendations for parents, educators, and platforms such as Roblox, in an effort to inform the design of appropriate regulatory measures.

References

1. Alanko, D.: The health effects of video games in children and adolescents. Pediatr. Rev. **44**(1), 23–32 (2023)
2. Baughan, A., et al.: Investigating attention and normative dissociation in children's social video games. In: Proceedings of the 23rd Annual ACM Interaction Design and Children Conference, pp. 30–43. ACM, New York (2024)
3. Cruzes, D.S., Dyba, T.: Recommended steps for thematic synthesis in software engineering. In: 2011 International Symposium on Empirical Software Engineering and Measurement (ESEM), pp. 275–284. IEEE, Washington, DC (2011)
4. Darvesh, N., et al.: Exploring the prevalence of gaming disorder and Internet gaming disorder: a rapid scoping review. Syst. Rev. **9**, 1–10 (2020)
5. Lacey, C., Caudwell, C.: Cuteness as a 'dark pattern' in home robots. In: 2019 14th ACM/IEEE International Conference on Human-Robot Interaction, pp. 374–381. IEEE, Daegu (2019)

6. Monge Roffarello, A., De Russis, L.: Towards understanding the dark patterns that steal our attention. In: CHI Conference on Human Factors in Computing Systems Extended Abstracts, pp. 1–7. ACM, New York (2022)
7. European Parliament: Regulating dark patterns in the EU: Towards digital fairness. https://tinyurl.com/ydjmryu7. Accessed 01 June 2025
8. Livingstone, S., Pothong, K.: Child Rights by Design: Guidance for Innovators of Digital Products and Services Used by Children. 5Rights Foundation (2023)
9. The Verge: Roblox is the latest target of state kids online safety bills. https://tinyurl.com/3kdx7ep5. Accessed 15 May 2024
10. Bloomberg: The Pedophile Problem on Roblox. https://tinyurl.com/yeyt36m9. Accessed 16 May 2024
11. Brazilian Internet Steering Committee: ICT Kids Online Brazil: Survey on Internet Use by Children in Brazil. https://tinyurl.com/7pe4k8ye. Accessed 16 June 2025

Operationalizing Radiant Patterns: A Refined Definition and Pattern Structure to Mitigate Deceptive Game Design Practices

Luiz Santos Filho$^{(\boxtimes)}$ and Ticianne Darin

Universidade Federal do Ceará, Fortaleza, Ceará, Brazil
luis.gsantosf@alu.ufc.br, ticianne@virtual.ufc.br

Abstract. Deceptive design patterns in digital games often prioritize developer interests at the expense of player well-being by manipulating behavior in potentially harmful ways. While the concept of Radiant Game Design Patterns (RPs) was introduced as a positive alternative to counteract deceptive patterns in games, its initial theoretical framing presented challenges for consistent practical application and operationalization. This paper addresses this gap by proposing two core contributions to advance ethical game design. First, we provide a refined definition of Radiant Patterns, grounded in Self-Determination Theory (SDT), which emphasizes ensuring that foundational player well-being is not significantly compromised by avoiding a decrease in players' autonomy, competence, and relatedness. Second, we present a detailed documentation structure—a practical template—for defining, instantiating, and sharing RPs that adhere to this refined definition. The application of this definition and structure is illustrated through an in-depth example of an RP. By providing these tools for operationalization, this work aims to equip the Human-Computer Interaction (HCI) community and game developers with a systematic way to collaboratively identify, develop, empirically validate, and implement ethical alternatives to deceptive patterns.

Keywords: Game Design · Self-Determination Theory · Digital Well-Being · Deceptive Patterns · Dark Patterns · Game Design Patterns · Positive Design · Healthy Game Design · Ethical Game Design and Countermeasure

1 Introduction

Deceptive design strategies have become a widespread problem in today's digital environment, significantly impacting user interactions across various platforms, including social media, online shopping [27], mobile applications [23], cookie consent interfaces [47], and video games [16]. As research on player well-being in HCI continues to advance, studies have investigated the consequences of negative design patterns in players' daily lives, especially as the digital gaming industry has evolved over the years [18,56].

T. Darin et al. (Eds.): WIPlay 2025, CCIS 2623, pp. 112–131, 2026.
https://doi.org/10.1007/978-3-032-01426-9_8

Although games are designed to engage players and provide an enjoyable experience [11], the gaming industry has been increasingly affected by practices that do not prioritize players' best interests [26]. Patterns of deception in digital games have been highlighted in studies over the last few years, mainly due to their negative consequences and potential to trigger disorders and malicious behavior [46,49,58].

While the HCI community has taken great steps forward in improving our understanding of dark patterns [1,31], and despite the existence of relevant studies that provide essential frameworks [12], evaluation instruments [32,34], and targeted design suggestions [42], such research predominantly emphasizes identifying issues or offering broad guidance instead of showcasing the development and thorough empirical assessment of practical and beneficial game design pattern applications.

The development of *practical* and *positive* design solutions for games requires further targeted efforts. Some steps have been taken in proposing design patterns to counteract dark patterns in general-purpose applications, such as the Bright Patterns [15]; and Fair Patterns [35]. In games, Lewis [22] presented a comprehensive set of 'Motivational Design Patterns,' grounded in psychological theory and offering a "language" for motivational design, substantiated through analytical case studies. Also, Miranda [30] developed on a new pattern concept called Radiant Patterns, offering game designers an alternative to lead the players to a state of well-being, satisfying one or more basic psychological needs. These contributions by [22] [30] provide relevant conceptual bases for actionable ethical design in games.

However, proposals such as the 'Radiant Game Design Patterns' and 'Motivational Design Patterns', although they are design patterns intended for implementation, are presented mainly at a conceptual or theoretical level. While offering principles, they often lack detailed, empirically validated examples of implementation within specific game mechanics and interfaces, as well as assessments of their performance regarding both player well-being and developer goals.

The consequence of positive patterns being largely abstract conceptual frameworks is an ongoing gap between ethical ideals and specific design strategies. Designers may grasp the concept of a 'radiant' pattern that enhances autonomy, but be unable to translate this concept when redesigning problematic mechanisms [41], such as daily quest mechanisms or in-app purchasing flows.

While theoretical frameworks are essential for advancing knowledge in the field, a critical gap exists between these concepts and their empirically validated, real-world instantiation in game design. This issue demands attention, as practitioners often lack specific, tested guidance on translating such ethical principles into concrete, effective design solutions. Thus, with this paper, we aim to help bridge this divide. We shed light on the concept of Game Radiant Patterns by refining its original definition, proposing a concrete framework for defining new patterns, implementing this framework, and guiding its practical application.

Through our work, we aim to contribute to both the game industry and the HCI community by revisiting and reshaping game design patterns that promote players' well-being. By developing a more refined definition, we proposed a more applicable and operational concept for use by the game industry. For a better understanding of how this pattern is structured, we present a practical template. This template is exemplified by an example that enables game developers to identify and empirically validate patterns that can serve as alternatives to deceptive ones. Through this template, we invite researchers and game designers to foster the development of game design patterns grounded in ethical principles and oriented toward promoting player well-being.

2 How Deceptive Patterns in Digital Games Affects Players and Player-Experience

The negative effects of using deceptive patterns have been extensively studied in the literature [5,17,28]. Regardless of the context in which they are applied, it is clear that these patterns not only affect the player's interactions with electronic devices [17,24,57], but also negatively impact their lives out of screen [5,45]. This is no different from the context of digital games as well, where deceptive patterns are associated with issues such as the engagement-addiction dilemma [58], gaming disorder [49] and screen addiction disorder [46] - the latter two are already recognized as clinical disorders by the World Health Organization.

In his work, Zagal [59] addressed the use of deceptive patterns in digital games—referred to at the time as *dark patterns*. He not only identified groups of patterns that negatively affect players but also compiled a catalog outlining harmful design practices—essentially, a guide on "what not to use" in game design to avoid causing harm to players. Among these patterns are mechanics frequently found in famous digital games like *Genshin Impact*[1] and *Clash of Clans*[2], such as *Daily Rewards*—which encourage players to return every day and punish them for missing a day—and *Pay to Skip*—which allows players to spend money to bypass waiting periods enforced by timers. However, this raises a critical question: if a catalog of deceptive design patterns already exists, why do such patterns persist in being used?

One of the main reasons for the continued use of deceptive patterns is their ease of implementation. These patterns can be implemented at low cost [28], on a large scale [5], and still remain highly effective in capturing and manipulating players [7]. By exploiting cognitive biases [29], such patterns undermine players' autonomy, inducing individuals to spend time and money in ways that may ultimately be detrimental to their well-being [55]. Furthermore, popular titles known to incorporate deceptive patterns, such as *Genshin Impact* [19], *Final Fantasy XIV* [54], and *League of Legends* [13], serve as influential models within the industry. Following the commercial success of these games, other developers frequently attempt to replicate their mechanics and design strategies

---

[1] MiHoYo. 2020. Genshin Impact. Game [Android, iOS, PlayStation 4, Windows, PlayStation 5, Xbox Series X/S].

[2] Supercell. 2012. Clash of Clans [iOS, Android].

without fully understanding their negative consequences, just for financial gain and engagement.

From the player's perspective, their individual experience and level of digital literacy significantly influence how they perceive these patterns. Players who are aware of the ethics in digital games can recognize these patterns and avoid participating in games that involve them [41]. This level of literacy has a direct impact on the effectiveness of deceptive design. Many players who are unaware of the consequences of these patterns may remain active in games that use them due to the manipulation they experience, resulting in frustration and compromising their autonomy [50].

In addition to players' literacy and experience, the effectiveness of these patterns depends on players' perception of how frequently these patterns appear in games and how they are presented in the UI [25]. Due to the complexity of the consequences of deceptive patterns' use, it is necessary to study and adopt practices that are ethical and promote healthy player interactions [22].

A significant number of articles in the literature already seek to identify deceptive practices in digital games [19, 48, 50] and although they identify these patterns, there is still a gap in the literature regarding ways to mitigate the negative effects of deceptive game patterns and focus on a more ethically driven set of patterns.

Therefore, it is necessary to build upon the work of [59], which specifies which standards should *not be used*, and provide designers with a deeper understanding of *what should be used*. In this way, it enables game developers to adopt more ethical practices in their work. The Self-determination theory has been explored alongside human-computer interaction (HCI) as an alternative in the development of patterns that support players' well-being [4, 10, 30].

3 Well-Being Applied to Game Design

Over the years, video games have often been associated with negative aspects of well-being, such as aggression, reduced academic performance, and psychological disorders [36]. However, more recent studies have begun to emphasize their positive effects, particularly by referencing theories related to intrinsic motivation, such as Self-Determination Theory (SDT) [40].

According to SDT, a eudaimonic life is more likely to fulfill basic psychological needs -autonomy, competence and relatedness-, thereby enhancing well-being [38]. Psychologists have drawn on the distinction between hedonia and eudaimonia to differentiate two overlapping but distinct perspectives on well-being. Hedonic approaches define well-being primarily in terms of pleasure and happiness. In contrast, eudaimonic approaches conceptualize well-being as a multidimensional construct that goes beyond pleasure, emphasizing meaning, self-realization, and the pursuit of intrinsically valuable goals [51].

Studies grounded in SDT have shown that video games can satisfy these needs, thereby increasing intrinsic motivation. Specifically, fulfilling these needs during gameplay enhances enjoyment, the motivation to continue playing, life satisfaction, and overall psychological well-being. When these needs are met, both the gaming experience and social interactions within games tend to be evaluated more positively [52]. On the other hand, when these needs are unmet, thwarted, or when gameplay is driven by external pressures, it is linked to diminished psychological functioning [37]. In other words, the impact of playtime on well-being likely depends on the player's underlying motivations and the extent to which the game supports need satisfaction. In this context, the player's experience (PX) serves as a moderating factor: when individuals are intrinsically motivated and derive enjoyment from gameplay, increased playtime is more likely to be positively associated with well-being [20].

Recently, Self-Determination Theory has been increasingly explored in the context of digital game development [43,53,60]. Grounded on SDT, [30] introduced the concept of Radiant Patterns—design patterns intended to support player well-being by satisfying their basic psychological needs. These patterns were conceived as the antithesis of dark patterns. However, as research on radiant patterns progressed [41], it became clear that there was a need to make these patterns more practical and easier to operationalize.

4   Revisiting and Reshaping Game Radiant Patterns

While the existing literature has a solid point on deceptive patterns and how they affect users [7,28,29], it remains scattered when it comes to identifying and presenting positive and ethically designed *actionable* approaches. There are design patterns that work for the construction of specific games, such as for serious games [3], reflective games [44], and empathy games [14].

Particularly addressing DPs in games, [30] first proposed a concept of design patterns that seeks to stimulate the positive potential of human beings, mitigate adverse effects, and called them Radiant Patterns. Their goal was to help fulfill humans' basic psychological needs through design, contributing to the individual's physical and mental health by proposing alternatives that stimulate the player's well-being. [30] proposes the definition:

> *Radiant Game Design Patterns (RPs) are patterns intentionally used by a developer in the creation of digital games to preserve the player's well-being, prevent negative experiences, and support the satisfaction of the player's basic psychological needs.*

This definition was initially intended to serve as an antithesis to the concept of Game Dark Patterns defined by [59], while also referring to intentional design practices in game development that address essential aspects of player well-being and the fulfillment of intrinsic psychological needs. While useful for contrast, we argue that this framing is ultimately too limiting for the full potential of Radiant Patterns. It was a straightforward definition committed to a player-centered, ethically-driven approach to safeguarding psychological well-being, and could provide a positive framework for ethical and positive game design. For instance, in an expert opinion report for the Kommission für Jugendmedienschutz (KJM; in English, Commission for the Protection of Minors in the Media) [21], RPs were mentioned as a way to support the designation of positive patterns, intended to counteract dark patterns and offer game developers an alternative to guide players into a state of well-being. They were also considered a starting point to avoid unethical practices in game design in the Grand Research Challenges in Games and Entertainment Computing in Brazil - GranDGamesBR 2020–2030 [9].

However, their use remains theoretical, as do many other proposals for countermeasures for DPs. The nature of the RP's definition makes their practical operationalization difficult. Key terms such as "preserve the player's well-being" and "prevent negative experiences" remain broad and somewhat open to individual interpretation, making it challenging for designers to apply or assess them consistently. Besides, the goal of preventing negative experiences—although they can harm players—is an ideal that may not always align with the inherent challenges and emotional range often integral to engaging gameplay. Furthermore, the definition offers limited guidance on empirically verifying that a pattern truly "supports the satisfaction" of basic psychological needs, or how to resolve the inevitable design trade-offs where the satisfaction of one aspect might affect another.

The absence of actionable clarity and quantifiable criteria renders designers unable to convert the noble aspiration of Radiant Patterns into tangible, verifiable design choices, thereby underscoring the need for a more refined and actionable framework. This is supported by studies that applied the concept, Santos [41], showed that the original concept was challenging to implement due to the absence of clear operational parameters.

So, building directly upon the definition established by [30], we propose a **refined definition of Game Radiant Patterns** that keeps the fundamental principles of intentionality and well-being priority, but brings more specificity. It focuses on avoiding a decrease in SDT needs, acknowledges developer goals, minimizes predictable risks, and provides more precise criteria for evaluation (e.g., does it decrease autonomy, relatedness, or competence? Does it utilize known problematic patterns?). It's also more actionable for designers, giving them negative constraints and a preventative focus.

Thus, the refined definition we propose is:

Radiant Game Design Patterns (RPs) are interaction patterns intentionally selected and implemented during the digital game design process to allow the pursuit of development goals while ensuring foundational player well-being is not significantly undermined. Specifically, RPs avoid decreasing the player's autonomy, relatedness, and competence. An RP represents a conscious design choice focused on minimizing predictable risks of psychological harm and avoiding design patterns known to consistently frustrate these basic psychological needs, thereby establishing ethical boundaries for player experience.

Instead of "aiming to satisfy," the new definition shifts the emphasis to a more preventative function that includes preserving current levels of need satisfaction from being undermined by design choices. Hence, the improbable goal of avoiding all negative experiences is replaced with more specific goals: "minimizing predictable risks of psychological harm" and "avoiding design patterns known to frustrate these basic psychological needs consistently." This focuses on anticipated adverse effects directly associated with psychological harm and SDT frustration, giving designers concrete criteria based on known risks and established anti-patterns.

Therefore, the new definition does not replace the ethical core of the original, but rather *puts it into practice*, providing the clarity and practical structure needed to make it more applicable as a concept for ethically guided game design. The concept evolves from a basic moral stance to a more detailed and actionable design guideline. While the original definition of Radiant Patterns was more conceptual, the revised version is more practical and achievable.

To imply that being 'not dark' does not inherently make a pattern 'radiant.' Our refined definition emphasizes a proactive stance: Radiant Patterns are not just about avoiding the frustration of basic psychological needs (which many dark patterns explicitly cause), but about somewhat stimulating well-being, which is not significantly undermined while allowing for the pursuit of development goals. This means an RP is *actively* designed around principles that support (or at least do not detract from) autonomy, competence, and relatedness in a constructive way.

5   Crafting Radiance: A Guide to Propose Radiant Patterns

Following the refinement of the definition of radiant patterns, a format is proposed for documenting and instantiating these patterns, as a means of operationalizing the definition and making them more accessible to the industry. To develop a functional approach to applying Radiant Patterns in game development, we propose a structure to create a Radiant Pattern that follows our refined definition, as game design patterns must have clear structures that distinguish them from one another to provide game designers with additional tools to influence gameplay [22].

To achieve that, we rely on [6] proposal that builds upon [2]'s patterns definition: "*Each pattern describes a problem which occurs over and over again in our environment, and then describes the core of the solution to that problem, in such a way that you can use this solution a million times over, without ever doing it the same way twice*". Björk and Holopainen extend this idea through the lens of game design, defining game design patterns as "*semi-formal, interdependent descriptions of commonly reoccurring parts of the design of a game that concern gameplay.*"

We then identified patterns commonly used in games that promote player well-being, based on the new Radiant Pattern definition introduced in this work. These patterns were identified through the gameplay experiences of the research team, which consisted of two students (one undergraduate and one postgraduate). Each pattern was then structured and validated by an experienced researcher in the field of HCI with a background in game research.

To develop a radiant pattern model, the research team identified components that would make the pattern as operationable as possible. This would ensure that, when other researchers replicate the model, no questions or doubts would arise about how to apply it. Initially, the pattern followed [22] model of motivational patterns. However, it had to be redesigned to align with the refined definition of a Radiant Pattern grounded on self-determination theory.

The first step in structuring the template was to define the **problem** that a radiant pattern aims to address—typically, situations in digital games that affect players' gameplay. Since deceptive patterns are often used as solutions in such cases, identifying a radiant pattern that achieves the same goal without causing harm can offer a more ethical alternative in a way that could possibly mitigate any negative consequences. However, a pattern is not present in all games; its **context** varies. Therefore, a detailed description of the scenarios and styles in which it can be used is required. After presenting the problem and defining the context, we discussed how the pattern can solve the problem in that context through a **proposed solution**. As the refined definition of a radiant pattern is no longer about satisfying basic psychological needs, but rather about mitigating the frustration associated with these needs, it is necessary to explain how the pattern can promote players' well-being by avoiding a decline in autonomy, relatedness, and competence. Therefore, it is essential to demonstrate how each pattern impacts each basic psychological need individually, providing specific information on how it promotes each need without having a negative effect.

As we design this structure, we consider scenarios in which applying this pattern irregularly could cause the opposite effect of its intended purpose. Therefore, we have identified situations in which the developer must **what for** so that the pattern does not actually harm players. For a more expanded and applicable of how these patterns can either benefit or harm players, we present **examples of implementation**. These examples illustrate situations in which the patterns may be negative—failing to meet the refined definition of RP —or positive, aligning with that refined definition. To finish the template, as the patterns were initially identified through the research team's previous gaming experience, we present the community with a list of **good examples** where this pattern is applied. To better demonstrate and clarify the pattern, this example can be accompanied by an illustration of its practical application.

5.1   Radiant Pattern Structure

Following the validation. We propose a consistent structural template to support the operationalization of this refined R P definition and to guide the identification, development, and documentation of specific Radiant Patterns. This template, detailed in Table 1, outlines the essential components to be considered and described when articulating an RP. By providing a standardized format, we aim to facilitate clear communication, enable comparative analysis between different patterns, and support the creation of a robust, shareable repository of these beneficial design elements. Each identified Pattern as an RP should follow the same structural template.

Table 1. Structural Template for Radiant Game Design Patterns (RPs)

Template Component	Brief Description
Name	Evocative title for the RP.
Problem	Game design issue the RP addresses.
Context	Recommended scenarios for RP application.
Proposed Solution	Core mechanic/interaction of the RP.
Avoiding Decrease in SDT Needs	How the RP supports Autonomy, Competence, and Relatedness.
Watch For	Potential pitfalls and misapplications.
Implementation Examples (Failing/Matching)	Contrasting correct and incorrect uses.
Good Examples	Illustrative games/features using the RP.

Name. The name of a Radiant Pattern may be a single word or a phrase that describes its fundamental concept. To establish a direct association between the pattern and a positive experience for the player, it is recommended that names be selected that evoke autonomy and a sense of accomplishment. Examples of suitable names include creation, free, and evolution.

Problem. As [2] noted, patterns function as solutions to recurring problem situations. Given that the objective of Radiant Patterns is to promote player well-being, the problems they seek to address pertain to game design issues that have a detrimental effect on players' well-being or that fail to satisfy their basic psychological needs. Consequently, each Radiant Pattern should be accompanied by a description of the game design issue that this pattern aims to address.

Context. Each pattern should be accompanied by a description of recommended scenarios and game styles in which it can be applied. Given that patterns possess distinct characteristics, it is essential to define their recommended use within the game context to ensure the pattern's effectiveness in achieving its intended positive outcomes.

Proposed Solution. As a solution to a recurring problem, each description should present how the RP can effectively address the identified problem. The proposed solution outlines how game mechanics can be implemented to enable the pursuit of development goals while ensuring foundational player well-being.

Avoiding Decrease in Autonomy, Relatedness and Competence. The pattern then continues with a description of how it supports the player's basic psychological needs. The three fundamental needs—autonomy, competence, and relatedness—are addressed individually, with a thorough exposition of how each pattern positively impacts them. These descriptions elucidate the manner in which the needs are supported independently, thereby ensuring that the fulfillment of one need does not interfere with the fulfillment of others.

Watch For. If implemented improperly or outside of the intended context, the efficacy of patterns may be compromised. Therefore, it is essential to include a description of how to minimize predictable risks, avoid frustrating implementations, and highlight examples of poor applications of the pattern. Additional warnings should also be provided to help designers recognize and prevent potential issues.

Example of Implementations: Failing and Matching the RP Criteria. As an extension of the "watch for" section, it is important to present examples of pattern implementations that align with the criteria defined for Radiant Patterns. Likewise, it is necessary to provide examples where the implementation does not meet these criteria. This enables a more in-depth discussion on implementation strategies and key considerations to help mitigate potential obstacles.

Good Examples As the identified patterns are based on mechanics already present in existing games, it is essential to present a comprehensive list of games that effectively incorporate these patterns. A visual representation of the pattern's practical application within a game can enrich the definition and offer game developers a better understanding of its practical implementation.

5.2 Radiant Pattern Example

In this subsection, we demonstrate the application of the proposed RP structure and present a game mechanic found in existing games that meets the criteria for a Radiant Pattern. This Radiant Pattern is called World Creation. Below, we present its documentation as a Radiant Pattern following the structure (Table 2).

Name. World Creation - Allows players to create and customize scenarios and stages.

Problem. Players may have too little agency, creative paths, or channels of meaningful expression within the boundaries of a game's pre-determined parameters. Inert game worlds can limit long-term play and social interaction based on shared experiences.

Context. Digital games where players interact with game systems and potentially each other. Applicable across various genres (sandbox, platformers, creative suites).

Proposed Solution. Allows players to create, customize, and collaborate on or share scenarios using readily accessible tools and resources, deliberately avoiding

Table 2. Example of a Radiant Pattern: World Creation (Summary)

Template Component	Example - World Creation Summary
Name	World Creation
Problem	Addresses limited player agency, creativity, and expression in pre-defined game worlds.
Context	Digital games (sandbox, platformers, creative suites) allowing player interaction with systems and others.
Proposed Solution	Provides accessible tools for players to create, customize, collaborate, and share scenarios without core functions depending on payment or excessive grind.
Avoiding Decrease in SDT Needs	**Autonomy:** Player control over creations. **Competence:** Mastery of tools, creative achievement. **Relatedness:** Sharing, collaboration, experiencing others' content.
Watch For	Gating core tools behind payment/grind; poorly designed/obfuscated tools; restrictive sharing; insufficient scaffolding for complex tools.
Implementation Examples (Failing/Matching)	**Failing:** Core tools paywalled/grind-locked; buggy tools. **Matching:** Accessible core suite; intuitive tools; easy sharing.
Good Examples	*LittleBigPlanet* (Create Mode), *Super Mario Maker*, *Dreams*.

dependencies on direct payment or excessive repetitive grinding for core creative functions.

Avoiding Decrease in Autonomy, Relatedness, and Competence

Autonomy - World Creation promotes autonomy by giving players plenty of control and freedom (the autonomy to customize their own environments) over their creations and their interaction with the game world. It prevents reducing autonomy by definition.

Competence - The pattern enables players to learn, master tools, be creative, and overcome design challenges (harnessing their creativity, sense of 'accomplishment'). Successfully creating and sharing content builds a sense of competence. It prevents a loss of competence by offering the opportunity for skill development.

Relatedness - Being able to share creations, collaborate, or play others' work (share these creations and invite other players to join, encouraging social interaction) satisfies relatedness needs. Facilitating social connection through collaborative, creative activities helps prevent a decrease in relatedness.

Watch For. A properly designed World Creation pattern would go out of its way not to make fundamental creative tools conditional on excessive grinding or direct payment. These are predicted risks for psychological harm (frustration, exploitation) and are set patterns that necessarily thwart autonomy (loss of liberty to create) and competence (progress feels hindered or artificial). The bottom line for maintaining the World Creation framework as an RP is that fundamental creative tools, basic elements, and the main ability to save and share creations should not be expressly limited by financial constraints or only provided through substituting payment for excessive grind. Monetization should target optional enhancements, platform access, or adjacent community offerings, all while keeping the basic act of creation separate and proficiency-dependent, without creating financial pressure as a barrier to core activity.

Example of Implementations

Implementations Failing to Meet RP Criteria

To gate key components, required mechanisms, or the storage and sharing of works behind boring, repetitive gameplay cycles (grind) or outright financial expenditure. Imposing costs on essential tools would directly hinder autonomy, as players are unable to realize their creative vision and competence freely, given that the capacity to construct is unjustly restricted by external factors unrelated to creative ability.

Poor implementations or Obfuscated Tools. The presentation of creation tools that are poorly designed, buggy, lack basic features (like precise positioning or undo functions), or are poorly documented undermine the player's feeling of competency, making them feel hampered in their ability to realize their ideas because of limitations imposed by the tools instead of limitations imposed by their skill level. Additionally, this reduces autonomy by rendering specific forms of creative expression effectively impossible.

Restrictive Sharing and Discovery Mechanisms. When sharing works is difficult, discovery of the works of others is inadequately supported (e.g., no search/curation), or there are arbitrary restrictions on what or how much can be shared, the relatedness dimension of the pattern is strongly negated. This can be annoying, as many creators' motivations include sharing and communicating with the community. Restricting this diminishes the value of creation.

Insufficient Scaffolding of Sophisticated Tools. Very sophisticated creation environments can overwhelm users if not backed up by solid tutorials, progressive feature unlocking, or overt guidance (scaffolding). Unveiling tremendous complexity without help can consistently lead to frustration and abandonment, precluding competence.

Implementations In line with RP Criteria

Accessible Core Creative Suite. To make a robust set of core creation elements and tools immediately available to the player. Though some extra pieces may be gated behind an upfront barrier, the core capacity for creation and expression is untethered from unreasonable grinding or monetary expenses. This strongly encourages autonomy and establishes a foundation for competency development.

Intuitive Design and Clear Feedback. Offering user-friendly, responsive tools with clear feedback and adequate tutorials (integrated into the gameplay itself) gives players a sense of empowerment. This directly supports competence by making the tools learnable and usable and minimizing frustration with the interface.

Facilitating Sharing and Community. Emphasize being able to post and discover/play community content easily. Making sharing and discovery easy and satisfying enhances the entire creative ecosystem and avoids the frustrating trend of isolating creators. This might include sharing full games and experiences.

Optional Unlocks By Engaging Play. While fundamental tools ought to be readily available, providing optional cosmetic qualities, upgraded parts, or thematic elements as rewards for participation in many of the game's aspects (which do not solely revolve around grinding) might suit the RP model. This would provide room for progress objectives without restricting required creativity, perhaps augmenting players' senses of competence as they acquire fresh creative possibilities.

Good Examples. The LittleBigPlanet game franchise has a "Create Mode" that allows players to create levels using tools provided by the developers. These levels can be accessed by other players if they are published to the community. Similarly, the Super Mario Maker franchise allows players to create levels using items and resources from other games in the Mario franchise (Fig. 1). Dreams goes even further, allowing players to create entire games and experiences, both visually and musically.

Fig. 1. Super Mario Maker as an example of World Creation Pattern.

6   Challenges, Perspectives and Limitations

As we refined the definition and template of Radiant Patterns, we encountered challenges related to their perception, application, and evaluation. Key issues included variations in player interpretation, measuring their impact on well-being, and balancing industry goals with ethical design. We also highlighted the importance of collaboration between academia and developers for their effective adoption.

6.1   Players Perception on Radiant Patterns

Our perception of radiant pattern is grounded in the intention behind their design: to counteract the harmful effects of deceptive patterns. We expect this mitigation to occur because radiant patterns align with Self-Determination Theory, a fundamental theory for promoting player well-being. However, we acknowledge that each player's perception can affect their experience of these patterns.

First, as [41] highlighted, digital literacy regarding ethics in game development directly affects understanding of these patterns. Player who are familiar with the SDT are more likely to distinguish between positive and deceptive patterns. Second, experienced players may already be familiar with deceptive patterns from their gameplay history. As such, they recognize these patterns as commonly used strategies to engage players, often without fully understanding their consequences.

We cannot be overly confident that these patterns will work in every context which they were designed. Since these patterns were developed empirically, further evaluation is necessary to understand their actual effects, especially when considering different player profiles. Players with certain profiles may react differently to the present of such patterns. Some players may even prefer these patterns, despite the potential negative consequences, while other players didn't even download the game if they know that these patterns are presented in the game.

6.2   A Balance Between Deceptive and Radiant Patterns

We recognize that the terms "deceptive patterns" and "radiant patterns" may reflect a dualistic perspective that associates radiance with virtue and darkness with harm or unethical behavior. However, our goal is not to undermine the industry by proposing these patterns, but rather to create a balance between industry interests and player well-being – an ongoing challenge in developing such design approaches.

Our refined definition comes from the understanding that, while the initial conceptualization of Radiant Patterns positioned them partly as an antithesis to Game Dark Patterns, we believe this perspective warrants refinement. Viewing Radiant Patterns solely as the opposite of Dark Patterns might inadvertently restrict their scope. In our novel proposed perspective, a design could avoid dark patterns yet fail to be 'radiant' if it does not consciously engage with principles supporting foundational well-being, such as actively considering player autonomy, competence, and relatedness.

Radiant design is more than the absence of harm; it is the presence of thoughtful, ethically-grounded design choices to ensure player well-being is not significantly undermined while pursuing engaging experiences. True radiance implies a constructive, positive orientation that may go beyond simply counteracting manipulative techniques. This nuanced understanding is crucial as we advocate for their broader adoption and exploration. A pattern could be neutral, neither dark nor particularly radiant. Radiant Patterns aim higher, representing a conscious, positive design orientation focused on fostering healthier player-game interactions, rather than merely existing as a negation of harmful practices. This broader, more constructive view allows Radiant Patterns to be a guiding principle for innovative game design, not just a corrective measure.

6.3   The Challenge to Evaluate Players Well-Being

Evaluating the well-being that these patterns may promote in players presents significant challenges. [41] demonstrate that radiant patterns, in contrast to deceptive ones, can raise awareness of ethical principles in digital games. However, evaluating the well-being that these patterns cause in players can be challenging. [41] work shows that radiant patterns, as opposed to deceptive ones, can raise awareness of ethical precepts in digital games. However, it has not yet been possible to investigate the real effects these patterns can have on well-being since they need to be inserted into the context of a game to directly affect gameplay. For gameplay to be complete, other factors affecting the player's experience must be considered, such as visual, sound, and graphic elements. Therefore, there is a need to develop evaluation metrics that focus on radiant patterns in isolation from other gameplay elements.

There is still no methodology to directly evaluate the well-being that these patterns can cause in users. However, it is possible to assess aspects of intrinsic motivation, such as autonomy, competence, and relatedness, which belong to self-determination theory. This can be done mainly through instruments such as the PENS scale [39] and the Intrinsic Motivation Inventory (IMI) [33]. As [8] describes, positive intrinsic motivation and need satisfaction are fundamental to Player Experience because they affect the gameplay moment and the broader impact on player well-being. However, what results from the pattern itself or the experience resulting from all the aspects present in gameplay? We invite academia and the gaming industry to investigate methodologies that can determine whether motivation is genuinely positive due to its connection with the game or the result of using radiant patterns.

6.4   A Radiant Pattern Repository

Radiant Patterns face the challenge of market acceptance, as deceptive patterns are designed strategies that are already well established, widely used, and profitable, despite being ethically inappropriate. They are employed, even when developers recognize their potential harm [1], which illustrates a complex industry conflict. A next step in the evolution of Radiant Patterns would be to explore how they can generate a return for the game industry, addressing the advantages of Deceptive Patterns and making them more attractive to game developers.

This progress can be collaborative as Radiant patterns can be identified based on players' and researchers' experiences with game mechanics. Applying the template structure proposed in this work makes it possible to systematize the creation and documentation of these patterns. Thus, the Human-Computer Interaction (HCI) community and game developers can collaborate to identify and refine new Radiant Patterns. This collaboration could lead to the development of an open repository of standards, strengthening the creation of a gaming industry guided by ethical principles and committed to promoting player well-being.

6.5   Study Limitations

Although a refined definition and a detailed structure for operationalization is presented, no evaluations with players have yet been conducted to validate the direct effects of Radiant Patterns on well-being. The difficulty in isolating the effects of design patterns from other gameplay elements such as graphics, sound, and narrative also compromises the accuracy of such assessments. Generalizing these results may also be affected, as players' perceptions of the patterns can vary depending on their gaming experience, personal profiles, prior exposure to games, and awareness of the consequences of digital design patterns.

Another important limitation concerns the practical adoption of these patterns by the game industry. Although they offer an ethical alternative to deceptive patterns, Radiant Patterns have not yet demonstrated concrete commercial viability. The adoption of such patterns may not offer game designers an immediate return in terms of their key objectives, including engagement metrics and financial performance.

7   Conclusion

This paper presents a refined definition of radiant patterns and a documentation structure that serve as a template to help game developers as well researches to identify and empirically validate radiant patterns for his operationalization. This structure is exemplified through the implementation of a example of a refined defined Radiant Pattern.

As a refined pattern built upon the Self-Determination Theory, we reinforce that the basic psychological needs of players—autonomy, competence, and relatedness—are not compromised by detrimental design decisions, preserving current levels of need satisfaction as well avoiding adverse effects directly associated with psychological harm. In this work, the authors extend an invitation to the Human-Computer Interaction community to contemplate the development of ethical alternatives to deceptive patterns by employing our systematic tool to collaboratively identify those alternatives.

Acknowledgement. This paper is a partial result of the project Digital Well-Being supported by CNPq (CNPq/MCTI No 10/2023 - UNIVERSAL) under grant number 404559/2023-9.

Disclosure of Interests. The authors declare that they have no competing interests.

References

1. Aagaard, J., Knudsen, M.E.C., Bækgaard, P., Doherty, K.: A game of dark patterns: designing healthy, highly-engaging mobile games. In: CHI Conference on Human Factors in Computing Systems Extended Abstracts, pp. 1–8 (2022)
2. Alexander, C.: A Pattern Language: Towns, Buildings, Construction. Oxford University Press (1977)
3. Arnab, S., et al.: Mapping learning and game mechanics for serious games analysis. Br. J. Edu. Technol. **46**(2), 391–411 (2015)
4. Ballou, N., Deterding, S.: 'i just wanted to get it over and done with': a grounded theory of psychological need frustration in video games. Proc. ACM Hum. Comput. Interact. **7**(CHI PLAY), 217–236 (2023)
5. Baroni, L.A., Pereira, R.: Deceptive patterns under a sociotechnical view. In: Proceedings of the XXIII Brazilian Symposium on Human Factors in Computing Systems, pp. 1–13 (2024)
6. Bjork, S., Holopainen, J.: Patterns in Game Design (Game Development Series). Charles River Media. Inc., Rockland, MA, USA (2004)
7. Bongard-Blanchy, K., Rossi, A., Rivas, S., Doublet, S., Koenig, V., Lenzini, G.: " i am definitely manipulated, even when i am aware of it. it's ridiculous!"-dark patterns from the end-user perspective. In: Proceedings of the 2021 ACM Designing Interactive Systems Conference, pp. 763–776 (2021)
8. Borges, B., Darin, T.: Does it make you shiver under your skin? Stating the importance of psychophysiological measures of well-being in player's experience. In: Workshop sobre Interação e Pesquisa de Usuários no Desenvolvimento de Jogos (WIPlay), pp. 1–11. SBC (2024)
9. Darin, T., Carneiro, N., Miranda, D., Coelho, B.: Challenges in evaluating players' interaction with digital games. In: Forum on Grand Research Challenges in Games and Entertainment, pp. 1–24. Springer (2020)
10. Darin, T., Carneiro, N., Miranda, D., Coelho, B.: Challenges in evaluating players' interaction with digital games. In: Santos, R.P.d., Hounsell, M.d.S. (eds.) Grand Research Challenges in Games and Entertainment Computing in Brazil - GranDGamesBR 2020–2030, pp. 1–24. Springer, Cham (2023)
11. Dhiman, D.B.: Games as tools for social change communication: a critical review. Glob. Media J. **21**, 61 (2023)
12. Fitton, D., Read, J.C.: Creating a framework to support the critical consideration of dark design aspects in free-to-play apps. In: Proceedings of the 18th ACM International Conference on Interaction Design and Children, pp. 407–418 (2019)
13. Fredriksson Friman, E., Zätterlund, O.: The dark patterns of battle passes: Investigating player attitudes to a growing type of microtransaction (2023)
14. Galvão, V.F., Maciel, C., Da Hora Rodrigues, K.R.: How to promote empathy in games? An analysis of the structural elements to be considered in the interaction design. In: Proceedings of the XXII Brazilian Symposium on Human Factors in Computing Systems, pp. 1–12 (2023)

15. Graßl, P., Schraffenberger, H., Zuiderveen Borgesius, F., Buijzen, M.: Dark and bright patterns in cookie consent requests (2021)
16. Gualeni, S., Van de Mosselaer, N.: Ludic unreliability and deceptive game design (2021)
17. Hannula, K.: Deceptive designs in UX: investigating the impact of dark patterns. B.S. thesis (2023)
18. Hsiung, H.H., Lin, C.Y., Zhu, G.Y.: The impact of intellectual capital efficiency on value creation in video game industry—an evidence from Taiwan. J. Infrastruct. Policy Dev. **7**(3) (2023)
19. Ječius, D., Frestadius, A.: How do players experience a gacha game depending on their perspective as a starting or a veteran player?: A case study of Genshin Impact (2022)
20. Johannes, N., Vuorre, M., Przybylski, A.K.: Video game play is positively correlated with well-being. R. Soc. Open Sci. **8**(2), 202049 (2021)
21. Kammerl, R., Kramer, M., Potzel, K., Wartberg, L.: Förderung von exzessivem Nutzungsverhalten bei Games: Gutachten für die Kommission für Jugendmedienschutz (KJM), December 2023. abrufbar unter einer URL, falls bekannt
22. Lewis, C.: Motivational Design Patterns. Ph.d. dissertation, University of California, Santa Cruz (2013). proQuest ID: Lewis_ucsc_0036E_10365. Merritt ID: ark:/13030/m5bp06nc. https://escholarship.org/uc/item/30j4200s
23. Li, W., Flatla, D.R., Arndt, F.: Divergent deceptions: comparative analysis of deceptive patterns in iOS and Android apps. Behav. Inf. Technol., 1–30 (2025)
24. Luguri, J., Strahilevitz, L.J.: Shining a light on dark patterns. J. Legal Anal. **13**(1), 43–109 (2021)
25. Bhoot, A.M., Shinde, M.A., Mishra, W.P.: Towards the identification of dark patterns: an analysis based on end-user reactions. In: Proceedings of the 11th Indian Conference on Human-Computer Interaction, pp. 24–33 (2020)
26. Malaquias, R., Cardoso, P.: Deception in video games: nine game design patterns. In: International Conference on Design and Digital Communication, pp. 106–120. Springer (2024)
27. Mathur, A., et al.: Dark patterns at scale: findings from a crawl of 11k shopping websites. Proc. ACM Hum. Comput. Interact. **3**(CSCW), 1–32 (2019)
28. Mathur, A., Kshirsagar, M., Mayer, J.: What makes a dark pattern... dark? Design attributes, normative considerations, and measurement methods. In: Proceedings of the 2021 CHI Conference on Human Factors in Computing Systems, pp. 1–18 (2021)
29. Mildner, T., Inkoom, A., Malaka, R., Niess, J.: Hell is paved with good intentions: the intricate relationship between cognitive biases and deceptive design patterns. In: Mitigating Dark Patterns Through Responsible Design, p. 223 (2024)
30. Miranda, D.M., Pontes, R.M., de Gois Ribeiro Darin, T.: It's dark but just a game: towards an ethical and healthy game design practice. In: Proceedings of the 21st Brazilian Symposium on Human Factors in Computing Systems, pp. 1–7 (2022)
31. Niknejad, S., Mildner, T., Zargham, N., Putze, S., Malaka, R.: Level up or game over: exploring how dark patterns shape mobile games. In: Proceedings of the International Conference on Mobile and Ubiquitous Multimedia, MUM 2024, pp. 148–156. Association for Computing Machinery, New York (2024). https://doi.org/10.1145/3701571.3701604
32. van Nimwegen, C., Bergman, K., Akdag, A.: Shedding light on assessing dark patterns: introducing the system darkness scale (SDS). In: 35th International BCS Human-Computer Interaction Conference, pp. 1–10. BCS Learning & Development (2022)

33. Nunes, C., Darin, T.: Cross-cultural adaptation of the intrinsic motivation inventory task evaluation questionnaire into Brazilian Portuguese. In: Proceedings of the XXII Brazilian Symposium on Human Factors in Computing Systems, pp. 1–11 (2023)
34. Nyström, T., Stibe, A.: When persuasive technology gets dark? In: European, Mediterranean, and Middle Eastern Conference on Information Systems, pp. 331–345. Springer (2020)
35. Potel-Saville, M., Da Rocha, M.: From dark patterns to fair patterns? Usable taxonomy to contribute solving the issue with countermeasures. In: Annual Privacy Forum, pp. 145–165. Springer (2023)
36. Prescott, A.T., Sargent, J.D., Hull, J.G.: Metaanalysis of the relationship between violent video game play and physical aggression over time. Proc. Natl. Acad. Sci. **115**(40), 9882–9888 (2018)
37. Przybylski, A.K., Weinstein, N.: Investigating the motivational and psychosocial dynamics of dysregulated gaming: evidence from a preregistered cohort study. Clin. Psychol. Sci. **7**(6), 1257–1265 (2019)
38. Rigby, C.S., Ryan, R.M.: Time well-spent?: Motivation for entertainment media and its eudaimonic aspects through the lens of self-determination theory. In: The Routledge Handbook of Media Use and Well-Being, pp. 34–48. Routledge (2016)
39. Rigby, S., Ryan, R.: The Player Experience of Need Satisfaction (PENS) Model, pp. 1–22. Immersyve Inc. (2007)
40. Ryan, R.M., Deci, E.L.: Self-determination Theory: Basic Psychological Needs in Motivation, Development, and Wellness. Guilford Publications (2017)
41. Santos Filho, L., Sousa Junior, A., Ribeiro, G., Darin, T.: They say that the world was built for two but deceptive patterns say otherwise: a critical game for player empowerment. In: Proceedings of the XXIII Brazilian Symposium on Human Factors in Computing Systems, pp. 1–15 (2024)
42. Sas, M., Denoo, M., Mühlberg, J.T.: Informing children about privacy: a review and assessment of age-appropriate information designs in kids-oriented F2P video games. Proc. ACM Hum. Comput. Interact. **7**(CHI PLAY), 425–463 (2023)
43. Sevinçli, M.C., Aydoğmuş, M.E.: Video games as a part of intervention programs based on self-determination theory. Psikiyatride Guncel Yaklasimlar **14**(2), 207–220 (2022)
44. Shaheen, A., Fotaris, P., Fallahkhair, S.: A systematic review of using reflective design features in game-based learning. In: 15th European Conference on Game Based Learning ECGBL, vol. 2021, pp. 638–645 (2021)
45. Shi, Z., Sun, R., Chen, J., Sun, J., Xue, M.: The invisible game on the internet: a case study of decoding deceptive patterns. In: Companion Proceedings of the ACM Web Conference 2024, pp. 521–524 (2024)
46. Sigman, A.: Screen dependency disorders: a new challenge for child neurology. J. Int. Child. Neurol. Ass. **17**, 119 (2017)
47. Soe, T.H., Nordberg, O.E., Guribye, F., Slavkovik, M.: Circumvention by design-dark patterns in cookie consent for online news outlets. In: Proceedings of the 11th Nordic Conference on Human-Computer Interaction: Shaping Experiences, Shaping Society, pp. 1–12 (2020)
48. Sousa, C., Oliveira, A.: The dark side of fun: Understanding dark patterns and literacy needs in early childhood mobile gaming. In: European Conference on Games Based Learning, vol. 17, pp. 599–610 (2023)
49. Stevens, M.W., et al.: Global prevalence of gaming disorder: a systematic review and meta-analysis. Aust. New Zealand J. Psychiatry **55**(6), 553–568 (2021)

50. Stockman, C., O'Connell, A., Nottingham, E.: When it's cute but also dark: critical analysis of Farmcute but also Darkille 3's game design in the digital economy. Int. Rev. Law Comput. Technol., 1–23 (2024)
51. Thorsteinsen, K., Vittersø, J.: Now you see it, now you don't: Solid and subtle differences between hedonic and eudaimonic wellbeing. J. Posit. Psychol. **15**(4), 519–530 (2020)
52. Türkay, S., Lin, A., Johnson, D., Formosa, J.: Self-determination theory approach to understanding the impact of videogames on wellbeing during COVID-19 restrictions. Behav. Inf. Technol. **42**(11), 1720–1739 (2023)
53. Tyack, A., Mekler, E.D.: Self-determination theory in HCI games research: current uses and open questions. In: Proceedings of the 2020 CHI Conference on Human Factors in Computing Systems, pp. 1–22 (2020)
54. Veiga, E., Silva, N., Gadelha, B., Oliveira, H., Conte, T.: Dark patterns in games: an empirical study of their harmfulness (2025)
55. Waldman, A.E.: Cognitive biases, dark patterns, and the 'privacy paradox'. Curr. Opin. Psychol. **31**, 105–109 (2020)
56. Wijman, T.: Newzoo's year in review: the 2023 global games market in numbers. https://newzoo.com/resources/blog/video-games-in-2023-the-year-in-numbers
57. Willis, L.E.: Deception by design. Harv. JL Tech. **34**, 115 (2020)
58. Yang, Q., Gong, X.: The engagement-addiction dilemma: an empirical evaluation of mobile user interface and mobile game affordance. Internet Res. **31**, 1745–1768 (2021). https://doi.org/10.1108/INTR-11-2020-0622
59. Zagal, J.P., Björk, S., Lewis, C.: Dark patterns in the design of games. In: Foundations of Digital Games 2013 (2013)
60. Zhao, C., et al.: The effects of active video game exercise based on self-determination theory on physical fitness and cognitive function in older adults. J. Clin. Med. **11**(14), 3984 (2022)

Practical Methods and Frameworks
for Game Design and Evaluation

A Non-functional Requirements Catalog of Aesthetics for Digital Games

Rafael Felipe Colloca Carrion, Henrique Prado de Sá Sousa, and Tadeu Moreira de Classe(✉)

Research Group on Games to Complex Contexts (JOCCOM), Graduate Program in Informatics (PPGI), Federal University of the State of Rio de Janeiro (UNIRIO), Rio de Janeiro, RJ, Brazil
rafael.carrion@edu.unirio.br, {hsousa,tadeu.class}@uniriotec.br

Abstract. Aesthetics is an important qualitative aspect of games that can significantly influence players' experience; however, its conceptualization as a Non-Functional Requirement (NFR) in game software remains underexplored. In this paper, we mapped a catalog of NFRs focused on the aesthetics of digital games. This represents an initial step toward providing a structured foundation that helps developers and designers treat aesthetics as a fundamental aspect of design, rather than a final refinement stage, thereby fostering richer and more satisfying aesthetic experiences for players. The catalog development was based on an analysis of key aesthetic theories, including MDA, GUESS, and Schell's Elemental Tetrad. Additionally, it was refined and validated with the input of experts in related fields. The NFRs were modeled using the Softgoal Interdependence Graph (SIG), enabling a conceptual knowledge map that helps to understand and operationalize aesthetic requirements.

Keywords: Game Aesthetics · Requirements Engineering · SoftGoal Interdependence Graph · Digital Games

1 Introduction

Games have been an integral part of human life since the dawn of civilization, serving as tools for socialization, entertainment, and even learning [6]. With technological advancements culminating in the digital revolution, new types of games emerged: digital games. This format has become a new form of cultural and artistic expression, revolutionizing the entertainment industry and impacting the global economy [11]

In the 1990s, 3D technology revolutionized game design, enabling the creation of explorable environments and dynamic camera angles. Today, the combination of technologies such as artificial intelligence, machine learning, and realistic graphics continues to transform digital games. This evolution allowed digital games to become increasingly complex, as well as enabling their use in many contexts beyond entertainment [18].

T. Darin et al. (Eds.): WIPlay 2025, CCIS 2623, pp. 135–147, 2026.
https://doi.org/10.1007/978-3-032-01426-9_9

For example, serious digital games include categories such as educational, training, and awareness games, with objectives beyond just entertainment. These games leverage simulations to teach content, develop skills, or raise awareness related to socially relevant topics, utilizing the interactivity and engagement of digital games to offer players a way to explore, understand, and even transform aspects of reality and social challenges [15].

The development of digital games is a multidisciplinary practice that combines skills in programming, design, narrative, and digital art. In the context of games, the terms "art" and "aesthetics" take on similar meanings in the industry, often associated with the player's visual experience [24], however, aesthetics is a broader concept in the academic context. Although there are various formal definitions of aesthetics in video game studies, they mainly involve sensory elements (usually visual and auditory) that interact with the player's senses and aspects of their perception and responses [19]. In this research, we expanded the concept by consolidating knowledge from different authors and theories.

The aesthetics of digital games play a fundamental role in the immersion and engagement of the player [22]. The sensory and emotional aspects of the gaming experience are strongly influenced by choices related to aesthetics, for example, the color palette can evoke different emotional states, while sound design can heighten tension or provide relaxation [12]. Aesthetics can also contribute to the narrative, connecting the player to the game's world on deeper levels and creating an experience beyond visual and auditory interaction [1].

Therefore, aesthetics in digital games constitute the initial layer of interaction between the player and the game, serving as a gateway to other aspects of digital games and their design [26]. Studies such as [3] indicate that well-designed aesthetic elements can enhance player satisfaction and engagement, with potential effects on cognitive performance.

Aesthetics can be understood as a Non-Functional Requirement (NFR) due to its conceptual lack of clarity, which is a well-known challenge in the software engineering field [4,8]. While functional requirements directly describe what the system must do, NFRs have specific characteristics that make it complex to determine and evaluate (other examples: performance, security, and usability).

In digital games, aesthetics plays a significant role, as its absence can severely compromise the player experience [23]. To better formalize aesthetics as a software NFR, it is necessary to deeply study its concept and understand in detail what it means in the game's domain. As a qualitative characteristic, aesthetics is an abstract concept that can not be defined per se, but it exists as a sum of many other qualitative elements. These elements can contribute positively or negatively to each other. The mapping of these elements and their relationships leads to an NFR catalog, commonly modeled using the Softgoal Interdependence Graph (SIG) model, proposed in the NFR Framework [5] (in this paper, references to the aesthetics SIG model or catalog indicate the same artifact).

As a first step to elicit knowledge, we made a systematic literature review (SLR) in the digital game literature [2] that revealed a lack of studies addressing aesthetics as an NFR; most works focus on other aspects such as technology and design, highlighting the need for a structured study. After this first step, we evaluate the catalog's content through interviews with experts in requirements engineering and game development.

The SIG model is used in Requirement Engineering as a catalog of knowledge that supports the conceptual understanding of mapped NFRs and guides their operationalization. Improving the specification of requirements contributes to the success of software projects by enhancing various intended impacts of games beyond entertainment, such as education, training, and awareness-raising, among other applications [6].

The remainder of this paper is structured in the following sections: Sect. 2 presents our research background, considering essential definitions to understand our proposal. Section 3 shows the methodology we followed to develop our catalog. Section 4, we presented the aesthetics NFR catalog for digital games using a SIG model, and in Sect. 5, we present a discussion of the study. Finally, Sect. 6 presents the final remarks and future works.

2   Backgrounds

2.1   Aesthetic Theories and Theoretical Lens

Various academic theories approach the aesthetics of digital games in different ways, as mentioned earlier. The MDA framework (Mechanics, Dynamics, Aesthetics) [7] categorizes the aesthetics of games as the emotional experience that players undergo through interaction with the game's mechanics and dynamics, consisting of three main components: mechanics (rules and systems), dynamics (interactions and processes), and aesthetics (experience and emotions). The GUESS theory (Gameplay, User experience, Environment, and Story) [21] integrates aesthetics with user experience and narrative, focusing on evaluating player satisfaction with great attention to usability as one of the critical factors. It categorizes aesthetic experience primarily based on visual, auditory, and interface elements. Jesse Schell's Elemental Tetrad [25], popularized through his book The Art of Game Design, defines aesthetics as the emotional feedback provided to the player, transmitted through sensory aspects such as visual, auditory, and tactile elements of the game. Each of these approaches, and others not mentioned, offers a unique perspective on aesthetics and its elements, but they fundamentally agree that aesthetics are crucial to the player's experience, directly influencing immersion through interaction with other game elements [29].

To conduct a comprehensive analysis of the aesthetics of digital games, we used the three main aesthetic theories mentioned: MDA [7], GUESS [21], and Jesse Schell's Elemental Tetrad [25]. These theories were identified as the most influential during a systematic literature review [2], encompassing different approaches to aesthetic elements and their interactions with other aspects of game design. The integration of these theories aims to help developers reflect on all relevant aesthetic aspects

Aesthetics play an important role in the design of digital games, shaping how players perceive and engage with the game world. By synthesizing the insights of the theories mentioned, developers can gain a comprehensive perspective on the aesthetic dimensions of games and their interplay with other elements of the game. This integration supports the creation of more complete game experiences, enriching the overall interaction between players and the game environment [30].

2.2   Requirements Engineering

Requirements Engineering (RE) is fundamental to software development, acting in the definition, analysis, and management of the requirements that the system must meet from the elicitation with stakeholders [13] to the end of the software life cycle, when no further evolution of the requirements is expected.

One of the challenges in the field is dealing with quality requirements, which have specific characteristics, such as the subjectivity of perception [4]. These requirements play a special role in the construction of games, since these types of software explore various dimensions of human perception, which increases the need for attention to the specifications of these requirements, as well as the qualitative impact they may have on users. Therefore, these requirements may be directly linked to the outcome of the players' experience, potentially impacting positively or negatively the success of the games, especially in meeting their primary objectives, for example, training [10] and learning [17].

In software engineering, qualitative requirements are defined as NFRs [4]. Some NFRs are abstract and require study to appropriately determine their concept and, subsequently, ways to operationalize them. For example, requirements such as transparency [14] and accessibility [20] are extensively studied and instantiated for different domains. Legal requirements of a qualitative nature are also investigated to be better addressed [16,27].

As said before, abstract requirements are characterized by being correlated with others of the same nature, being elements resulting from the composition of these correlations. Through this mapping, it is possible to better understand the concept of the main requirement, which will help when studying better ways to operationalize it in the different dimensions of game software.

3   Construction Process of the Aesthetics Catalog

The process of building the SIG was segmented into three phases: the elicitation of NFRs, the SIG graph modeling, and finally, the evaluation of the SIG. The diagram in Fig. 1 illustrates the SIG construction process.

The initial phase was dedicated to examining the NFRs based on the research results. We considered results from a systematic literature review [2] and reading definitions and books. The subsequent phase focused on developing the catalog, organizing, elaborating, and refining the identified NFRs by SIG modeling, using game design specialists. During the evaluation phase, the catalog was presented to academic experts and professionals from relevant sectors related to game

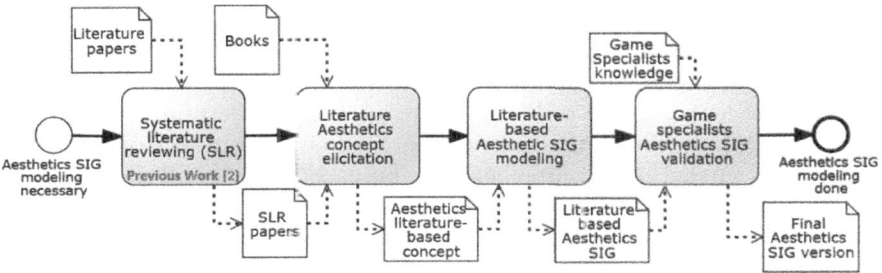

Fig. 1. SIG development methodology.

development. Then, the catalog was refined, representing the final phase of its construction, when we created the final SIG version.

3.1   Systematic Literature Mapping (SLM)

In previous work [2], we conducted a Systematic Literature Mapping (SLM) to identify the aesthetic aspects discussed by the authors of primary studies and consequently elicit the NFRs based on the findings. Among the 758 articles identified, 18 studies were selected after applying the inclusion and exclusion criteria.

3.2   Literature Aesthetics Concept Elicitation

Before starting the research, we realized that the aesthetics of digital games is a promising academic area, but with limited research compared to other domains. It was also noted that aesthetic elements, although present, are usually not the main focus of researchers' discussions. Therefore, we began the research by looking for requirements in non-primary academic studies.

During the first two steps, no structured guidelines were found addressing aesthetic qualities in digital games from a requirements engineering perspective. Existing studies tend to focus on comments on aesthetic operationalizations and specific challenges related to these aspects [2]. The organization of aesthetic requirements followed these comments and observations for the completion of the next step.

However, the systematic review revealed the most applied aesthetic theories in the study of digital games, which will serve as the foundation for this research by offering varied perspectives on aesthetic requirements and player experience.

3.3   Literature-Based Aesthetic SIG Modeling

Subsequently, the actions to build the catalog were planned. First, three main domains covered by the catalog were defined, based on the main aesthetic definitions mentioned earlier: MDA [7], GUESS [21], and the Elemental Tetrad [25], thus encompassing a broader range of relevant aspects for the development of the aesthetics of a digital game, according to the knowledge elicited in [2]. Additionally, the authors, whose combined expertise spans requirements engineering and game development (more than 10 years of academic and professional experience), elicited and reviewed requirements based on their collective knowledge, ensuring a grounded and comprehensive approach. Finally, all elicited NFRs were organized with their respective definitions.

Developing the catalog involved organizing the information at this stage. The NFR Framework [5] notation was adopted, and a Softgoal Interdependence Graph (SIG) was created to represent the NFRs catalog. Furthermore, the catalog is designed to encompass broad and widely applicable terms, ensuring that it captures the essential elements present in most digital games.

3.4   Game Specialists Validation

To validate the version of the catalog's SIG graph specific based on the literature, we carried out the dissemination and evaluation steps with six experts in game development. Each expert evaluated the completeness and satisfaction of the graph concerning the aesthetic requirements, self-assessing their knowledge in the related areas. During the interviews, opinions on removing, adding, and modifying requirements were also collected, which provided feedback to improve the catalog.

After validation with experts, the catalog was refined to incorporate suggestions for adjustments in the structure and content of the requirements. This aimed to ensure a representation more aligned with the essential aesthetic aspects for digital game development.

4   Catalog of Aesthetics in Digital Games

This section presents the research artifact developed to support the development of aesthetic NFRs in the context of digital games. This catalog aims to provide a structured foundation for the development of aesthetics in digital games, an area that is under-researched compared to other areas of game development in the academy, serving as a reference for game developers and designers by considering aesthetics as an essential design element rather than just a final refinement phase.

4.1   Identification and Justification of NFRs

To construct the SIG, NFRs that emerged from the literature review [2] and readings of books specialized in the subject were considered. The approach for building the SIG was based on three aesthetic theories of digital games found in the literature review—MDA [7], GUESS [21], and Jesse Schell's Elemental Tetrad [25].

The concept of aesthetics as an NFR for digital games is a recent and underexplored perspective in academic literature. Due to the lack of studies directly addressing qualities of aesthetics and requirements in this context, it was necessary to interpret based on established theories in the field of game development previously mentioned. This approach allowed for the validation of the qualities of aesthetics. The Table 1 represents the relationship between non-functional requirements that are linked to aesthetics and their respective sources of information. Additionally, the initial opinions of authors with combined knowledge in game development and requirements engineering will be compared.

Table 1. The presence of NFRs in the theories and analysis of the authors

NFRs	MDA	Elementary Tetrad	GUESS	Authors' initial analysis
Environmentality	Yes	Yes	Yes	Yes
Immersiveness	Yes	Yes	Yes	Yes
detailability	No	Yes	No	Yes
Visuality	Yes	Yes	Yes	Yes
Sonority	Yes	Yes	Yes	Yes
Interactivity	Yes	Yes	Yes	Yes
Narrativity	Yes	No	Yes	Yes
Expressiveness	Yes	Yes	No	Yes
Emotional Range	Yes	No	No	No
Synchrony	Yes	No	No	Yes
Authenticity	No	No	No	Yes
Relatability	No	No	Yes	Yes
Depth	Yes	No	No	No
Usability	No	No	Yes	Yes
Adaptability	No	No	Yes	Yes
Comprehensibility	No	Yes	Yes	No
Accessibility	No	No	Yes	Yes
Clarity	No	Yes	No	Yes
Responsiveness	No	No	Yes	No
Consistency	Yes	No	No	Yes

The analysis of the results reveals that, although the three theories cover various important qualities of aesthetics, some were not explicitly addressed but remain relevant in supporting the other mentioned requirements. Additionally, the authors, leveraging their combined expertise in requirements engineering and game development, elicited and reviewed requirements. The table reflects on the theories, highlighting aspects of aesthetics such as emotional response, usability, and immersive sensory experience. Based on these, we identified and justified the inclusion of the key non-functional requirements, considering how each theory emphasizes the connection between aesthetics and the player experience. The NFRs and their respective definitions are represented in Table 2. These definitions were primarily derived from the three theories of aesthetics presented in Table 1, except for the quality 'authenticity,' whose definition can be found in the book [28].

The Concepts are merged from different sources to reach a broader understanding of the concept studied. Incorporating different perspectives helps identify a wider range of qualities that may contribute to a higher level of aesthetics.

Table 2. NFRs' definitions

NFRs	Definition
Environmentality	The ability to immerse the user in the game's setting
Immersiveness	The ability to sensorially insert the user into the current moment of the game
detailability	The ability to present details that enrich the environment
Visuality	The ability to visually represent the game's elements and actions
Sonority	The ability to represent the game's elements and actions through sound
Interactivity	The ability to interact with various game elements
Narrativity	The ability to convey the game's story
Expressiveness	The ability to evoke emotional responses from the user
Emotional Range	The ability to portray a variety of emotions
Synchrony	The ability to use aesthetic elements consistent with emotional tone
Authenticity	The ability to depict emotions and feelings realistically
Relatability	The ability to involve the user in the characters' emotions
Depth	The ability to represent complex emotions
Usability	The ability to optimize and enhance player interactions
Adaptability	The ability to tailor the game to the player's individual preferences and needs
Comprehensibility	The ability to communicate the meaning of interactions clearly
Accessibility	The ability to accommodate users with diverse needs and limitations
Clarity	The ability to present information clearly and unambiguously
Responsiveness	The speed and precision of interactive responses to the user
Consistency	The ability to present interactions with predictable patterns

4.2   Structuring the SIG

The SIG graph was structured into three main branches, each representing the peculiarities of each theory and their interdependencies with game design elements. These initial branches correspond to key dimensions: expressiveness (emotional aspects), environmentability (sensory aspects), and usability (functional aspects). In this way, the graph encompasses aesthetic experience in a multidimensional manner.

With the requirements identified and justified through the theoretical lenses mentioned, a preliminary version (Fig. 2 – just white clouds) of the SIG graph was developed.

4.3   SIG Evaluation and Refinement Process

Evaluation Phase. The SIG was examined through interviews with six experts in digital game development and requirements engineering during an academic conference on digital games. This evaluation process sought to assess the artifact's structure and completeness as a potential guide for applying aesthetic concepts in game development, while also exploring its possible utility as a support artifact.

Experts were invited to share their perspectives on the preliminary graph, offering suggestions for possible modifications, exclusions, or additions. As part of the process, they completed self-assessments using a Likert scale (1 = totally disagree to 5 = totally agree) [9] covering three relevant domains: game development, game aesthetics, and requirements engineering. The NFR catalog's adequacy was similarly evaluated Table 3.

Table 3. Self-assessment and Satisfaction according to Specialists.

Questions	Specialist 1	Specialist 2	Specialist 3	Specialist 4	Specialist 5	Specialist 6
What is your level of knowledge in game development?	3	4	4	4	5	5
What is you level of knowledge in aesthetics of games?	3	2	3	3	4	3
What is your level of knowledge in requirements engineering?	5	1	1	3	3	4
Is the catalog satisfactory for its purpose?	**4**	**4**	**5**	**4**	**4**	**3**

Refinement Phase. The experts' suggestions were considered during the refinement process, which involved reviewing possible additions, removals, and modifications to requirements. One notable discussion point centered on the inclusion of usability as an aesthetic aspect. Although some experts expressed reservations about this connection, the theoretical framework (particularly the GUESS theory) supported considering usability as one component of aesthetic experience.

The resulting version Fig. 2 (white and gray clouds - after refining) appears to reflect several enhancements compared to the initial graph. This artifact offers a preliminary framework for examining aesthetic requirements in digital games from an RE perspective. Although representing progress in this area, the catalog naturally raises questions that could benefit from further investigation. The study may serve as a starting point for future work that might expand and develop this approach.

5   Discussion

The research highlights the scarcity of studies connecting non-functional requirements (NFRs) to aesthetic challenges, an area that requires greater attention and development. While the catalog created by the authors represents progress, it is important to acknowledge that the expert's evaluation involved six participants, with particular underrepresentation of specialists in game aesthetics compared to other domains, mirroring the broader academic landscape where this area receives less attention than technical aspects of game development.

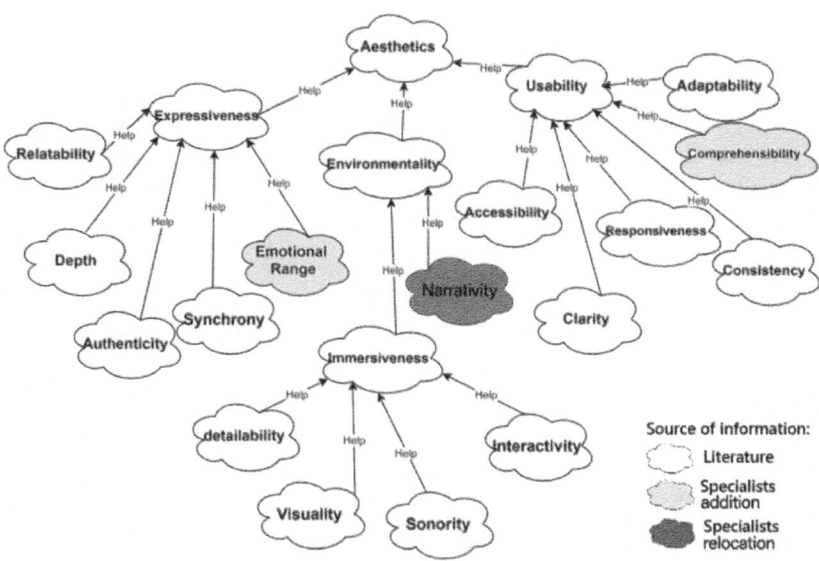

Fig. 2. Aestethics Catalog.

Additionally, the inherently subjective nature of aesthetic experiences presents fundamental challenges for systematic categorization. These considerations suggest the catalog would benefit from further refinement and expansion in future work.

The analysis of key aesthetic theories provides a solid foundation for discussing aesthetics in digital games. However, the integration of these theories and the practical application of aesthetic NFRs still require validation and refinement. The research suggests that, while it represents a relevant first step, further developments and revisions will be essential to expand and refine this approach. This indicates that the field is in its early stages and that more work is needed to mature the understanding of aesthetics in digital games.

Moreover, the importance of this article lies precisely in its ability to open a dialogue about aesthetics in games, an aspect often overlooked in game design. Aesthetics is not merely a superficial element; it directly influences the player's experience and immersion in the game, as discussed in the presented theories. Thus, the research not only contributes to the existing literature but also serves as a call to action for more academics and developers to engage with this topic.

In summary, aesthetics is a powerful element in digital games, shaping emotional impact and player engagement. While the industry recognizes and leverages the value of aesthetics to create visually appealing and immersive experiences, academics often underestimate its potential. This oversight limits opportunities for deeper exploration into how aesthetics enhance not just entertainment but also the effectiveness of serious games.

In the context of serious games, a stronger grasp of aesthetics by developers could lead to significantly improved user experiences, aligning with the social and educational goals these games often aim to achieve. Given that many serious games are developed in academic environments, incorporating aesthetic considerations more effectively could amplify their impact, ensuring they are not only functional but also deeply engaging and purpose-driven. This article represents an important step toward addressing this gap, serving as a starting point for future research to explore and expand the role of aesthetics in the development of digital games.

6 Final Remarks and Future Work

This study explores the importance of integrating non-functional requirements of aesthetics into the development of digital games, highlighting a gap in the academic literature, which often prioritizes technical and design aspects over aesthetics, a crucial element for the player's experience. The research aims to explore the concept of aesthetics in depth and then map the interrelated qualities as NFRs using the SIG model. This model helps to visualize the complexity of the main concept (aesthetics) and provides developers with a clear and practical tool to guide the operationalization of it in digital games.

The catalog was mapped from different sources, including literature and Specialists in game design. The catalog was evaluated by a small set of experts in these domains, suggesting its usefulness. In future work, other rounds of evaluation will be implemented to better validate the catalog's usefulness. It is not easy to reach a final version of an NFR catalog due to the qualitative concepts that compose it and which may have different meanings within domains. This catalog is a first effort to help game software requirement professionals understand aesthetics and then better operationalize it for digital games. Additionally, the fact that this is an underexplored research area highlights the existence of hidden challenges, leading to the need for future studies to deepen the understanding of aesthetics in digital games, aiming for more robust and integrated development.

The mapping of the aesthetics catalog helps professionals to better understand the aesthetics concept, consequently enabling them to analyze how to operationalize it in game software. The catalog also demonstrates that aesthetics is a multidimensional element composed of different aspects of the game art. Such an approach may pave the way for scholars in areas such as game design, user experience, and software engineering to further explore how aesthetic aspects can enhance player experience and development guidelines.

As future steps, we intend to expand the catalog of non-functional requirements by conducting research in the context of serious games, with a particular focus on educational games. This development could directly benefit the design of educational games, offering a robust aesthetic foundation for developers who often lack expertise in aesthetics due to the multidisciplinary nature of games.

Acknowledgment. The authors thank Coordination for the Improvement of Higher Education Personnel (CAPES) and Carlos Chagas Filho Foundation for Research Support of the State of Rio de Janeiro – FAPERJ (proc. E-26/204.478/2024) for partially funding this research.

References

1. Atkinson, P., Parsayi, F.: Video games and aesthetic contemplation. Games Cult. (2021). https://doi.org/10.1177/1555412020914726
2. Carrion, R.F.C., de Classe, T.M.: Como estética é utilizada e aplicada no design de jogos educativos? um estudo sistemático da literatura. In: Anais do XXIII Simpósio Brasileiro de Jogos e Entretenimento Digital, pp. 25–37. SBC, Porto Alegre, RS, Brasil (2024). https://doi.org/10.5753/sbgames.2024.241046
3. Casanova, F., Oliveira, J., Williams, M., Garganta, J.: Expertise and perceptual-cognitive performance in soccer: a review. Revista portuguesa de Ciencias do Desporto **9**(1), 115–122 (2009)
4. Chung, L., do Prado Leite, J.C.S.: On non-functional requirements in software engineering. In: Borgida, A.T., Chaudhri, V.K., Giorgini, P., Yu, E.S. (eds.) Conceptual Modeling: Foundations and Applications. LNCS, vol. 5600, pp. 363–379. Springer, Heidelberg (2009). https://doi.org/10.1007/978-3-642-02463-4_19
5. Chung, L., Nixon, B.A., Yu, E., Mylopoulos, J.: Non-Functional Requirements in Software Engineering, vol. 5. Springer, New York (2012). https://doi.org/10.1007/978-1-4615-5269-7
6. Huizinga, J.: 1938: Homo Ludens: A Study of the Play-Element in Culture (1955)
7. Hunicke, R., LeBlanc, M., Zubek, R., et al.: MDA: a formal approach to game design and game research. In: Proceedings of the AAAI Workshop on Challenges in Game AI, San Jose, CA, vol. 4, p. 1722 (2004)
8. Jarzębowicz, A., Weichbroth, P.: A systematic literature review on implementing non-functional requirements in agile software development: issues and facilitating practices. In: Przybyłek, A., Miler, J., Poth, A., Riel, A. (eds.) LASD 2021. LNBIP, vol. 408, pp. 91–110. Springer, Cham (2021). https://doi.org/10.1007/978-3-030-67084-9_6
9. Joshi, A., Kale, S., Chandel, S., Pal, D.K.: Likert scale: explored and explained. Br. J. Appl. Sci. Technol. **7**(4), 396–403 (2015)
10. Júnior, R.R., de Classe, T.M., de Castro Lima, C.: Games with safety training purposes in the industry: game design method and its demonstration. J. Interact. Syst., 434–449 (2024)
11. Kaur, A., Behki, P.: The evolution and impact of game development in the digital era. In: 2024 International Conference on Emerging Technologies in Computer Science for Interdisciplinary Applications (ICETCS), pp. 1–6. IEEE (2024)
12. Kehm, O.: Mystery Through Visual Detail: How Video Game Art Impacts Emotion. Master's thesis, Toronto Metropolitan University (2022)
13. Kotonya, G., Sommerville, I.: Requirements Engineering: Processes and Techniques. Wiley Publishing (1998)
14. Leite, J.C.S.P., Cappelli, C.: Software transparency. Bus. Inf. Syst. Eng., 127–139 (2010)
15. de Matos Lima, S., Otero, P.: Serious games are more than just games. Archivos Argentinos De Pediatria (2024). https://doi.org/10.5546/aap.2023-10218.eng
16. Mendes, J., Viana, D., Rivero, L.: Developing an inspection checklist for the adequacy assessment of software systems to quality attributes of the Brazilian general data protection law: an initial proposal. In: Proceedings of the XXXV Brazilian Symposium on Software Engineering, pp. 263–268 (2021)

17. de Menezes, G.J., Hatherly, R.M., de Oliveira, E.G., de Classe, T.M.: Sqland: aprendendo sql com suporte de um jogo digital educacional. In: REVISTA NOVAS TECNOLOGIAS NA EDUCAÇÃO, pp. 426–435 (2024)

18. Mudryk, S.: Variability of games in the process of human development. Naukovij časopis Nacional'nogo pedagogičnogo universitetu ìmenì M.P. Dragomanova (2024). https://doi.org/10.31392/udu-nc.series15.2024.5(178).26

19. Niedenthal, S.: What we talk about when we talk about game aesthetics. In: Proceedings of DiGRA 2009 Conference: Breaking New Ground: Innovation in Games, Play, Practice and Theory (2009)

20. Oliveira, R., Silva, L., Leite, J.C.S.P., Moreira, A.: Eliciting accessibility requirements an approach based on the NFR framework. In: Proceedings of Annual ACM Symposium on Applied Computing, pp. 1276–1281. ACM (2016)

21. Phan, M.H., Keebler, J.R., Chaparro, B.S.: The development and validation of the game user experience satisfaction scale (GUESS). Hum. Fact. **58**(8), 1217–1247 (2016)

22. Ramirez Gomez, A., Lankes, M.: Eyesthetics: making sense of the aesthetics of playing with gaze. Proc. ACM Hum.-Comput. Interact. **5**(CHI PLAY), 1–24 (2021)

23. Saadatmand, M., Tahvili, S.: A fuzzy decision support approach for model-based tradeoff analysis of non-functional requirements. In: 2015 12th International Conference on Information Technology-New Generations, pp. 112–121. IEEE (2015)

24. Santaella, L.: Game arte no contexto da arte digital. DAT J. **2**(1), 3–14 (2017)

25. Schell, J.: Tenth Anniversary: The Art of Game Design. CRC Press, Boca Raton (2020)

26. Schlüter, A., Waldkirch, M., Burmeister-Lamp, K., Auernhammer, J.: No second chance for a first impression: the role of aesthetics in early access video games. Int. J. Innov. Manag. **25**(10), 2140002 (2021)

27. de Sá Sousa, H.P., Almentero, E.K., de Classe, T.M., dos Santos, R.J., Leite, J.C.S.P.: Uma abordagem baseada no catálogo de requisitos não funcionais para conformidade à lgpd. In: Workshop de Engenharia de Requisitos 2023 (2023)

28. Tettegah, S., Huang, W.D.: Emotions, Technology, and Digital Games. Academic Press (2015)

29. Vella, D.: Beyond agency: games as the aesthetics of being. J. Philosophy Sport **48**(3), 436–447 (2021)

30. Vuksanovic, D.: Aesthetics, media, games. Biblioteka Diogen **30**(2), 142–157 (2022). https://doi.org/10.54664/rdrd7616

ThinkPlay: Integrating Learning Indicators in Educational Digital Games

Eric Carvalho da Silveira[1]([✉]), Matheus Soppa Geremias[2],
Taynara Cerigueli Dutra[3], Eleandro Maschio[4], and Isabela Gasparini[1]

[1] Universidade do Estado de Santa Catarina (UDESC), Joinville, SC, Brazil
eric.cvsilveira@gmail.com, isabela.gasparini@udesc.br
[2] Universidade Federal do Paraná (UFPR), Curitiba, PR, Brazil
[3] Instituto Federal de Santa Catarina (IFSC) - Campus Caçador, Caçador, SC, Brazil
taynara.dutra@ifsc.edu.br
[4] Universidade Tecnológica Federal do Paraná (UTFPR) - Campus Guarapuava,
Guarapuava, PR, Brazil
eleandrom@utfpr.edu.br

Abstract. This paper describes the development of the ThinkPlay tool, designed to assist developers in applying Game Learning Analytics (GLA) indicators in Educational Digital Games (EDG). The tool aims to address the lack of standardization in the collection of data related to user learning in games, providing guidelines for implementing indicators that were identified through a review of the literature. The development process included a theoretical framework and involved the identification of GLA indicators from existing research. Employing the Interaction Design methodology, the project progressed from a validated low-fidelity prototype to a fully functional web-based platform. The tool was subsequently evaluated by experts in the fields of EDG and GLA using the Technology Acceptance Model (TAM) questionnaire. The results demonstrate high acceptance in terms of usefulness, ease of use, and intention of use, and it is expected that game developers can benefit from the tool to include the capture of learning data in their games.

Keywords: Educational Digital Games · Game Learning Analytics · Data Indicators

1 Introduction

Data collection is a fundamental step in software development, as it enables the extraction of information and the transformation of actions into measurable data through methodologies and monitoring models. From these data, analysis can identify patterns and trends with applications ranging from the healthcare

---

Supplementary Information The online version contains supplementary material available at https://doi.org/10.1007/978-3-032-01426-9_10.

T. Darin et al. (Eds.): WIPlay 2025, CCIS 2623, pp. 148–160, 2026.
https://doi.org/10.1007/978-3-032-01426-9_10

sector to digital game development [4]. Therefore, ensuring precise and efficient data collection is essential for the success of analytical processes.

An application of data collection lies in Educational Digital Games (EDG), which have gained prominence as tools to enhance users' learning. Through players' interactions with these games, it is possible to collect relevant data that allow evaluation of the learning process, an area known as *Game Learning Analytics* (GLA) [5]. However, the implementation of these capture techniques faces challenges due to a lack of standardization, which often results in the absence of effective data collection mechanisms [3].

ThinkPlay, a tool developed during an undergraduate Computer Science thesis project, was designed to facilitate the implementation of GLA indicators in EDG. Serving as a guideline framework for developers, it also provides secondary benefits for educators and students by enabling analysis of learning behaviors, progress tracking, and performance evaluation. The tool's creation involved comprehensive identification, extraction, analysis, and categorization of EDG indicators from existing literature.

This article is structured as follows: Sect. 2 presents the Theoretical Framework; Sect. 3 discusses related works; Sect. 4 details the process of identifying and selecting the indicators incorporated into the tool; Sect. 5 describes the development stages of the solution; Sect. 6 presents the evaluation process conducted with experts; and finally, Sect. 7 outlines the final considerations.

2   Theoretical Framework

This section presents the core concepts that underpin the study of EDG and the data analysis methodologies applied in this context. It addresses the main approaches of Learning Analytics (LA), Game Analytics (GA), and GLA, highlighting their contributions to understanding and improving the teaching-learning process.

2.1   Educational Digital Games

According to [14], new generations, known as digital natives, quickly adapt to emerging technologies while simultaneously showing resistance to traditional teaching methods. This phenomenon challenges educators to incorporate digital tools into the pedagogical process, aiming to enhance both effectiveness and student engagement. In this context, EDG emerge as playful resources capable of promoting a more dynamic and motivating learning experience, fostering the development of skills such as critical thinking, problem-solving, and interdisciplinary collaboration [1,2].

2.2   Data Analytics

LA is the field dedicated to measuring, collecting, and analyzing data related to learners and their contexts, aiming to understand and optimize both the learning process and the educational environments in which it occurs [4]. The benefits of LA extend to students, who gain a more conscious reflection on their own learning, as well as educators, who can identify specific difficulties and adjust their pedagogical strategies to better meet students' needs [11].

Within the realm of digital games, GA refers to the collection and analysis of data aimed at understanding player behavior, providing essential insights to support decisions related to game development and improvement [12]. Through GA, it is possible to identify usage patterns and significant events that reveal how players interact with the game, directly contributing to enhancing the user experience.

Integrating the concepts of LA and GA, GLA applies specific data analysis techniques to assess the learning process in educational digital game environments [5]. While traditional GA primarily focuses on commercial aspects and player experience, GLA directs its attention to knowledge retention and acquisition, prioritizing the educational impact of games.

In this context, GLA involves the collection and analysis of multiple indicators, such as temporal logs, specific player actions, and contextual states, which allow detailed monitoring of students' interactions with the game, identification of difficulties, and provision of targeted feedback to enhance the teaching-learning process [10,13]. Despite its promising potential, significant challenges remain regarding the standardization of these indicators and the widespread adoption of these practices in the development of EDG.

3   Related Work

The study conducted by [3] addresses the creation of an interaction model to analyze learning in Serious Games (SG) and highlights the lack of standardization in the representation of these interactions. This model proposes metrics associated with common events in SG, categorizing them accordingly. It then stores player information such as the current level, frequency of level completion, selected options, scores, among others.

In a related effort, [7] emphasized the challenge of lack of contextualization in the data provided by games and proposed the use of xAPI (Experience API) to map events in digital games. In this sense, the study explored gameplay metrics of three games from different genres, aiming at the adoption of an open standard in the context of GA based on xAPI for gameplay metrics. Thus, the study highlights the potential of contextualizing gameplay data in GA.

Further advancing, [6] proposes the GLBoard system, which aims to standardize data originating from EDG through an architecture that captures generic data such as timestamps and user interactions. This system provides a control panel that allows the visualization and manipulation of player action data within the game. From GLBoard, the collected data can be easily transferred and handled within the control panel, enabling developers to visualize information from the games.

After reviewing the related work, relevant aspects were identified within the context of the present study. Table 1 presents a comparison between the studies analyzed in this section, highlighting their objectives, focus areas, and application domains in relation to the proposed tool. While prior works have explored data collection in EDG and digital games broadly, they primarily address the capture of predefined indicators, assuming developers already know which metrics to collect. In contrast, ThinkPlay tackles a more foundational challenge: the lack of familiarity among developers with GLA indicators. Unlike existing solutions, ThinkPlay not only assists in implementing indicators but also guides the selection of appropriate metrics. These differences underscore the uniqueness of the proposed work.

Table 1. Comparison between related work and the proposed study

Title	Objective	Focus	Application Area
Applying standards to systematize learning analytics in serious games	To construct an interaction model for learning analysis in serious games.	To propose metrics for standardizing GLA implementation in serious games.	EDG, LA, GA
GLBoard: um sistema para auxiliar na captura e análise de dados em jogos educacionais	To systematize data collection in educational games to integrate GLA into the game.	To propose a generic model for data collection in educational games.	EDG, GLA
Towards an Open Standard for Gameplay Metrics	To create an open standard to make gameplay metrics more accessible.	To propose an open standard for collecting gameplay metrics.	GA
Proposed Work	To design and apply a set of data indicator guidelines to support GLA in EDG.	Creation of a set of guidelines aimed at standardizing the collection and analysis of data in educational games.	EDG, GLA

4   Indicators Selection

The GLA data indicators incorporated into *ThinkPlay* were identified through a literature review and complemented by our research group's mapping study [22]. From the analyzed works, a structured categorization system organized the indicators based on their functional and analytical purposes. Below we detail all categories, with the complete indicator table available via *link*[1].

- **Completable**: This category captures repeatable player achievements, reflecting mastery of game mechanics. Adapted from [3], it includes metrics like *number of attempts* [16] and *completed levels*.
- **Learning Curves**: Indicators such as *player progress over time* [5] visualize skill development trajectories through longitudinal analysis, enabling educators to identify learning plateaus or breakthroughs.
- **Player Data**: Individual progression metrics like *level reached* [15] provide personalized insights.
- **Level Data**: This indicators analyzes level-specific interactions (e.g., *number of players per level*), revealing design strengths or difficulty spikes that may require instructional intervention.

---

[1] https://thinkplay.tiiny.site.

- **Data Requiring External Devices**: This category comprises indicators that require specialized hardware or software tools for data collection, such as: *fixation time (eye-tracking)* [17].
- **User Experience**: Interface interactions (*menu selections, resource accesses* [18] map engagement strategies, focusing more on user behaviors than on the actions themselves.
- **Time Tracking**: Temporal analytics (*idle time, time to dropout*) help optimize session structures and identify time related data.

5   Development

Prioritizing user-centered design, the project adopted Interaction Design and its simplified lifecycle (Fig. 1) to systematically address user needs [8]. The process consisted of four phases:

1. Discovering Requirements: Identification of system requirements through stakeholder analysis and literature review, defining core functionalities for the final product.
2. Designing Alternatives: Development of multiple design solutions based on gathered requirements, with iterative feedback loops allowing revisitation of previous stages as new needs emerged.
3. Prototyping: Creation of both low-fidelity and high-fidelity versions for progressive validation.
4. Evaluation: Rigorous testing of prototypes against requirements before final system development.

5.1   Discovering Requirements and Designing Alternatives

In order to understand user needs, a brainstorming session was conducted during a research group meeting consisting of seven researchers with experience in EDG and GLA. The goal was to identify user demands and behavior to support the development of the tool. During the process, three key questions regarding the design of the tool emerged, as presented in Table 2. Based on these questions, design alternatives for the tool were proposed, with their respective responses also shown in Table 2.

5.2   System Flow

The overall system flow, shown in Fig. 2, describes the user's journey within the tool and their behavior. It begins with the user accessing the tool and logging in, if already registered; otherwise, a new account is created. Then, any existing projects are displayed. The user then begins the creation of a new project by providing the requested information (name, goal, target audience). Following this, the user selects the relevant GLA indicators for their game under development.

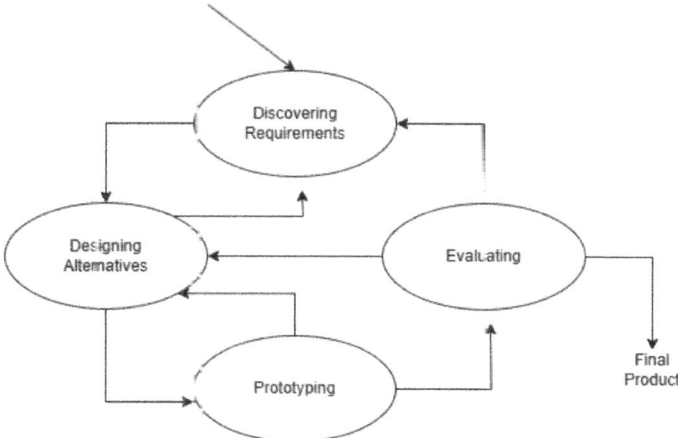

Fig. 1. Interaction Design Process. Adapted from [8]

Table 2. Questions and Answers Regarding the Tool

Question	Answer
How will GLA indicators be presented to users?	By structuring them into categories and subcategories, minimizing cognitive load and organizing the information [9].
How will users be able to select GLA indicators for their game?	An addition system was implemented, allowing users to select and register indicators for their project.
What user and game information needs to be stored?	The following data will be stored: name, email, password, date of birth, occupation, prior experience with GLA, and registered projects.

In this context, a detailed view of this selection process is shown in Fig. 3, in which the tool displays the indicator categories to the user. The user navigates through these categories, explores their definitions, and reviews the registered indicators. For the indicators of interest, various information is provided, including definitions, implementation methods, and usage examples from the literature. Finally, the user selects the relevant indicators for their game and adds them to the project.

After selection, the tool processes the data provided by the user and presents the finalized project with the selected indicators. The user then has the opportunity to review and make adjustments to the project as needed.

5.3 Prototyping and Evaluation

The tool's prototyping followed an iterative process, beginning with the development of a low-fidelity prototype. Starting from the initial prototype, it was

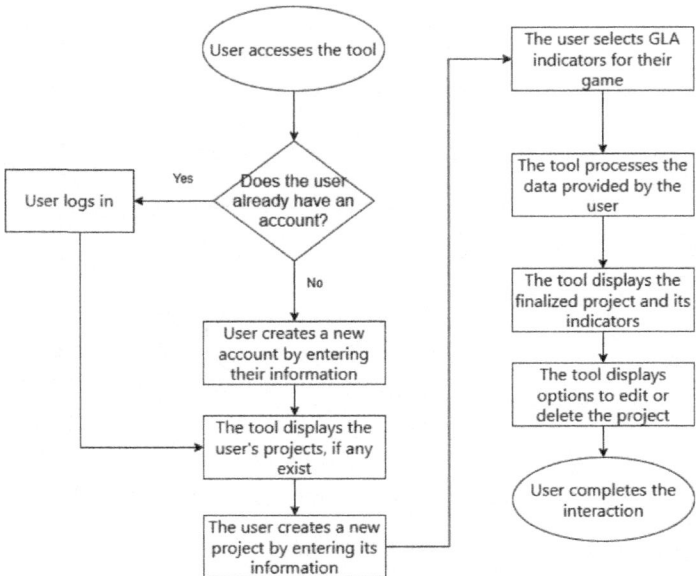

Fig. 2. General Flow of the Tool

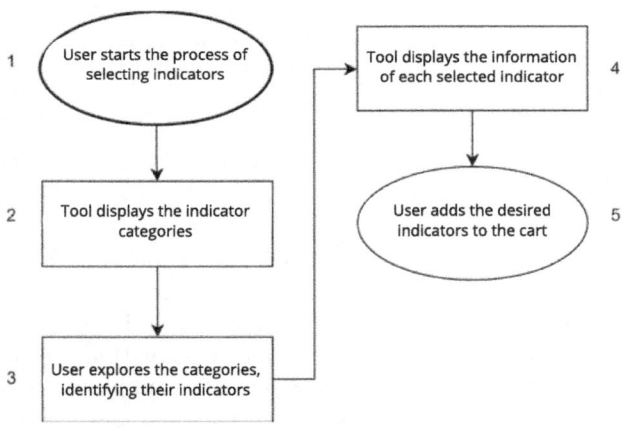

Fig. 3. Flow of GLA Indicator Selection

evaluated by the research group and iteratively updated until reaching the final version, which can be accessed at $link^2$.

In the final stage of Interaction Design, evaluation, the tool was reviewed by three EDG developers with no prior experience in GLA. The evaluation process involved: (1) introducing the tool's purpose and methodology, (2) demon-

---

[2] https://thinkplayprototype.tiiny.site.

strating the low-fidelity prototype, and (3) collecting structured feedback. While responses were overwhelmingly positive, developers suggested usability improvements particularly regarding form data entry and requested additional features for experienced users familiar with indicators. All initial requirements were met, and interaction with the game developer users provided a foundation for project improvements and refinements.

Following the evaluation, a high-fidelity prototype was developed as a fully functional web platform with integrated database. The implementation leveraged Nuxt.js and Vue.js for front-end development, enabling server-side rendering and responsive interfaces through Tailwind CSS. For back-end operations, SQLite3 was adopted due to its lightweight architecture, simplicity for development projects, and effective relational data management capabilities. Development followed the agile Kanban methodology, enabling prioritization of tasks and ensuring clear project progress tracking [21]. Figures 4 and 5 illustrate, respectively, the information screen of a selected indicator and the summary screen of the indicators chosen for the project. The final version of the tool, including all implemented features, can be viewed in detail in the video available at the following $link^3$.

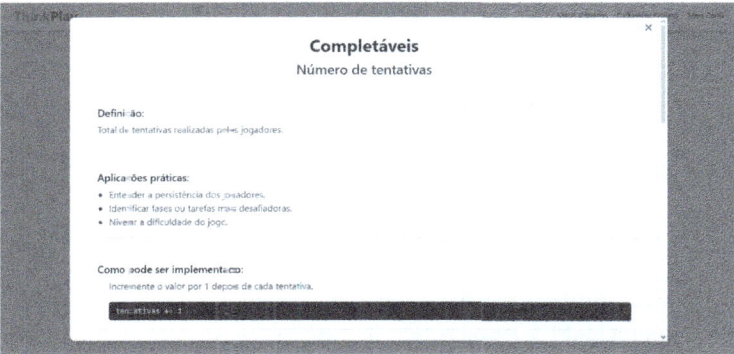

Fig. 4. Information screen of selected indicator (Context in Brazilian Portuguese)

6   Evaluation with Experts

The tool was evaluated through an empirical assessment involving experts, conducted in two stages. In the first stage, the experts interacted with the tool, exploring its functionalities. In the second stage, a Technology Acceptance Model (TAM) questionnaire was administered, consisting of a demographic profile section, questions adapted from the original model, and a section for suggestions, doubts, and criticisms.

---

^{3} https://bit.ly/3XuB7B7.

Fig. 5. Summary screen of the indicators selected for the project (Content in Brazilian Portuguese)

The TAM questionnaire was adapted according to the study by [19], using the structure proposed by [20]. It consisted of 14 questions, distributed across the three main constructs of the model. The questionnaire used a 5-point Likert scale, where 1 means "strongly disagree", 3 is neutral, and 5 means "strongly agree". Table 3 presents the adapted questionnaire.

Table 3. Adapted TAM Questionnaire

TAM Construct	Question	ID
PU	ThinkPlay would allow me to find data indicators more quickly.	Q.UP-01
PU	Using ThinkPlay would increase my productivity.	Q.UP-02
PU	Using ThinkPlay would improve my job performance.	Q.UP-03
PU	Using ThinkPlay would increase my work effectiveness.	Q.UP-04
PU	Using ThinkPlay would make my job easier.	Q.UP-05
PU	Overall, I believe ThinkPlay would be useful in my work.	Q.UP-06
PEU	I found ThinkPlay easy to use.	Q.FUP-01
PEU	Learning to operate ThinkPlay was easy for me.	Q.FUP-02
PEU	My interaction with ThinkPlay was clear and understandable.	Q.FUP-03
PEU	ThinkPlay was flexible to interact with.	Q.FUP-04
PEU	I did not need much effort to become skilled at using ThinkPlay.	Q.FUP-05
PEU	Overall, I found ThinkPlay easy to use.	Q.FUP-06
BI	I see myself using ThinkPlay.	Q.IU-01
BI	I intend to use the data indicators from ThinkPlay.	Q.IU-02

The experts selected to evaluate the developed tool had varied backgrounds, all with experience in the field of education and specific interest in EDG. The team consisted of five experts: three PhD holders/PhD candidates and two Master's holders/Master's candidates. They were chosen based on their involvement and experience in EDG, with most having between 3 and 5 years of experience, and one with over 10 years. Furthermore, their primary areas of expertise included EDG and Education, with a focus on Serious Games, while two experts also had experience with GLA. Regarding demographic data, the sample included three men and two women. Age distribution was balanced, covering different age ranges: one participant under 25, one between 25–35, one between 35–45, and two between 45–55.

The TAM results, presented in Fig. 6, indicate positive acceptance by the experts. The "Partially Agree" and "Strongly Agree" categories predominated, with 88.57% (62/70) of responses falling into these two categories combined. Only 8 responses were neutral, and no responses indicated disagreement. In the Perceived Usefulness (PU) construct, agreement reached 80%, reflecting a favorable evaluation of the tool's utility. The Perceived Ease of Use (PEU) construct received the highest level of agreement, with 96.66%, indicating that the experts found the tool intuitive and easy to use. Lastly, the Behavioral Intention (BI) construct reached 81.81% agreement, showing that most experts intend to use the tool in the future. Overall, the TAM results reveal a very positive evaluation, with experts recognizing its usefulness, ease of use, and adoption potential.

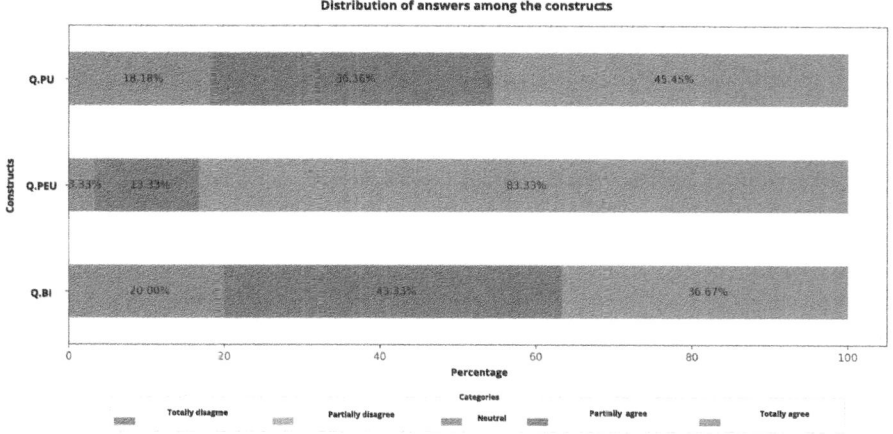

Fig. 6. Distribution of Responses by Construct

In the feedback section (suggestions, critiques, and open discussions), participants proposed both granular and systemic improvements. Minor adjustments—such as textual clarifications, color palette refinements, and optimized information architecture—were implemented iteratively. Strategic suggestions emerged from qualitative feedback:

- *"There could be explicit linkages between indicators and the tools needed to implement them"* (SG Expert);
- *"The system could store more game-related information"* (GLA researcher).

While immediate updates addressed usability concerns, broader feature proposals like these have been documented for future development cycles.

The TAM questionnaire results reveal positive acceptance of the tool, especially in the constructs of Perceived Ease of Use (96.66%) and Behavioral Intention (81.81%). These results indicate that the tool was well received by the experts, who acknowledged its usefulness, ease of use, and intention of use. The expert evaluation phase thus consolidated the tool's success and guided improvements for the next stages of the project.

The evaluation, while providing meaningful validation of the tool's acceptance, presents certain limitations that should be acknowledged. The expert sample size was limited to only five specialists, which may affect the generalizability of the results. Methodologically, the exclusive use of TAM - despite being a validated instrument - could benefit from complementary approaches.

7   Final Considerations

This article reported the research and development process of the *ThinkPlay* tool, designed to assist developers in applying GLA indicators in EDG. The tool emerges as an alternative to the lack of standardization in the use of data resulting from user interaction with games – a recurring challenge in the GLA field. By providing a structured set of indicators, accompanied by definitions, applications, and implementation guidelines, *ThinkPlay* aims to support developers in collecting and analyzing relevant data for learning assessment within games. Thus, the tool seeks to address a gap in the field, making the application of GLA more accessible to professionals developing EDG.

For the development of the tool, several studies from the literature were initially identified, in which indicators used in EDG and their application guidelines were analyzed. Based on this analysis, the most relevant indicators were selected and structured for integration into the tool. The construction of *ThinkPlay* followed the Simple Design methodology, which, through an iterative process, resulted in the development of a high-fidelity prototype: a web platform with an integrated database, meeting all previously defined requirements. To validate the tool, an evaluation was conducted with experts in the fields of EDG and GLA, in which an adapted version of the TAM questionnaire was applied. The result was a high level of acceptance from the experts, who positively evaluated its usefulness, ease of use, and intention of use, indicating the effectiveness and relevance of the tool in the context of EDG development.

It is important to note, however, that these encouraging results should be interpreted considering the study's limitations, particularly the expert sample size (N=5) and the exclusive reliance on TAM methodology, which suggest the need for broader validation in future studies.

For future work, three main directions are envisioned: (1) public deployment of the tool to make it accessible to EDG developers, (2) implementation of selected improvements suggested during the evaluation phase, and (3) expansion of validation studies to address the current limitations through mixed-methods approaches with larger, more diverse samples. Currently, the tool remains private, accessible only to authorized users, while these refinements are being implemented. The positive reception from experts, coupled with the planned enhancements, positions *ThinkPlay* as a promising solution to bridge the gap between GLA research and practical implementation in educational game development.

Acknowledgments. This work was developed as part of the undergraduate thesis in the Computer Science program at Universidade do Estado de Santa Catarina (UDESC), in partnership with Universidade Federal do Paraná (UFPR), Instituto Federal de Santa Catarina (IFSC) - Campus Caçador and Universidade Tecnológica Federal do Paraná (UTFPR) - Campus Guarapuava. The Artificial Intelligence tool ChatGPT version 4o was used to assist in translating the text into English.

The study was financed in part by the Coordenacção de Aperfeiçoamento de Pessoal de Nível Superior - Brasil (CAPES) - Finance Code 001, and also partially supported by CNPq grant 302959/2023-8 (DT2), FAPESC Edital no 60/2024 research project "Metodologias inovadcras e technologies educacionais para o processo de ensino e aprendizagem", and PROMOP/UDESC.

References

1. Hoelfmann, C., et al.: O uso dos jogos digitais educacionais no processo de ensino e aprendizagem. Florianópolis, SC (2016)
2. Savi, R., Ulbricht, V. Jogos digitais educacionais: benefícios e desafios. Renote **6** (2008)
3. Serrano-Laguna, á., Martinez-Ortiz, I., Haag, J., Regan, D., Johnson, A., Fernández-Manjón, B.: Applying standards to systematize learning analytics in serious games. Comput. Stan. Interfaces **50**, 116-123 (2017)
4. Drachen, A., Seif El-Nasr, M., Canossa, A.: Game analytics–the basics. In: Game Analytics: Maximizing the Value of Player Data, pp. 13–40 (2013)
5. Alonso-Fernandez, C., Calvo, A., Freire, M., Martinez-Ortiz, I., Fernandez-Manjon, B.: Systematizing game learning analytics for serious games. In: 2017 IEEE Global Engineering Education Conference (EDUCON), pp. 1111–1118 (2017)
6. Silva, D., Pires, F., Melo, R., Pessoa, M.: GLBoard: um sistema para auxiliar na captura e análise de dados em jogos educacionais. In: Anais Estendidos Do XXI Simpósio Brasileiro De Jogos E Entretenimento Digital, pp. 959–968 (2022)
7. Charleer, S., Gutiérrez, F., Gerling, K., Verbert, K.: Towards an open standard for gameplay metrics. In: Proceedings of the 2018 Annual Symposium On Computer-Human Interaction in Play Companion Extended Abstracts, pp. 399–406 (2018)
8. Rogers, Y., Sharp, H., Preece, J.: Interaction Design: Beyond Human-Computer Interaction. Wiley (2023). https://books.google.com.br/books?id=E26yEAAAQBAJ
9. Santos, L., Tarouco, L.: A contribuição dos princípios da teoria da carga cognitiva para uma educação mediada pela tecnologia. In: V Congresso Brasileiro De Ensino Superior A Distância. Gramado, RS. ESUD (2008)

10. Chung, G.: Guidelines for the design and implementation of game telemetry for serious games analytics. In: Serious Games Analytics: Methodologies for Performance Measurement, Assessment, and Improvement, pp. 59–79 (2015)
11. Scheffel, M., Drachsler, H., Stoyanov, S., Specht, M.: Quality indicators for learning analytics. J. Educ. Technol. Soc. **17**, 117–132 (2014)
12. Drachen, A., Mirza-Babaei, P., Nacke, L.: Games User Research. Oxford University Press (2018)
13. Perez-Colado, I., Alonso-Fernandez, C., Freire, M., Martinez-Ortiz, I., Fernandez-Manjon, B.: Game learning analytics is not informagic! In: 2018 IEEE Global Engineering Education Conference (EDUCON), pp. 1729–1737 (2018)
14. Prensky, M.: Nativos digitales, inmigrantes digitales. On the Horizon **9**, 1–7 (2001)
15. Slimani, A., Elouaai, F., Elaachak, L., Yedri, O., Bouhorma, M., Sbert, M.: Learning analytics through serious games: data mining algorithms for performance measurement and improvement purposes. Int. J. Emerg. Technol. Learn. (iJET). **13**, 46–64 (2018)
16. Melo, D., Melo, R., Bernardo, J., Pessoa, M., Rodrıguez, L., Pires, F.: Uma estratégia de game learning analytics para avaliar level design em um jogo educacional. In: Anais Do XXXI Simpósio Brasileiro De Informática Na Educação, pp. 622–631 (2020)
17. Avila-Pesantez, D., Usca, B., Angamarca, B., Avila, L.: Improving the serious game design using game learning analytics and eye-tracking: a pilot study. In: 2021 IEEE URUCON, pp. 536–540 (2021)
18. Feltrero, R., Hernando, S., Ionescu, A.: E-learning strategies for media literacy: engagement of interactive digital serious games for understanding visual online disinformation. Am. J. Distance Educ. **37**, 276–293 (2023)
19. Corrêa, A.: Um [Re]design Centrado no Usuário da Visualização de Informação no Contexto da Avaliação de Competências. Universidade do Estado de Santa Catarina - UDESC (2022)
20. Davis, F.: A technology acceptance model for empirically testing new end-user information systems: theory and results. Massachusetts Institute of Technology (1985)
21. Silva, D., Santos, F., Neto, P.: Os benefícios do uso de Kanban na gerência de projetos de manutenção de software. In: Anais Do VIII Simpósio Brasileiro De Sistemas De Informação, pp. 715–725 (2012)
22. Geremias, M. S., Dutra, T. C., Maschio, E., Gasparini, I.: O uso de Game Learning Analytics em Jogos Digitais Educacionais: Um Mapeamento Sistemático da Literatura. In: Simpósio Brasileiro De Informática Na Educação (SBIE), pp. 737–749 (2024)

Experience Report on Using HybridGamePX

José Olinda da Silva[1] and Paulyne Matthews Jucá[2]

[1] Instituto Federal de Educação, Ciência e Tecnologia do Ceará, São Paulo, Brazil
jose.olinda@ifce.edu.br
[2] Universidade Federal do Ceará, Campus de Quixadá, Quixadá, Brazil
paulyne@ufc.br

Abstract. There is a growing interest in HCI, especially in Game User Research, in understanding and evaluating aspects such as fun, motivation, playability, and player experience throughout the development process, focusing on the interactions during game sessions. Game evaluation can be performed using techniques such as observation, heuristics, interviews, or playtests. Hybrid board games mix tangible and intangible components, bringing new challenges to evaluating the player experience. Some research investigates different aspects of the development and evaluation of hybrid games. However research shows that there is still a research gap to evaluate the challenges of the hybrid experience. HybridGamePX was proposed to help researchers and game designers plan the playtest of hybrid games. This article presents the experience report of students of the Federal University of Ceará using HybridGamePX to evaluate different hybrid games. The research is empirical and qualitative. Data were collected in the form of questionnaires. The results highlight situations where the use of the model helped, points of improvement, and suggestions for the evolution of HybridGamePX.

Keywords: HybridGamePX · Player experience Playability · Playtest

1   Introduction

Hybrid games are described as a category that integrates elements from different domains to create more interactive experiences [28]. Hybridity in games is characterized by combinating physical and digital aspects and can expand to other domains [12], for example, geolocation and the use of augmented reality in real environments. This integration challenges traditional design approaches, requiring solutions that balance the dynamism of the digital medium with the tangibility of physical elements [22].

Given the variety of domains that can be combined, restricting the definition of hybrid to the physical-digital model may prove limiting [10–12]. However, this approach remains the most common in the literature [20], especially in the context of board games integrated with digital applications [7,17,23–25,33,34],

T. Darin et al. (Eds.): WIPlay 2025, CCIS 2623, pp. 161–178, 2026.
https://doi.org/10.1007/978-3-032-01426-9_11

which are often referred to as hybrid board games (HBG) or board games with app [26].

The design of hybrid games requires that the digital project respect and amplify the material attributes of the physical game, such as the manipulation of pieces, cards, and boards, rather than replacing them [23,26]. The introduction of digital applications and resources must preserve the management and sociability of the in-person game, functioning as a complement that expands the playful experience without disarticulating its essential physicality [25].

Regarding usability, attention must be paid to the risk of cognitive overload when digital components are poorly integrated or add excessive complexity to the player experience (PX) [24]. This requires special attention to balancing technological innovation and accessibility, especially for audiences less familiar with digital devices [31].

These challenges demonstrate that hybrid game design is not just about adding technologies to physical games [10,12] but about building a cohesive experience [8], where analog and digital aspects are integrated in a fluid, sensitive and meaningful way [15].

Unlike digital or analog games [1,2,4,16,18,32], hybrid games require an approach that takes into account the simultaneity of interfaces and supports, as they mix real, fictional and digital worlds blended through physical interactions and richer sensory experiences, uncommon in video games [19]. Therefore, it is required that the evaluation and testing process be planned in such a way as to cover tangible aspects (physical components) and digital aspects (applications, automated mechanics, devices, etc.) [34].

Despite the consolidated practices of playtesting in games [3,5,6], few studies specifically address the blend between physical and digital dimensions [20]. This opens space for investigations on how the transition between media affects the player's experience. HybridGamePX was proposed to address this gap. It consists of a set of perspectives and key questions to help plan the testing of hybrid games [9].

This paper presents the results of evaluating the use of HybridGamePX carried out by students in the planning of hybrid game playtests.

2   HybridGamePX

The main objective of *HybridGamePX* is support the planning of playtests in hybrid games [9].

HybridGamePX seeks to assist the process of evaluating hybrid games, encouraging reflections on the points at which physical and digital elements come together during the gaming experience. It is aimed at designers, evaluators, researchers, playtesters, and others interested in understanding how the hybrid characteristics of the game influence the player experience.

Given its nature, *HybridGamePX* should not be seen as a measurement tool or as a closed set of instructions to conduct a playtest. It is a qualitative guide that suggests what can be observed or investigated from different perspectives when a game mixes analog and digital components, focusing on helping in the test planning stage. This implies that using all perspectives is not mandatory: It is up to the tester to select those relevant for each project or test stage. The guiding questions associated with each perspective can also be adapted according to the context, and there is no need to use the complete set in every playtest.

HybridGamePX relies on two main concepts to help organize and conduct the playtesting process in hybrid games: perspectives and guiding questions. These concepts provide a framework for observing and evaluating the different aspects of playability and player experience.

Inspired by the idea of "lenses" proposed by [27], each perspective represents a domain or point of view to evaluate the game. The perspectives are divided into two broad categories: (i) playability, focused on dimensions such as mechanics, usability, and functional aspects, and (ii) player experience, focused on perceptions, reactions and engagement during the game. In this way, each perspective indicates *what* to observe or evaluate when planning a hybrid game playtest.

Playability perspectives include Timing (1), Randomising (3), Housekeeping (4), Informing (7), Storytelling (9), and Teaching (11).

Player experience perspectives Timing (2), Housekeeping (5), Artificial Intelligence âĂŞ AI (6), Informing (8), Storytelling (10), Teaching (12), Personalization (13), Longevity (14), Digital Device Flow (15), App as Support (16), Privacy and Individuality (17), Dispensability (18), Player-Game Interaction (19), Player-Player Interaction (20), Gameplay (21), and Environment (22).

For each perspective, guiding questions are proposed that serve as a reference for data collection and observation of player behavior and game functionality. These questions can be adapted according to the evaluation methodology adopted in the playtest, for example, by transforming them into interview topics or characteristics to be observed.

The purpose of the guiding questions is to help the designer/playtester to focus on the fundamental elements of each perspective and, in this way, better understand how the components, players, and interactions are articulated in the game's experience.

3   Related Work

Until the development of this research, no studies were found whose main focus was the planning of playtests for hybrid games. The existing studies focus on the definition of guidelines for the development of hybrid games, on the analysis of the interaction between physical and digital components, on the discussion of ethical dilemmas, such as privacy and inclusion, on the durability of games, and on the importance of clearly defining objectives for playtests.

The paper *Hybrid Board Game Design Guidelines* [12] proposed a set of 17 design guidelines for hybrid board games, resulting from an iterative process involving workshops with industry experts, interviews with developers and research with players. The guidelines address accessibility, added value, automation, aesthetics, sociability and, integration between physical and digital components, seeking to guide the development of products that take advantage of the potential of hybridization without compromising the player experience.

The paper *More Than a Gimmick - Digital Tools for Boardgame Play* [25] investigated the use of digital tools in board games, exploring how these technologies impact design and PX. The research was based on semi-structured interviews with 18 professionals in the board game industry, including designers, publishers, and developers, using a qualitative approach of reflexive thematic analysis to extract patterns and concerns related to the use of digital components. The main objective of the study was to understand how digital tools are incorporated into board games and how they influence design practices and the player experience. As a result, five design principles for hybrid games were proposed: traceability, completeness, integration, privacy, and materiality.

In *Unpacking "Boardgames with Apps": The Hybrid Digital Boardgame Model*, [26] presents a systematic classification of the functions performed by digital tools in hybrid board games. The research was conducted through a mixed-methods approach, which combined critical playtests, a survey with 237 players, and interviews with 18 game designers and publishers. Using affinity mapping and card sorting validation techniques, the authors identified eight main domains— timing, randomizing, housekeeping, informing, storytelling, remembering, calculating, and teaching—that describe how digital elements support and shape the gaming experience. The central objective was to understand and categorize the specific functions performed by digital technologies, going beyond the generic view of "games with apps" and offering an analytical framework independent of the technology used. This classification supported the formulation of several perspectives of HybridGamePX.

The paper *Core or Chore? How Hybridity Impacts Player Experience* [30] analyzes the influence of hybridization on *player experience* in hybrid games, comparing hybrid and nonhybrid versions of the same board game. The research was conducted through an A/B study with mixed methods. The results highlight that hybridization can be well received when it facilitates interaction with the core of the game, reducing the cognitive load associated with operational activities. Furthermore, the study reinforces the need for specific measures to assess PX in hybrid games, since traditional instruments developed for video games do not adequately capture the particularities of the experience in hybrid board games. These observations reinforce the importance of developing specific approaches for planning and evaluating playtests in hybrid games, justifying the creation of specific models and perspectives, such as the one proposed in this research.

4   Methodology

This work has an applied nature, and aims to report the experience of students who used HybridGamePX in evaluating hybrid games. The methodology consists of two big steps: Performing the playtests and collecting the experience of each student. Therefore, first, it is necessary to conduct the playtest following the recommendations in the literature and HybridGamePX itself and then interview the students about this experience. Thus, to conduct the playtest, the steps were: 1)

Selection of the hybrid games to be evaluated. They had to be available, preferably in Portuguese. 2) Preparation of the material necessary to play. 3) Planning the playtest in its sub-steps: 3.1) Exploratory and preliminary gameplay among the researchers who would conduct the research (students), to identify the hybrid aspects of the game and select the perspectives of HybridGamePX present in the game; 3.2) Formalization of the details of the playtest, the definition of the objective ("Why?"), target audience ("Who?"), location and date ("Where?"), aspects to be evaluated with the support of HybridGamePX ("What?") and instruments ("How?") selection for each playtest/game. In addition, this stage generated the appropriate terms of commitment for each game; 4) Conducting the playtest according to the demands raised for each game. After the playtest, a report and final evaluation of the results were prepared based on the researchers' observations and the answers the players gave in the interviews.

After the playtest, the students answered a questionnaire about their experience, reporting positive and negative factors using HybridGamePX. The data in this study, therefore, are qualitative and their analysis is empirical.

5   Students' Experience in Applying the HybridGamePX

In this section, we analyze the perceptions of students who applied the HybridGamePX model in case studies conducted at the Federal University of Ceará - Campus of Quixadá. These studies were published in the article entitled "Evaluating Player Experience in Hybrid Games Using HybridGamePX" [14], presented at SBGames24, covering the games Codenames, The Search for Planet X, and Unlock!: Escape Adventures. The playtests of the games Forgotten Waters, Codenames, and Pokémon Go were presented as course completion works, described respectively in [13, 21, 29].

The analysis is based on data on the students' experience in applying the HybridGamePX model, which was collected through a structured questionnaire which investigated aspects such as suitability, usefulness, and applicability of the model in planning playtests.

Characterization of Participants

Five undergraduate students participated in the evaluation and were members of the research group at the Federal University of Ceará - Campus Quixadá, where this research was developed. Among the respondents, four identify as male and one as female. All of them have some relationship with the research group that created HybridGamePX, which represents a risk to the validity of the research. However, this is a report of experience using HybridGamePX and not a final validation of the model.

– **STUDENT 01**: Studying Software Engineering, aged between 18 and 24 years old, had already participated in playtesting sessions before applying the model and evaluated the game Codenames.

- **STUDENT 02**: Also studying Software Engineering, aged between 25 and 34 years old, and had no previous experience with playtesting and evaluated the game *Forgotten Waters*.
- **STUDENT 03**: Software Engineering student, aged between 25 and 34 years and had already participated in other playtesting sessions and evaluated the game *Pokémon GO*.
- **STUDENT 04**: Digital Design student, aged between 25 and 34 years old, with previous playtesting experience and also evaluated the game *Forgotten Waters*.
- **STUDENT 05**: Software Engineering student, aged between 18 and 24 years old, and had no previous experience with playtesting and evaluated the games *In Search of Planet X*, *Codenames*, *Chronicles of Crime* and *Unlock!*.

Regarding the types of playtests performed, participants adopted different strategies according to the resources available and the characteristics of the games analyzed. Participants STUDENT 01 and STUDENT 03 responded that they conducted tests with people close to them, such as friends and colleagues, while STUDENT 02 and STUDENT 04 chose to conduct sessions with experienced users familiar with the games. STUDENT 05 conducted tests with different audiences, including people close to them and participants with or without experience in board games.

The analyses presented in the following subsections consider the individual perceptions of these students about the application of the HybridGamePX model, as well as the specific contexts of the games evaluated by each.

5.1 Frequency of Use and Perceived Usefulness of Perspectives

The students' answers to the questions below allowed us to assess the frequency of use of the HybridGamePX model perspectives during playtest planning, and their usefulness in guiding data collection.

Regarding the frequency of consultation of the HybridGamePX perspectives during the planning of their playtest [E-01], four of the five students stated that they used the model frequently. STUDENT 01, STUDENT 03, STUDENT 04, and STUDENT 05 indicated that they consulted the perspectives frequently, while STUDENT 02 said they always used them.

Regarding the usefulness of the HybridGamePX model defining the focus of data collection in the playtesting [E-02], four students gave it the maximum score (5 - essential). In contrast, one gave it a score of 4 (very useful). STUDENT 04's answer was the only one that differed slightly from the others, giving it a score of 4 instead of 5. Even so, no answer indicated the low usefulness of the model.

5.2 Application of Categories, Model Adaptation and General Evaluation

The following questions addressed aspects related to the practical application of the perspective categories, any adaptations made by the students, their general opinion about the model, and their report on using HybridGamePX in planning the playtesting.

Regarding question [E-03] ("Which category (set of perspectives) did you find easiest to apply in your planning using the model"), students were asked to indicate which category—Playability or Player Experience—they found easiest to apply during the planning of playtesting. Three students directly indicated the category Player Experience, one student mentioned Playability, and another stated that they had used both equally.

Regarding question [E-04] ("Did you adapt or modify the guiding questions provided by the model?"), four students indicated that they had adapted or modified the guiding questions provided by the model. STUDENT 01 mentioned adaptation to the context of the game and the participants. STUDENT 02 reported following the model with minor adjustments. STUDENT 03 indicated using the questions as a basis, adapting them to the interviews. STUDENT 04 reported using the model before and after the sessions without detailing changes. STUDENT 05 sought to identify, based on the questions, aspects of difficulty for the players during the test.

In the overall evaluation of the HybridGamePX model [E-05], three students gave it a score of 5 (Excellent), and two gave it a score of 4 (Very good). STUDENT 01, STUDENT 02, and STUDENT 05 gave it a score of 5, while STUDENT 03 and STUDENT 04 gave it a score of 4. The response scale was composed of the following possibilities: 1) Bad   2) Average   3) Good   4) Very good   5) Excellent.

The responses to question [E-06] ("Briefly describe how you used the HybridGamePX model in planning your playtesting") indicate that all students used the model in planning the playtesting but also to guide interviews and post-test evaluations. STUDENT 01 reported using perspectives to develop questions. STUDENT 02 described following the model step by step. STUDENT 03 used the guiding questions as a basis for interviews. STUDENT 04 used the model at different times, before and after the sessions. STUDENT 05 looked for elements in the questions to observe the difficulties and reactions of the participants.

5.3   Most Relevant Perspectives, Difficulties, Limitations and Comparison

The following questions addressed the most relevant perspectives, difficulties in use, and comparison with other approaches.

In question [E-07], students reported the most relevant perspectives. STUDENT 01 mentioned player-game interaction, player-player interaction, and housekeeping. STUDENT 02 highlighted storytelling housekeeping, and player-game interaction. STUDENT 03 pointed out the environmental perspective. STUDENT 04 mentioned gameplay and storytelling. STUDENT 05 stated that he had used all the perspectives, and this was because he had performed playtests with very different games.

In question [E-08] ("Did you encounter any difficulties in understanding or using any of the perspectives? Which one(s) and why?"), three students reported difficulties in using some perspectives. STUDENT 01 mentioned difficulties in adapting the perspectives to the game context and the profile of the participants without describing which difficulties. STUDENT 02 reported limitations in the applicability of the perspectives to certain types of games but did not mention which games. STUDENT 05 highlighted difficulties with the Longevity and Personalization perspectives, indicating a lack of explicit content for direct application. STUDENT 03 responded that he encountered no difficulties, and STUDENT 04 did not responded the question.

The responses to question [E-09] ("How did the model help (or not) identify problems in your game design? Give examples") indicate that four students reported that the model contributed to the identification of problems in the game design. The mentions focus on using guiding questions as an instrument for observation and directing the analysis during the playtests. STUDENT 01 stated that "the model helped guide the interview questions and the points of attention during the observation.". STUDENT 05 highlighted that "the most central point of Hybrid is how it makes us reflect on the elements of the game and, consequently, observe points that would previously go unnoticed". STUDENT 02 mentioned that the application of the model helped in the perception of aspects that were not evident before its application. STUDENT 03 reported that the model contributed to identifying potential problems and flaws in the game's logic. STUDENT 04 did not answer this question.

In question [E-10] ("To what extent did the model help ensure that the playtest objectives were achieved?"), all students indicated that the model helped ensure that the playtest objectives were achieved, although in different ways of application. STUDENT 01 highlighted that "in the planning phase, the perspectives helped define the focus and the data that should be collected, which helped achieve the playtest objectives". STUDENT 02 stated that "the model was very useful in achieving the proposed objectives, mainly by allowing better direction of actions and observation during the game". STUDENT 03 reported that "the model can be used as a basis for planning any playtest, including helping to conduct interviews with players and analyze what was observed". STUDENT 04 summarized his perception by stating that the model helped to "standardize the evaluation and interviews". STUDENT 05 responded objectively: "Yes", without further details.

In question [E-11] ("How does the HybridGamePX model compare to other game playtesting approaches that you know or have used?"), three students stated that they were not familiar with or had not used other playtesting approaches, which may be related to the fact that they were still in academic training. STUDENT 01 stated: "I am not familiar with any others". STUDENT 02 reported: "I have not used any other approaches for playtesting, only empirical group practices". STUDENT 04 mentioned: "I have only used Hybrid". Students who indicated some basis for comparison, such as STUDENT 03 and STUDENT 05, stated that the HybridGamePX model proved more targeted and objective. STUDENT 03 noted that "some models may lack possible deeper questions, which Hybrid proposes". In contrast, STUDENT 05 highlighted that the model "is more precise and objective than some approaches I have used".

These responses to question [E-11] reflect the lack of specific models for hybrid games. Although more generalist approaches, such as that of [6], offer valuable and applicable guidelines for planning tests in different types of games, no previous methodologies with a specific focus on playtesting hybrid games were identified. The responses also point to the need to evaluate HybridGamePX with a professional audience and less related to the research group to reduce bias.

In question [E-12] ("Do you feel that any perspective is missing from the model? If so, which aspect should be included?"), three students explicitly stated that they did not feel any perspective was missing from the model. STUDENT 01 responded: "I did not feel that any were missing." STUDENT 03 simply wrote: 'No.'. In contrast, STUDENT 02 considered that "he believes that there is no lack of perspectives but that the model could provide more detail for certain games" which may indicate a demand for practical examples or a more contextualized application of existing perspectives. STUDENT 05 suggested the inclusion of aspects related to game feel, indicating that "perhaps including issues more closely linked to game feel would be useful", suggesting that more sensorial or subjective dimensions of the player experience were not yet fully covered by the current perspectives of the model. STUDENT 04 did not respond to this question.

In question [E-13] ("Comment on the usefulness of the guiding questions. Did they help direct your observation and analysis during the playtest?"), all students reported that the guiding questions in the model helped direct the observation and analysis during the playtest. The answers varied in terms of level of detail but indicated a common perception of usefulness. STUDENT 01 stated that "HybridGamePX also guided the formulation of interview questions and points of attention during the observation". STUDENT 02 stated that "the guiding questions were essential to guide the analysis and maintain focus during the process". STUDENT 03 reported that "the guiding questions assist in the planning process and in the focus of the observation", reinforcing the structuring function of the model. STUDENT 04 responded succinctly that "they helped", adding that "they are also essential to provide clarity and focus". STUDENT 05 highlighted that "they help, in addition to being a great starting point for thinking about what to observe in the playtest".

In general, the responses analyzed in this section reveal how students used the HybridGamePX model in different stages of planning and executing their playtests, highlighting aspects they considered most relevant, difficulties encountered, comparisons with other approaches, and perceptions about the guiding questions.

5.4   Suggestions for Improvement of the HybridGamePX

The following questions sought to identify suggestions for improvement based on students' experiences while applying the model.

In question [E-14] ("If you could suggest an improvement to the HybridGamePX model, what would it be? Justify."), four students suggested possible improvements to the HybridGamePX model based on their experiences. The responses revealed varied suggestions, mainly focused on improving the guiding questions. STUDENT 03 did not answer the question.

STUDENT 01 suggested that "more guiding questions could have been made available per perspective". The suggestion indicates that, although the student used the existing questions, he realized that the number could be expanded to cover different aspects of each perspective in greater depth.

STUDENT 02 suggested that examples of adapted questions be included, stating: "I believe it is important to have examples of questions applied to game contexts". The statement suggests that the model, in its current version, presents questions at a generic level for the student's context and that the presence of examples in real or simulated contexts could facilitate its understanding and practical application.

STUDENT 04 pointed out the need to "develop more questions and approaches that allow for personalized application", which indicates an expectation of greater flexibility in the model by offering alternatives that could be adjusted to different types of games or playtest objectives.

STUDENT 05 suggested including questions related to game feel writing: "a possible improvement would be to include questions more focused on game feel, such as physical response or tactile sensations during the experience". This response draws attention to the perceived absence of elements linked to the sensory dimension of the player's experience, especially relevant in hybrid games that involve physical components.

The contributions presented highlight distinct and specific suggestions, concentrated in three main axes: (i) the expansion of existing guiding questions, (ii) the contextualized example of their use, and (iii) the incorporation of sensory aspects into the player's experience. The responses do not indicate rejection of the model but rather specific suggestions for refinement based on concrete uses.

Three students responded to the open question [E-15] ("Leave a free comment about your experience using the model: what was it like to work with it, what surprised you the most, or what worked least in your context.") freely reporting their general impressions about using the model. The answers reinforce perceptions already presented in other questions and add subjective elements about the experience.

STUDENT 01 evaluated that "it does what it proposes well" but reiterated that the difficulties occurred when using the model outside the context of hybrid games: "My biggest difficulties were because I used the model for other platforms that are not hybrid, but it still worked well".

STUDENT 04 described the experience as positive: "It was great. I thought it allowed me to see user experience evaluation differently", suggesting that the model broadened his view of the evaluation process.

STUDENT 05 stated that "working with the HybridGamePX model was an interesting experience", highlighting as the most surprising aspect "the depth that some questions can end up bringing to a playtest, thus stimulating a detailed reflection on aspects that often go unnoticed during a pre-playtest".

Table 1 summarizes the main responses.

Table 1. Summary of main responses.

	1	2	3	4	5
Game	Codenames	Forgotten Waters	Pokémon GO	Forgotten Waters	In Search of Planet X, Codenames, Chronicles of Crime and Unlock!
Usefulness	5	5	5	4	5
Most relevant perspectives	player-game interaction, player-player interaction, and housekeeping	storytelling, housekeeping, and player-game interaction	environmental	gameplay and storytelling	all perspectives
Difficulties	adapting the perspectives to the game context	limitations in the applicability of the perspectives	no difficulties	-	longevity and personalization
Help	define the focus and the data	direction of actions and observation	helping to conduct interviews and analyze data	standardize the evaluation and interviews	-
Overall evaluation	5	5	4	4	5

6   Discussion of Results

This section discusses the results obtained with the application of the HybridGamePX model, based on the case studies and the perceptions of students who used the model. The objective is to analyze the empirical data critically in light of the proposed research questions (RQ), emphasizing those directly related to the practical application of the model.

RQ: What dimensions and parameters are relevant to guide the planning of playtests and the evaluation of the player experience in hybrid games?

The case studies show that different dimensions were selected from Hybrid-GamePX according to the type of game analyzed, evidencing the flexibility of the model in adapting to different contexts. In the case of games with strong narrative integration, such as *Forgotten Waters*, the prioritized perspectives included governance (perspectives 4 and 5), storytelling (perspectives 9 and 10), and interaction between players (perspective 20). These choices reflected the centrality of the collective construction of the narrative and the need for a balance between rules and interpretative freedom in the game. In games such as *Codenames* and *Unlock!*, perspectives such as information (8), personalization (13), teaching (12), and gameplay (21) were selected, which proved to be appropriate for focusing on clarity of rules, variations in strategies, and dynamics between participants. The study of *Pokémon Go*, in turn, highlighted the importance of addressing geolocation and overlap between physical and digital maps, which was done through specific questions developed from the section focused on locative games in the model itself (perspective 22 - environment).

The choices made in the case studies were guided by previous analyses of the games and their contexts, as well as the objectives defined for the playtests, as reported by the students in their response to question E-06. The responses indicate that the model worked as a structured starting point for identifying the most relevant elements in each situation, being used to delimit what to observe and to support and compose/elaborate the questions used in interviews. The diversity of perspectives cited in question E-07—such as player-game interaction (19), player-player interaction (20), storytelling (9 and 10), housekeeping (4 and 5), setting and personalization (13)—suggest that students did not follow a single pattern but mobilized different dimensions according to the specificity of the object analyzed. An example of this was the response of STUDENT 05, who stated that he used all perspectives due to the variety of games evaluated, reinforcing the scope of the model.

The responses to question E-03 also provide an important clue about the users' understanding of the dimensions: three students indicated greater ease with the perspectives of the "Player Experience" category. At the same time, only one mentioned "Playability" and another equivalently used them. This may indicate that, in the planning process, aspects related to the subjective experience of the player—such as storytelling, clarity of objectives, or flow—proved to be more tangible or accessible to students in training than more technical categories associated with game mechanics in the context of the playtests carried out.

Considering the students' data, it can be observed that HybridGamePX offers an initial set of dimensions considered pertinent but that empirical experience also points to opportunities for refinement and expansion, especially concerning to sensory, ergonomic, and interface aspects. However, it is important to highlight that HybridGamePX can be used in conjunction with other evaluation models with a more specific focus on interface and usability, for example. The adaptability demonstrated in the case studies, and the responses to question E-07 appears to be one of the main strengths of the model when it comes to guiding playtest planning in hybrid games.

RQ: How can a systematic set of dimensions or perspectives be applied in practice, and what challenges or adaptations emerge during their use in hybrid game playtests?

The practical application of the HybridGamePX model, as described by the students and evidenced in the case studies, demonstrates that their perspectives were used not only for planning the playtests (as indicated in the answers to questions E-01) but also as a structuring tool for observations during the game and formulation of post-session interviews (E-06 and E-13). In all reports, the model was mobilized in multiple stages of the evaluation process, revealing its methodological flexibility. In addition to guiding the focus of data collection, it also contributed to the formulation of research questions, used by some participants before, during, and after the game sessions, as stated by STUDENT 04.

However, the practical application did not occur homogeneously. The answers to question E-04 reveal that four of the five students adapted or modified the model's guiding questions. The motivations for this varied from adjusting to the specific context of the games and participants, as reported by STUDENT 01, to the need to redirect the questions to the particular objectives of the session, as reported by STUDENT 03. This pattern suggests that, despite providing a practical starting point, the model demands a certain degree of interpretation and customization on the part of users, always oriented towards the objective of the playtest.

The difficulties reported in question E-08 also help to understand the challenges encountered in the practical application of the model. Three students reported obstacles, emphasizing the difficulty in adapting specific perspectives to the type of game analyzed. STUDENT 05, for example, specifically mentioned the perspectives of longevity and personalization as difficult to apply, as he could not find clear examples to guide them. The lack of directly applicable content seems to have been an obstacle to the full use of some dimensions, especially those that require greater abstraction or are more related to the prolonged game experience, such as longevity.

These challenges are also noticeable in the case studies. In *Pokémon Go*, the locative nature of the game required the creation of a structured diary based on questions derived from HybridGamePX, a solution that differs from the approaches based on direct observation used in board games or games with more controlled physical components. This example highlights the need to adapt the model to the hybrid format of the game under analysis, highlighting its applicability in non-traditional contexts, as well as the methodological adjustments required. However, it is the nature and purpose of the model to be flexible and adaptable to different contexts, and users of the model are strongly encouraged always to adapt it in the best possible way. Thus, the adaptation of guiding questions, such as an observation diary, is welcome and can be used in the model as an example of an application.

In summary, the data suggest that HybridGamePX is used in practice in a versatile way, supporting the planning, observation, and analysis of playtests.

However, its application requires adaptations, especially in different contexts such as locative, analog, or games with different audiences. The adaptations made by the students point to the importance of a more detailed instructional process, with contextualized examples and guidelines that help customize the model according to the characteristics of the evaluated hybrid game.

RQ: To what extent does adopting a structured set of perspectives contribute to qualifying playtest planning and supporting the evaluation of the player experience in hybrid games?

The students' responses indicate that the HybridGamePX model significantly improved the planning and execution of playtests, especially by offering a systematic and adaptable structure to guide the evaluation process. The practical usefulness of the model was initially evident in the responses to question E-02, in which four of the five students gave the HybridGamePX a maximum score for defining the focus of data collection. In contrast, the fifth gave it a score of 4. This data indicates a high degree of agreement on the guiding function of the model, even among students with different levels of experience in playtesting.

The contribution of the model was also reiterated in the responses to question E-10, which investigated to what extent the model helped achieve the playtest's objectives. All students responded affirmatively, highlighting that using perspectives and guiding questions made it possible to delimit the points of attention and conduct the evaluation in a more targeted manner. STUDENT 01, for example, stated that the model helped define the focus of data collection, STUDENT 04 reported that the model helped "standardize" the evaluation and interviews, and STUDENT 03 mentioned that HybridGamePX could be used as a basis for planning and conducting the interviews with the players. Although with different levels of detail, the responses suggest that the model not only organizes the process but also generates confidence about what should be observed and analyzed.

Another relevant point was the perception that the model helps identify flaws or problems in the game design, as revealed in the answers to question E-09. Four students reported that using HybridGamePX helped them observe elements of the game that could go unnoticed without a prior analysis structure. STUDENT 05 highlighted, for example, that the model promotes detailed reflection on the game elements, allowing for the identification of previously overlooked issues. STUDENT 03 mentioned identifying flaws in the game logic, while STUDENT 02 stated that the model allowed them to perceive previously un evident aspects. These answers indicate that the adoption of the model promoted a more critical and observational approach on the part of users, even among those with little or no previous experience.

The positive perception of the model is also reflected in question E-05 regarding general opinion. Three students gave it the highest score (5 - Excellent), and two gave it a score of 4 (Very Good), demonstrating high acceptance. Although suggestions for improvement were made—such as more examples, expanding the guiding questions, and including sensory aspects (E-14)—these recommendations do not question the model's usefulness but rather point to desired refinements based on practical experience of use.

The data presented here suggest that adopting HybridGamePX was perceived as a factor in improving the planning and conduct of playtests in hybrid games. Students indicated that the model favors the focus of the analysis, helps identify design problems, and organizes the evaluation process with greater clarity. The limitations observed do not compromise its applicability but indicate opportunities for refinement, especially to make it more accessible to audiences less familiar with formal evaluation methodologies.

7   Final Considerations

The general objective of this paper was to report the experience of students who used the HybridGamePX model to support the planning of playtests in hybrid games, focusing on the evaluation of the player experience and playability.

The practical application of the model involved case studies with games such as *Codenames*, *Unlock!*, *Forgotten Waters*, *Pokémon Go*. The analysis of these applications demonstrated that the model's perspectives were used selectively and adaptively, according to the characteristics of the game and the objectives defined for each playtest. The discussion of the results also showed that the students adapted the guiding questions, used the model as a guide for observation and evaluation, and pointed out concrete contributions for identifying problems and the direction of the analysis.

8   Research Limitations

The main limitation of this research is related to the number of participants and the participation of students related to the research group in the evaluation stage. Despite efforts to make direct invitations through different channels, such as social networks and academic events, there was low participation of external participants. This difficulty is understandable given the nature of the object of study: it is a model aimed at a specific niche—hybrid games—whose production and analysis are still restricted to smaller groups within the game design community. Therefore, this work should be read as an experience report on the use of HybridGamePX and not as a final evaluation of the model. The evaluation still needs to be carried out with professionals in the area who are unrelated to the research group.

9   Future Work

The results achieved pave the way for further studies. The following are possible developments suggested for the research: Apply HybridGamePX in broader educational and commercial contexts, including its use by professional designers in real development cycles. Improve the model's guiding questions by incorporating contextualized examples, usage scripts, and more detailed instructions. Evaluate the possibility of including a new perspective focused on the sensory dimension of the player experience (game feel), as suggested by students.

Acknowledgments. The authors would like to thank Funcap and the Federal University of Ceará for their support during the execution of this work.

References

1. Borges, J.B., Juy, C.L., Matos, I.S.d.A., Silveira, P.V.A., Darin, T.d.G.R.: Player experience evaluation: a brief panorama of instruments and research opportunities. J. Interact. Syst. **11**(1), 74–91 (2020). https://doi.org/10.5753/jis.2020.765
2. Carter, M., Downs, J., Nansen, B., Harrop, M., Gibbs, M.: Paradigms of games research in HCI: a review of 10 years of research at CHI. In: Proceedings of the first ACM SIGCHI Annual Symposium on Computer-Human Interaction in Play. CHI PLAY '14, pp. 27–36. ACM (2014). https://doi.org/10.1145/2658537.2658708
3. Choi, J.O., Forlizzi, J., Christel, M., Moeller, R., Bates, M., Hammer, J.: Playtesting with a Purpose. In: Proceedings of the 2016 Annual Symposium on Computer-Human Interaction in Play. CHI PLAY '16. pp. 254–265. ACM (2016). https://doi.org/10.1145/2967934.2968103
4. Drachen, A., Canossa, A.: Towards gameplay analysis via gameplay metrics. In: Proceedings of the 13th International MindTrek Conference: Everyday Life in the Ubiquitous Era. MindTrek '09, pp. 202–209, ACM (2009). https://doi.org/10.1145/1621841.1621878
5. Drachen, A., Nacke, L.E., Mirza-Babaei, P. (eds.): Games User Research, 1st edn. Oxford University Press, Oxford, United Kingdom (2018)
6. Fullerton, T., Swain, C.: Playtesting. In: Game Design Workshop, pp. 248–276. Elsevier (2008). https://doi.org/10.1016/b978-0-240-80974-8.50016-6
7. Gómez-Maureira, M.A., Barbero, G., Freese, M., Preuss, M.: Towards a Taxonomy of AI in Hybrid Board Games. In: International Conference on the Foundations of Digital Games. FDG '20, pp. 1–6. ACM (2020). https://doi.org/10.1145/3402942.3409607
8. Günther, S., et al.: CheckMate: exploring a tangible augmented reality interface for remote interaction. In: Extended Abstracts of the 2018 CHI Conference on Human Factors in Computing Systems, pp. 1–6. ACM, Montreal QC Canada (2018). https://doi.org/10.1145/3170427.3188647
9. Jucá, P.M., Souza Filho, J.C.d., Silva, J.O.d.: Hybridgamepx: Uma proposta de modelo para a avaliação da experiência do jogador no uso de jogos híbridos. In: Anais Estendidos do XXII Simpósio Brasileiro de Jogos e Entretenimento Digital (SBGames Estendido 2023), pp. 213–223. Sociedade Brasileira de Computação (2023). https://doi.org/10.5753/sbgames_estendido.2023.233836
10. Kankainen, V.: The interplay of two worlds in blood bowl: implications for hybrid board game design. In: Proceedings of the 13th International Conference on Advances in Computer Entertainment Technology. ACE '16, pp. 1–7. Association for Computing Machinery, New York, NY, USA (2016). https://doi.org/10.1145/3001773.3001796
11. Kankainen, V., Arjoranta, J., Nummenmaa, T.: Games as blends: understanding hybrid games. J. Virtual Reality Broadcast. (2019). https://doi.org/10.20385/1860-2037/14.2017.4

12. Kankainen, V., Paavilainen, J.: Hybrid board game design guidelines. In: DiGRA Digital Library. Digital Games Research Association DiGRA (2019). https://doi.org/10.26503/dl.v2019i1.1098
13. Lima, D.D.: Explorando a narrativa em forgotten waters: avaliação da experiência do jogador com o método hybridgamepx. Master's thesis, Universidade Federal do Ceará, Quixadá (2025)
14. Marinho, B.O., Gama, M.A.H., Jucá, P.M.: Avaliando a experiência do jogador em jogos híbridos usando hybridgamepx. In: Anais do XXIII Simpósio Brasileiro de Jogos e Entretenimento Digital (SBGames 2024). SBGames 2024, pp. 194–204, Sociedade Brasileira de Computação (2024). https://doi.org/10.5753/sbgames.2024.240599
15. Maurer, B., Fuchsberger V.: Dislocated boardgames: design potentials for remote tangible play. Multimodal Technol. Interact. 3(4), 72 (2019). https://doi.org/10.3390/mti3040072, https://www.mdpi.com/2414-4088/3/4/72
16. Mirza-Babaei, P., Zammitto, V., Niesenhaus, J., Sangin, M., Nacke, L.: Games user research: practice, methods, and applications. In: CHI '13 Extended Abstracts on Human Factors in Computing Systems. CHI '13, pp. 3219–3222. ACM (2013). https://doi.org/10.1145/2468356.2479651
17. Mora, S., Fagerbekk, T., Monnier, M., Schroeder, E., Divitini, M.: Anyboard: a platform for hybrid board games. In: Wallner, G., Kriglstein, S., Hlavacs, H., Malaka, R., Lugmayr, A., Yang, H.-S. (eds.) ICEC 2016. LNCS, vol. 9926, pp. 161–172. Springer, Cham (2016). https://doi.org/10.1007/978-3-319-46100-7_14
18. Nunes, C., Darin, T.: Echoes of player experience: a literature review on audio assessment and player experience in games. Proc. ACM Hum.-Comput. Interact. 8(CHI PLAY), 1–27 (2024). https://doi.org/10.1145/3677069
19. Oliveira, A.P., Sousa, M. Vairinhos, M., Zagalo, N.: Towards a new hybrid game model: designing tangible experiences. In: 2020 IEEE 8th International Conference on Serious Games and Applications for Health (SeGAH), pp. 1–6. IEEE (2020). https://doi.org/10.1109/segah49190.2020.9201838
20. Paiva, F., Mendonça, G. Viana, W.: A systematic mapping of hybrid games in the academy. In: Anais Estendidos do XXI Simpósio Brasileiro de Jogos e Entretenimento Digital (SBGames Estendido 2022), pp. 128–137. SBGames Estendido 2022, Sociedade Brasileira de Computação (2022). https://doi.org/10.5753/sbgames_estendido.2022.225932
21. Queiroz, C.S.: Avaliação da experiência de jogadores no jogo híbrido Pokemon Go. Master's thesis, Universidade Federal do Ceará (2024). tCC
22. Rocha, C.S.: Jogos híbridos: um problema novo em design visual. Master's thesis, UE - Universidade Europeia (2019). http://hdl.handle.net/10400.26/31061
23. Rogerson, M.J., Gibbs, M., Smith, W.: "I love all the bits": the materiality of boardgames. In: Proceedings of the 2016 CHI Conference on Human Factors in Computing Systems. CHI'16, pp. 3956–3969. ACM (2016). https://doi.org/10.1145/2858036.2858433
24. Rogerson, M.J., et al.: Observing multiplayer boardgame play at a distance. In: Extended Abstracts of the 2021 Annual Symposium on Computer-Human Interaction in Play. CHI PLAY '21, pp. 262–267. Association for Computing Machinery, New York, NY, USA (2021). https://doi.org/10.1145/3450337.3483485
25. Rogerson, M.J., Sparrow, L A., Gibbs, M.R.: More than a gimmick - digital tools for boardgame play. Proc. ACM Hum.-Comput. Interact. 5(CHI PLAY), 1–23 (2021). https://doi.org/10.1145/3474688

26. Rogerson, M.J., Sparrow, L.A., Gibbs, M.R.: Unpacking "boardgames with apps": the hybrid digital boardgame model. In: Proceedings of the 2021 CHI Conference on Human Factors in Computing Systems. CHI '21, pp. 1–17. ACM (2021). https://doi.org/10.1145/3411764.3445077

27. Schell, J.: The Art of Game Design: A Book of Lenses, 3rd edn. CRC Press, Londres (2019)

28. Silva, A.D.F., Callado, A.d.C., Jucá, P.M.: Caracterizando Jogos Híbridos Segundo a Experiência dos Jogadores. In: Simpósio Brasileiro de Jogos e Entretenimento Digital (SBGames), pp. 307–317. SBC (2024). https://doi.org/10.5753/sbgames.2024.240166, iSSN 0000-0000

29. da Silva, W.I.V.: Avaliação da Experiência do Jogador no Jogo Codenames: Comparação entre as Versões Analógica, Híbrida e Digital. Master's thesis, Universidade Federal do Ceará, Quixadá (2025)

30. Soraine, S., Rogerson, M.J.: Core or Chore? How hybridity impacts player experience. In: Proceedings of the 20th International Conference on the Foundations of Digital Games. ACM, New York, NY, USA, Graz, Austria (2025). https://doi.org/10.1145/3723498.3723842

31. Sousa, M.: Informal adult learning and training sessions: playing modern board games in the digital age. Educ. Media Int. 61(1–2), 117–133 (2024). https://doi.org/10.1080/09523987.2024.2357958

32. Sweetser, P., Wyeth, P.: GameFlow: a model for evaluating player enjoyment in games. Comput. Entertain. 3(3), 3 (2005). Association for Computing Machinery (ACM). https://doi.org/10.1145/1077246.1077253

33. Tyni, H., Kultima, A., Mäyrä, F.: Dimensions of hybrid in playful products. In: Proceedings of International Conference on Making Sense of Converging Media, pp. 237–244. ACM, Tampere Finland (2013). https://doi.org/10.1145/2523429.2523489

34. Tyni, H., Kultima, A., Nummenmaa, T., Alha, K., Kankainen, V., Mäyrä, F.: Hybrid playful experiences: playing between material and digital - hybridex project, final report. Technical report 19, Tampereen yliopisto (2016). https://trepo.tuni.fi/handle/10024/98900

Player Experience with New Mechanics: A Mixed-Methods Study of Motivation, Emotion, and Engagement

Jamyle Teles[✉][iD], Mariana Castro[iD], Isabelle Reinbold[iD], Bosco Borges[iD], and Ticianne Darin[iD]

Federal University of Ceará, Fortaleza, CE 60455-760, Brazil
{jamyleteles,marianarangelcastro28,reinbold}@alu.ufc.br,
ticianne@virtual.ufc.br

Abstract. Understanding players' early gameplay experiences is crucial, especially in games with unconventional mechanics. Fez, a puzzle-platformer, introduces a perspective-rotation mechanic that transforms gameplay from 2D to a 3D-like experience. While prior studies have addressed soundtrack and usability, little is known about how such innovative design affects novice players during onboarding. This study investigated player experience using a mixed-methods evaluation grounded in Human-Computer Interaction and game design. We combined four validated instruments—SAM (emotion), IMI-Teq-Br (intrinsic motivation), UES-Br (engagement), and PX-Br (player experience) - with interviews and behavioral observations. Data from 27 participants revealed high pleasure, autonomy, and engagement, though perceived competence varied. UES-Br scores showed strong focused attention and perceived reward but lower aesthetic appeal. SAM responses indicated predominantly positive affect. Qualitative findings revealed that initial confusion and visual discomfort were often replaced by curiosity and cognitive adaptation. Participants described the core mechanic as creative and engaging, with curiosity about its technical aspects. These results emphasize the importance of well-designed onboarding in supporting motivation and cognitive flow in innovative games, offering insights for both evaluation methods and experiential design in game research.

Keywords: Player experience · Game Design · Evaluation · Human-Computer Interaction · Mixed-methods evaluation · Intrinsic motivation · Player engagement · Player emotion

1 Introduction

Self-Determination Theory (SDT) is a recognized macro-theory concerning human motivation, psychological growth, and well-being [34]. In the field of Human-Computer Interaction (HCI), SDT has been extensively adopted as a theoretical framework for understanding user experience from the perspective of intrinsic motivation, emphasizing the universal psychological needs for competence, autonomy, and relatedness [35] Although frequently referenced in digital game research, many of its core constructs remain underexplored, particularly in empirical evaluations of novice players' initial experiences [40]. This

© The Author(s), under exclusive license to Springer Nature Switzerland AG 2026
T. Darin et al. (Eds.): WIPlay 2025, CCIS 2623, pp. 179–199, 2026
https://doi.org/10.1007/978-3-032-01426-9_12

gap becomes even more relevant when considering games with unconventional mechanics, which may directly affect motivation and long-term engagement.

Intrinsic motivation plays a central role in game design, as games are inherently voluntary and engaging experiences. Enhancing this motivation is one of the most effective strategies to foster deep and lasting player engagement, surpassing the effectiveness of superficial rewards [2]. However, the way in which basic psychological needs are fulfilled—or thwarted—by specific design elements can significantly influence emotional responses and engagement, especially during the early stages of gameplay [11]. While gamification has expanded interest in the relationship between motivation and digital experiences in areas such as education [17], organizational engagement [12], and online learning [26], the gaming context requires a deeper understanding of how components of the player experience—such as affect, intrinsic motivation, and engagement [6]—interact when faced with innovative mechanics.

Fez is a puzzle platform game where the two-dimension world reveals a third dimension through the "Fez Hat," allowing players to rotate between four perspectives. This transforms the objective of the game: to explore and collect cube fragments in order to restore the balance of the universe. This mechanic alters how players interact with the environment and presents a unique onboarding challenge, requiring not only the assimilation of new rules but also a shift in spatial perception and navigation. Fez serves as an ideal case to study how innovative mechanics impact initial player motivation, affect, and engagement.

This study explores how novice players respond to the introduction of Fez, particularly its innovative perspective-shifting mechanic, by analyzing affective responses, intrinsic motivation, and engagement. Validated instruments in Brazil were employed—Self-Assessment Manikin (SAM) [41], IMI-Teq Br [28], UES-Br [24], and PX-Br [5]—alongside qualitative interviews and the use of the HEXAD-12 player typology [18], which allows for further an additional analytical layer of how different player types react to the same game mechanic.

Consequently, Fez serves as a compelling case study for examining how innovative mechanics impact novice players' early experiences. This study asks: How do affect, intrinsic motivation, and engagement shape the initial experience with Fez's perspective-shifting mechanic? It contributes by offering evidence to designers on how unusual mechanics influence player response and onboarding challenges. For HCI and game researchers, it shows how a mixed-methods approach with qualitative data enables nuanced insights. Finally, it adds to research on how players adapt to games that defy traditional spatial reasoning from the outset.

2   Related Work

Player Experience (PX) has been a focus of investigation within the field of Human-Computer Interaction (HCI), with efforts aimed at understanding aspects such as motivation, engagement, and affect [1]. Several instruments have been developed to measure these dimensions. Among them are the Intrinsic Motivation Inventory (IMI; [32]), its adapted version IMI-Teq [23], the User

Engagement Scale (UES; [20]), the Self-Assessment Manikin (SAM; [7]), and PX-Br [5]. While these tools are effective individually, few studies have combined them in an integrated and systematic manner to analyze different aspects of the player experience within a single context [22, 42]. This limitation in combining instruments may restrict multifaceted and in-depth analyses of PX.

Onboarding - the initial phase of interaction with a game - has been identified as critical for player engagement and retention [3]. In games with unconventional mechanics, this moment may pose even greater challenges. Recent studies have proposed mixed-method approaches to evaluate this process, such as the use of physiological and qualitative metrics [30], implicit instructions in low-complexity games [16], or adaptive systems supported by artificial intelligence [10]. However, few works address onboarding in games that deviate from conventional learning mechanics.

Fez is a notable example of a game with an innovative core mechanic, requiring a shift in three-dimensional perspective without explicit instructions. Although studies have already examined its dynamic soundtrack, educational potential [27] and usability [31], no empirical and multifaceted investigation has yet been conducted into how novice players experience its onboarding. Thus, a gap remains in the literature regarding how dimensions of intrinsic motivation—such as autonomy and competence [33]—affect initial engagement in games with unconventional mechanics. Addressing this gap may contribute to a more comprehensive understanding of PX in digital games.

3   Methodology and Materials

This study aims to explore how the interplay of affect, intrinsic motivation, and engagement shapes the initial player experience of novices encountering Fez's distinctive perspective-shifting mechanic for the first time. This section details the methodology and materials employed to investigate this objective.

General Procedure. The evaluation was performed in laboratory. Prior to evaluation, all participants received a briefing on the study's purpose and their rights, including voluntary withdrawal without consequence. Anonymity was ensured for all collected data to protect privacy. Participants then signed an Informed Consent Form outlining the study's nature, potential risks and benefits, and data protection measures to ensure full understanding and consent before testing began.

Participants used a headset and Xbox controller to play Fez on a computer. They needed to finish the first level (first cube) within 35 min to prevent long, uncomfortable sessions. If they finished early, they could play until around 30 min, at which point the observer would end the session after a significant in-game event (like getting a cube or unlocking something new) to avoid cutting them off during high engagement. Pilot tests showed 35 min was enough time to experience the game's start, the perspective-shifting mechanic, and finishing the first level, letting researchers study how players reacted and adapted. During gameplay, the game screen was recorded for observers, who used a template to note evaluation timing, milestones, and observations for follow-up interview questions. After playing, participants answered a profile questionnaire and the HEXAD-12. Then, they completed SAM (emotions), PX-Br (experience), IMI-Teq Br (motivation), and UES-Br (engagement) questionnaires in a random order. A follow-up interview explored their experience. Sessions averaged one hour.

Participants. The evaluation included participants over 18, available for in-person testing, and unfamiliar with Fez or its perspective-shifting mechanic. Recruitment was done via an online form shared on social media (e.g. Whatsapp and Instagram), collecting contact info, availability, and prior knowledge of the game. Those aware of the core mechanic were excluded. A total of 27 participants (13 men, 13 women, 1 non-binary), aged 18âĂŞ41, took part in the study. The research involving human participants described in this paper was conducted in accordance with ethical standards and was approved by the Research Ethics Committee (REC) of the Federal University of Ceará (UFC), under protocol number CAAE [87112524.6.0000.5054].

Game. Fez is a puzzle platform game developed by Polytron Corporation launched on May 1st, 2013. During gameplay, the player explores a 2D world with a two-dimensional character named Gomez. When the character receives the "Fez Hat," they gain the ability to rotate the 2D world through four perspectives, revealing a third dimension. The goal is to explore and collect cubes/fragments to restore cosmic order. **Data collection methods.** This study aimed to explore the potential relationship between participants' self-reported emotions and their intrinsic motivation or level of engagement during gameplay. Detailed descriptions of each methodological approach are provided in the subsequent sections.

The **Hexad-12** [19], a concise adaptation of the 24-item Hexad scale [38], assesses six user types (Philanthropist, Socializer, Achiever, Player, Free Spirit, Disruptor) via two statements per type rated on a seven-point Likert scale. It facilitates rapid user profiling, particularly when time is constrained or used in conjunction with other instruments. This study utilized a 24-item Portuguese translation [36] but only analyzed the standard 12 items of the Hexad-12.

The **PX-Br** [4] is a Brazilian Portuguese questionnaire using a 5-point Likert scale to assess player experience across immersion/presence, fun, and gameplay. The **Self-Assessment Manikin (SAM)** [7] is a non-verbal pictorial technique employing 9-point Likert scales to rate the affective dimensions of pleasure (valence), arousal, and dominance in response to stimuli, with each dimension represented by five figures illustrating a range of feelings. The **UES-Br** [25] is a 30-item Brazilian Portuguese adaptation of the User Engagement Scale (UES) [14], using a 5-point Likert scale to measure engagement in digital interaction through four subscales: Focused Attention (FA), Perceived Usability (PU), Aesthetic appeal (AE), and Reward (RW). The **IMI-Teq-Br** [28] is a 21-item Brazilian Portuguese adaptation of the Intrinsic Motivation Inventory Task Evaluation Questionnaire (IMI-TEQ) [29], utilizing a 7-point Likert scale to assess intrinsic motivation and self-regulation via four dimensions: interest/enjoyment, perceived choice, perceived competence, and pressure/tension.

The **Semi-structured interview** was made following a script which included 16 questions plus in-depth questions made according to the need seen by the interviewer (see Table 5 in Appendix section). The questions addressed the player's general experience, the effects of game elements on the experience, aspects of the experience that may have affected emotion, motivation and engagement and information about what the experience of completing the gameplay was like.

For the qualitative analysis of the interviews, a thematic analysis was performed following the 6-steps framework defined by [8], to identify themes relevant to the study's objectives. An inductive approach was used to categorize similar excerpts, resulting in six key themes: (1) **Aesthetics and Visual Perception**(3 subthemes), (2) **Perception about Soundtrack and Sound Effects** (2 subthemes),(3) **Clarity and Coherence of the Game** (5 subthemes), (4) **Player Profile and Behavior** (6 subthemes), (5) **Immersion and Engagement with the Experience** (9 subthemes), and (6)**Remarkable Moments of the Experience** (5 subthemes).

4 Results

In order to achieve the goal of this study, we collected data from 27 participants, using different research methods and instruments. We quantitatively analyzed the questionnaire data and also compared them with the qualitative data from the interviews. In this section, we present the general results about the profiles of the participating players, the results of the questionnaires applied (IMI-Teq BR, SAM, UES-Br, PX-Br and HEXAD 12) and also their answers to the semi-structured interview.

4.1 Participants' Profiles and HEXAD-12

The evaluation included participants who met the inclusion criteria: being over 18 years old; being available for an in-person test and having never played the game "Fez" before or having had limited interaction with it.

Among the 27 participating users, 13 (48.15%) declared themselves to be men, 13 (48.15%) women and one (3.7%) non-binary, with ages ranging from 20 to 41. Regarding the area of study or professional activity, the majority of users (18 users - 66 7%), reported working or studying in the area of Technology/Development. Health and Human Sciences were reported by three participants (11.1%). Education by two (7.4%), while Marketing, Illustration, Natural Sciences, Arts and Tattooing were mentioned, individually, each by one participant (3.7%).

Among the participants, most had incomplete higher education (70.37%), followed by completed higher education (14.81%), master's degrees (11.11%), and a doctoral degree (3.7%). In terms of gaming experience, levels were fairly distributed: beginner (25.9%), intermediate (48.1%), and advanced (25.9%). The most frequently mentioned game genres (participants could select multiple) were adventure (28.6%), RPG (19.5%), strategy (15.6%), and FPS (11.7%).

To identify player profiles and interpersonal preferences using the Hexad-12 scale, questionnaire data were organized and analyzed through descriptive statistics. Table 1 summarizes the results for the six user types: Socializer, Free Spirit, Achiever, Philanthropist, Gamer, and Disruptor.

Table 1. Results for each user type of the Hexad-12

Hexad Type	Mean	SD	Min	Max	Median	Mode
Socializer	9.93	2.02	4	14	10.00	11.00
Free Spirit	11.63	2.63	4	14	12	14
Achiever	11.30	2.74	5	14	12	14
Philanthropist	12.67	1.52	9	14	13	14
Player	10.67	2.99	3	14	11	14
Disruptor	5.93	2.93	2	14	6	6

It is observed that the most common user types, based on the highest averages, were Philanthropist (M = 12.67, SD = 1.54), Achiever (M = 11.30, SD = 2.74), and Free Spirit (M = 11.63, SD = 2.63). Philanthropist was the most prevalent, with 40.74% reaching the maximum score, indicating a strong drive to help others without personal gain. Free Spirits and Achievers also showed high averages but with moderate variation. Socializers had a lower average (M = 9.93, SD = 2.02), suggesting a less intense but still present motivation for social connection. Disruptors had the lowest average (M = 5.93) and high variability (SD = 2.93), indicating that most participants were not strongly motivated by challenge.

While the Hexad-12 scale captured varying degrees of player characteristics, participants in this sample exhibited relatively high scores for the Philanthropist, Free Spirit, Achiever, and Player types, contrasting with a notably lower average for the Disruptor profile. The sample indicated a leaning towards intrinsically motivated profiles: Philanthropists (purpose-driven), Achievers (competence-driven), and Free Spirits (autonomy-driven) showed averages between 11.30 and 12.67, with a mode of 14. Notably, the extrinsically motivated Player user type also presented a high average of 10.67 and a mode of 14.

4.2   IMI-Teq Br, UES-Br, SAM and PX-Br

The **IMI-TEQ-Br** results regarding the overall experience indicated a high level of Interest/Enjoyment, with an average score of 6.17 (SD = 1.57) on a 7-point scale, and a mode of 7. The range of responses was from 2.17 to 7. This suggests that the game was generally well-received by participants, who reported significant interest and appreciation for the experience. For the **Perceived Competence** dimension, the average response was 4.8 (SD = 1.39, mode = 5.6, range 1.6–6.6). This indicates a more varied perception of how competent participants felt while playing the game. The **Perceived Choice** dimension showed a high average of 5.8 (SD $=$ 0.83, mode $=$ 5.8, range 3.6–7), suggesting that participants generally felt a sense of autonomy in the decisions they made during the gameplay. The relatively low standard deviation indicates a consistent perception across participants. Finally, the **Pressure/Tension** dimension presented the lowest average score of 2.4 (SD $=$ 1.30, mode $=$ 2.4, range 1–5.8). This suggests that participants experienced low levels of stress or pressure during the game. The standard deviation indicates some variability in these feelings among the participants (see Table 2).

Table 2. IMI-TEQ Br score Results

IMI-TEQ Br	Interest Enjoyment	Perceived Competence	Perceived Choice	Pressure/Tension
Mean	6.16	4.8	5.8	2.4
SD.	1.57	1.38	0.83	1.29
Min	2.16	1.6	3.6	1
Max	7	6.6	7	5.8
Mode	7	5.6	5.8	2.4

Similar to the IMI-TEQ results, the statistical analysis of the **UES-Br** showed generally high scores across all scales, approaching the maximum value of 5. The **Aesthetic Appeal (AE)** scale presented the lowest average at 3.43. The **Focused Attention (FA), Perceived Usability (PU)**, and **Perceived Reward (RW)** scales exhibited higher average scores of 4.0, 4.12, and 4.6, respectively. The overall UES score for the experience averaged 4.3. The mode of responses for each scale also tended towards the higher end of the scale, reinforcing this pattern. Notably, the **Perceived Reward (RW)** scale had a mode of 4.6, indicating that most participants scored above the average on this aspect. Furthermore, the low standard deviations observed across all scales (below 1) suggest a high degree of consistency and low variability in the participants' responses (see Table 3).

Table 3. UES Br SF score Results

UES Er SF	Mean	SD	Min	Max	Mode
FA	4	0.66	2.14	5	4
PU	4.12	0.76	1,5	5	4,37
AE	3.42	0.68	0.71	3.57	3,57
RW	4.6	0.83	2.2	5	4.6
UES (score)	4.3	0.65	2.36	4.9	4 6

The analysis of the **Self-Assessment Manikin (SAM)** data indicated predominantly positive perceptions of the evaluated experience. SAM uses three

9-point scales, where 7–9 reflect positive, 1–3 negative, and 4–6 neutral affective responses. The **Pleasure/Valence** dimension showed the most positive results, with a mean of 7.67 (SD = 1.84). A significant majority (81.4%) of responses were positive, with only 3.7% negative and 14.8% neutral ratings. The **Arousal dimension** exhibited the greatest variation, with a mean of 4.22 (SD = 2.33). The distribution was heterogeneous: 40.7% negative, 37% positive, and 22.2% neutral responses. The median and mode were both 7, while the mean was lower, indicating an asymmetric distribution. The **Dominance dimension** showed moderate performance, with a mean of 5.19 (SD = 2.15). Positive responses accounted for 51.8%, neutral for 25.9%, and negative for 22.2% (see Table 4).

Table 4. SAM Dimensions Results

SAM dimensions	Mean	SD	Median	Mode
Pleasure/Valence	7.6	1.83	8	9
Arousal	4.22	2.32	7	7
Dominance	5.18	2.14	5	5

PX-Br responses indicate positive evaluations in **Gameplay** (23 participants - 85.2%) and **Immersion/Presence** (20 participants - 74.1%) dimensions. **Fun** was the dimension with the lowest positive percentage (59.3%) and the highest neutral percentage (25.9%), as shown in Fig. 1. For **Immersion/Presence**, a majority of participants (74.1%) reported a positive experience (29.6% very high, 44.4% high). This dimension also had the lowest negative ratings (7.4% low or very low). The **Gameplay** dimension received the most positive evaluations, with 85.2% of participants rating it highly (59.30% very high, 25.9% high). The **Fun** dimension had the lowest positive rating at 59.3% (48.1% very high, 11.1% high). Conversely, it also had a lower negative rating (14.8% low or very low) but a significant portion of moderate responses (25.90%), indicating that while many found the game fun, a substantial number had a neutral or negative experience regarding this aspect.

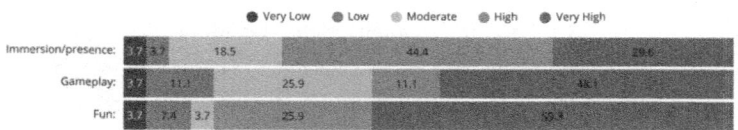

Fig. 1. Categorization of Player Experience Dimensions.

4.3 Interview Analysis

We qualitatively analyzed the users' answers for the interview questions (Table 5, in Appendix). The qualitative analysis involved the transcription and thematic analysis of interview data, resulting in the identification of six key themes. The **Visual Perception and Aesthetics** themes (1) addresses participant perceptions of the game's visual elements. This includes the subthemes: (i) visual discomfort, which reported players' feedback of flashing and overly bright colors during the new mechanic's introduction, as mentioned in the unit *"I think it was the phase transition that made the screen very flashy, that little transition in the animation"*. Additionally, some participants noted that the font used in the text exhibited low readability, as one marked *"The font was really bad; I couldn't read it properly"*.

The subthemes of (ii) opinions on aesthetics and (iii) visual elements that attracted attention showed that participants generally found the game's visuals appealing, praising the pixel art and the "cute" main character (*"I found it very cute. When he puts on the little hat.", "I really love this pixel art style. I found it very pleasant."*). However, some found the style confusing or not indicative of a challenging game (*"The game's style kind of makes it seem like you won't be punished for falling...", "I believe that in a game that starts with this visual style, you've created something more childlike, simpler, easier"*).

The **Perception of Soundtrack and Sound Effects** theme (2), which was subdivided in (iv) Perceptions about the soundtrack and (v) Perceptions of sound effects, examines participant feedback on the game's auditory components. The soundtrack was frequently described as pleasant, soft, enjoyable, and relaxing, often functioning as agreeable ambient sound within the gameplay experience, as expressed in the statement: *"I didn't dwell on the soundtrack. So, it was like an ambient sound that was pleasant to the game."*. However, during the introduction of the new perspective-shifting mechanic, the soundtrack became an important element for player immersion and engagement. This is reflected in the statements: *"When the music became more high-pitched and you became more immersed, I felt that I connected more with the game."* and *"In the introduction, he goes to another world, that was the most impactful part."*

Within the **Clarity and Coherence of the Game** theme (3), five subthemes explored participant understanding of the game's narrative and objectives. Subthemes (vi) and (ix) revealed that most participants understood the primary objective as collecting cubes (*"The objective was simple... find the cubes and open the doors..."*). However, subthemes (vii) and (viii) indicated that some players found the narrative confusing (*"I don't think I understood anything. The story, I didn't understand at all."*). Consequently, as highlighted in subtheme (x) moments of confusion, this lack of clear narrative context for the simple objective led to confusion and decreased motivation for some participants (*"I found going after the cubes perhaps a bit tedious because I thought the way the game worked was cool, but I wasn't understanding what these cubes are..."*).

The subtheme moments of confusion further highlighted instances where clear objectives were lacking. For example, participants reported disorientation after acquiring the second cube due to multiple emerging pathways, as illustrated by: *"That part was confusing for me because I started getting completely lost in the game's progression."* Additionally, the novel perspective-shifting mechanic itself elicited confusion for some players, as indicated by: *"One of the parts that frustrated me the most was because I didn't realize that changing the perspective would change my sense of space."*

The **Player Profile and Behavior** theme (4) encompassed six subthemes reflecting player preferences in the gaming experience. Exploratory players (xii) displayed interest and engagement with the mechanics and multiple pathways, stating *"I liked it a lot because, besides being something new, it still has plenty of questions and challenges. I don't know where I'm going or where I'm coming back from. So, I thought it was really cool."* Non-exploratory players (xiii), however, reported a preference for direct instruction and less interest in narrative or side content, noting *"I like (skipping cut-scenes); it's very rare for me to watch them. I'm not curious about the characters; So, in any game I play, I won't do side quests, for example. Very rarely. [...] I only tried to pay attention to what directly instructed me. And even that, sometimes, I didn't pay attention to."*

The **Immersion and Engagement in the Experience** theme (5) explored participant engagement, immersion, and perceptions of moments involving changes in the game's mechanics. The introduction of the perspective-shifting mechanic (xxiii) was identified as the most immersive moment by participants, as exemplified by *"So, when it exploded (the moment to change perspective) and he said, 'No, now you have to go after the cubes,' then I thought, 'Ah, now I know what to do.'"*. Consistent with earlier subthemes, the soundtrack (part of theme 2) also contributed to immersion, with one participant stating *"I think so, largely due to the sound design, like putting on the headphones. So much so that when I took them off, I was like, 'wow, I'm leaving this world, going to another.' But I think it was also a lot about the sound and the visual elements there that really held my attention."*

Regarding moments where the game felt like it might be breaking, some players described instances that led them to believe the game had glitched or lagged, as said in *"I really thought something had gone wrong, and I said, 'No, wait a minute, let's see.' And then he wakes up again with the little hat, and then I thought, 'ah,' and then the perspective-shifting aspect I found really cool, really out of the box"*. Furthermore, when discussing the point at which they stopped playing, most participants indicated that it was difficult to disengage, as an example in: *"It was (hard to stop). I wanted to continue. [...] I felt like I was already getting the hang of the game. And... that I was really progressing"*. Moreover, regarding the subtheme of player interest in continuing gameplay beyond the evaluation, participant opinions diverged, likely reflecting individual player profiles and perceptions, as evidenced by statements such as: *"That's the kind of game that captivates me"* and *"He didn't create a connection with me to the point where I wanted to play more"*.

In the **Memorable Moments of the Experience** theme (6), this section highlights the most significant points of the experience, subdivided into (xxvii) relevant moments of the experience, (xxviii) best moment of the game, (xxix) worst moment of the game, (xxx) moments of challenge, (xxxi) moments of satisfaction, and (xxxii) moments of frustration. One of the most remarkable moments, frequently aligned with peak immersion, was the perspective-shifting experience, as related in *"Then there's that dimension break, right? When you*

turn, he discovers a new world. So he can see something he couldn't see before".
However, some players also highlighted specific, time-consuming challenges, as in
"At the end when I was... that puzzle was good. That last [STONE PUZZLE] [....]
It's because it was the only moment I thought the game was actually difficult,
really challenging. When I really had to think about what I was doing and what
to do."

While opinions on the best moments and moments of satisfaction varied,
common instances included completing a cube ("I managed to acquire the first
whole cube to make the evolution.") or discovering hidden elements ("I managed
to solve the little stairs one... I felt clever for finding that place" and "I felt happy
when I started finding things. When I found the key to the chest"). Conversely,
the worst moments, moments of challenge, and frustration often stemmed from
difficulty with the game mechanics ("I started to realize that things were getting
a bit more difficult than what I was expecting... in terms of noticing... of solving
the problems of what angles there are...") or issues with character movement,
particularly during platforming sections ("When I fell and died, all the falls.
Every single fall. Because sometimes I wanted to jump from one spot to another...
and then I had to jump in some way and come back.").

5   Discussion

In this section, we consider these results together, integrating them with relevant literature to deepen the understanding of the player experience and their
implications for game design and future research.

5.1   Initial Excitement and Onboarding Challenges: How Players Reacted to Fez's Core Mechanic and Tutorial Absence

Fez stands out for its core mechanic that requires a significant cognitive shift
in spatial understanding. This study contributes to a relatively underexplored
area of player adaptation to such fundamentally novel interaction paradigms, as
noted in prior works on non-traditional gameplay experiences [13] and recent
explorations into onboarding with innovative mechanics [21]. Most participants
reported initial surprise upon encountering this mechanic, particularly during the
reset and in puzzles where rotation revealed new paths or hidden elements. These
"aha moments" were described with enthusiasm and expressions of surprise and
satisfaction, supported by the positive Gameplay ratings in the PX-Br (85.2%
positive responses).

However, while the novelty of the mechanic expressed a initial pleasure, when
analysing the qualitative responses, several players reported a decline in interest after the initial excitement faded. This was often attributed to a perceived
vagueness in both narrative and game objectives. Although players enjoyed the
mechanic, the often struggled to feel deep emotional connection to the purpose
of the game. As one participant noted "In reality, I considered it as a game
that was a bit meaningless [...] , it's assumed that it will connect you in some
way, it will keep you hooked in it [...] and the game's narrative itself didn't bring

that connection to me.". When asked about their interpretation of the objectives and narratives of the game, most of the participants gave vague answers and even reported they didn't see the meaning of their true purpose (*"I didn't really understand why he was going after these fragments (of cubes), what the objective was or for whom the was doing this."*). Moreover, when asked to describe the main character using a single adjective, participants tended to choose superficial descriptors, such as "normal" or "cute" .SZ

These results present a slight contrast with the positive score observed in the SAM Pleasure/Valence, Interest/Enjoyment in the IMI-Teq-Br, and the Focused Attention of the UES-Br. While these instruments indicated high levels of pleasure and engagement during gameplay, the qualitative data from interviews revealed that some participants still felt disconnected from the game's narrative and goals. This contradiction may suggest that some players can be momentarily engaged with aesthetic and mechanical novelties, but still feel a lack of purpose or deep emotional connection, while others need to be anchored in meaningful contexts and clear goals to maintain engagement over time. Another hypothesis that may explain this contrast—between high reported levels of interest, enjoyment, and focused attention on the one hand, and a disconnectedness from the narrative on the other—is that players can remain engaged and motivated by other elements of the game, such as opportunities for exploration or goals to achieve. For instance, some players with tendencies toward an Achiever profile (according to the Hexad typology) demonstrated high levels of enjoyment and interest on the IMI-Teq-BR and high focused attention on the UES-BR, even while reporting that they did not understand the game's narrative (*"I think there was something I was supposed to understand, but I didn't."*). This may indicate that pursuing goals that fulfill their needs as Achievers can keep such players engaged and motivated, even when other elements, such as the narrative, are not as significant for them.

Besides that, the IMI-Teq Br results reflect a motivational profile where players experienced high interest and enjoyment ($M = 6.17$) and strong perceived choice ($M = 5.8$), but only moderate perceived competence ($M = 4.8$). These results from IMI-Teq Br are also supported by the SAM questionnaire, where these users also reported high levels of pleasure and low or moderate levels of the dominance aspect. These users had in common a high tendency for Free Spirit and/or Philanthropist profiles according to the Hexad topology. This tendency may suggest that, while Fez supported autonomy through its open exploration and lack of detailed tutorials, it did not fully satisfy the need for competence in all participants.

Fez's lack of traditional onboarding—avoiding tutorials or direct instructions—led to mixed reactions among participants. Some players, particularly those identified as Free Spirits and Achievers in the HEXAD typology, reported that they appreciated the opportunity for autonomous discovery and felt competent while progressing, which is coherent with the usual preferences and personal goals of these profiles of players. These players tended to respond with a high score, to PX-Br, on the question about feeling disconnected from the real world while playing the game and they also reported moderated or high focused attention on the UES questionnaire. On the other hand, others participants, however, struggled with adaptation, reporting confusion or feeling lost early in the gameplay, unsure how or when to use the perspective-shifting mechanic. While a few participants found the challenges easy and did not require guidance, the overall low average and high variability in Disruptor scores (on the Hexad questionnaire) suggest that most were not primarily motivated by challenge. Instead, the data points to a predominance of players driven by autonomy, purpose, and competence—consistent with Tondello [39], who found that games with unconventional mechanics tend to attract players with these motivational profiles.

The varied reactions to the absence of tutorials in Fez illustrate how different players may respond based on their psychological. Players who value autonomy and discovery, such as Free Spirits and Achievers, as identified by the HEXAD typology, often enjoyed challenge and felt rewarded by figuring things out on their own. For these individuals, the design reinforced both autonomy and competence, fostering intrinsic motivation.

In contrast, participants who reported confusion, disorientation, or lack of understanding early in the game likely experienced a frustration of the competence need. This was echoed in the qualitative data and aligned with the lower scores in Perceived Competence and moderate SAM Dominance ($M = 5.19$). When onboarding fails to offer adequate guidance, players who are less tolerant of ambiguity or challenge may feel overwhelmed, which can lead to reduced motivation or early disengagement.

Understanding these initial adaptation processes is vital as game designers innovate with novel game interactions beyond established norms. The mixed reactions to Fez's tutorial absence suggest that unconventional mechanics may necessitate varied onboarding strategies tailored to player types. For players who value exploration and independent discovery, the lack of tutorials can boost autonomy and accomplishment. However, for those needing more guidance and less motivated by complex challenges, this absence can cause frustration. In such cases, more detailed or optional tutorials might be crucial for sustaining player interest.

5.2   A Multifaceted Look at Player Experience: Strengths and Tensions Across Instruments

The player experience is very complex and cannot be evaluated in a trivial way [6]. The use of multiple instruments in this study allowed for a richer characterization of the player experience than any single measure could provide, as evidenced by [37], who emphasize the importance of integrated approaches in evaluating player experience.

Several dimensions revealed consistent patterns of engagement and satisfaction. High scores in Pleasure/Valence (SAM), Interest/Enjoyment (IMI), and Focused Attention (UES-Br) suggests players found the experience intrinsically rewarding and cognitively absorbing. These results were further supported by the positive evaluations of Immersion/Presence and Gameplay in the PX-Br.

This convergence across instruments reflects the emotional and cognitive appeal of the game's core mechanic, particularly during early exploration. Qualitative excerpts reinforce this: participants described feeling "curious," "excited," or even "surprised" when discovering the perspective-shifting mechanic, aligning with the notion of "aha moments" observed during gameplay.

Despite high reported engagement, moderate scores in Perceived Competence (IMI) and Dominance (SAM) suggest a tension: players enjoyed the experience but didn't always feel fully in control or confident in mastering the core mechanic. Qualitative data helps explain this, indicating that enjoyment of the aesthetic and challenge could coexist with struggles in mastering the perspective-shifting mechanic, leading to confusion and a sense of lower control. One participant exemplified this by praising the aesthetics' positive impact on exploration (*"It had an impact, since the aesthetics kind of makes you want to explore the game environment."*) and expressing enjoyment of the challenges despite difficulty (*"I really liked it, but I couldn't do it."*). This participant also described initial confusion with the perspective changes but eventual adaptation through exploration (*"At first I was confused by how many perspectives there were, but then I started to adapt more to find them."*) and its role in achieving goals (*"I thought it was really cool. Because I wasn't able to get past the platforms. Then when I changed the perspective, I was able to get past it."*). This highlights that enjoyment and frustration can coexist, emphasizing the need for well-structured challenge to sustain motivation.

Another contradiction was revealed when comparing the qualitative and quantitative data. While several participants described the game's objectives as "repetitive" or even "boring", with one participant even stating that they began creating their own challenges to stay engaged, the quantitative instruments painted a different picture. The UES-Br revealed high scores in the Focused Attention dimension, suggesting that players remained absorbed during gameplay. Similarly, the IMI-Teq Br indicated high levels of intrinsic motivation, and the Immersion/Presence dimension from the PX-Br was also evaluated positively by most participants. The PX-Br Gameplay dimension was also very well evaluated, with over 80% of positive evaluations, which can indicate how well received was the mechanic, aesthetics and soundtrack of the game.

It was also noticed that many participants may had immersion peaks, mainly at moments when they were completing an objective, and satisfaction when they completed a goal. Since one of the gameplay stop moments in the evaluation was established as the completion of an objective in the game, when asked to stop playing the participants were in a moment of satisfaction. This may have positively affected the motivation, engagement and satisfaction instruments.

Moreover, the lab environment and task-based nature of the test may have contributed to elevated levels of focus and immersion (due to controlled conditions and time-limited play), which may not correspond to sustained engagement in a more natural or real-world gameplay context. This could explain why participants maintained attention and motivation during the test but still described the experience as repetitive or lacking purpose in the interviews.

Additionally, the HEXAD-12 typology, identifying most participants as intrinsically motivated Philanthropists, Free Spirits, and Achievers (valuing autonomy and competence), provides crucial context for interpreting the data. These motivational orientations help explain why participants reported high levels of Interest/Enjoyment (IMI) and Focused Attention (UES-Br), even when the game presented challenges or lacked explicit guidance. For these profiles, Fez's design, centered on exploration and problem-solving without traditional tutorials, aligns well with their preference for autonomy. Furthermore, the competence derived from mastering the perspective-shifting mechanic may have amplified the high satisfaction scores observed in both SAM and PX-Br, despite moments of confusion or unclear objectives. In this context, high satisfaction may have contributed to overall positive responses in the IMI and UES-Br instruments. Thus, the convergence between emotional satisfaction (SAM, PX-Br) and cognitive engagement (IMI, UES-Br) seems closely linked to both the game's design and the motivational characteristics of the participant group. Ultimately, these findings highlight the importance of a mixed-methods approach. While quantitative instruments are useful for identifying patterns of engagement and cognitive focus, qualitative data provide a deeper understanding of players' emotional responses, expectations, and needs—aspects that numerical scores alone cannot explain. The integration of both perspectives reveals not only what players experienced but also why and under what conditions those experiences may or may not be sustained. This approach aligns with the guidelines proposed by Carneiro [9], who emphasize the use of semi-structured interviews to capture subjective nuances of player experience, demonstrating the importance of combining methods.

5.3 Implications to the Game Design and Game Research

The study's findings offer key implications for game design and research, especially concerning novel mechanics and player experience evaluation. First, the diverse reactions to Fez's core mechanics and onboarding underscore the necessity of design strategies that accommodate varied player needs and preferences. Games introducing new mechanics should balance player autonomy with sufficient guidance. While some players benefit from explicit onboarding to build competence and avoid frustration (*"But [the game]... gave so many paths that I wanted to keep exploring more and more of the map."*), others prefer independent exploration for a sense of mastery (*"You have to keep exploring the place [...] and sometimes I waste time exploring."*).

This suggests the potential value of flexible tutorials that adapt to player types or offer optional guidance without hindering exploration. Second, the contrast between qualitative reports of vague goals/narratives and high engagement levels emphasizes the multifaceted nature of player motivation. Engagement with mechanics and visuals doesn't guarantee narrative connection, purpose, or emotional investment. To cultivate stronger emotional resonance and meaningful experiences, game designers should focus on effectively integrating innovative mechanics with clear and purposeful narratives and objectives.

Thirdly, the application of multiple complementary evaluation methods revealed insights that could have been missed if only a qualitative or quantitative approach had been used. The integration of questionnaires with qualitative feedback enabled a deeper understanding of the player experience. This reinforces the importance of using mixed-methods approaches in game research, as player responses are often complex and sometimes contradictory—especially when considering different player types who may react differently to gameplay, as also argued by Elson and Quandt [15] in their advocacy for combined methods to capture the multiple levels of user responses in digital games.

Finally, the motivational profiles emphasize the importance of considering the different player typologies in both design and research when considering games. Games that attract players with strong intrinsic motivation, autonomy and competence might benefit from simpler tutorials and challenges that require exploration on the part of the player. Games aimed at players who need detailed explanations to feel competent need more detailed guides. Future research could explore how diverse player motivations can influence their responses to game retention, emotional engagement and persist in learning curves.

The results of this study highlight the importance of considering players' needs and how they adapt to new mechanics. Furthermore, it demonstrates the need to consider employing multidimensional evaluation methods when evaluating a game in order to capture nuances in the player experience that often cannot be captured by a single type of evaluation. With these considerations, we hope that game designers and researchers can better create and evaluate experiences that are not only innovative, but also engaging, motivational, and emotionally satisfying for a variety of players.

6   Conclusion

This mixed-methods study explored how Fez's perspective-shifting mechanics influence player motivation, emotion, and engagement. The findings underscore the importance of thoughtful onboarding to ease player adaptation to unconventional mechanics, reducing confusion and enhancing engagement. By combining quantitative and qualitative data, the study revealed nuanced insights that might be missed by single-method approaches. Despite limitations, including a relatively small participant group predominantly composed mostly of individuals familiar with technology and game design, our results offer valuable contributions to game design research, particularly in understanding how to introduce innovative mechanics without compromising motivation.

Future work should explore onboarding strategies tailored to diverse player types (e.g., via HEXAD typologies), compare experiences across games with novel mechanics, and investigate how narrative and player preferences affect emotional connection and learning. Cross-analysis of multiple instruments could reveal patterns in how emotion, motivation, and engagement interact, supporting emotionally aligned design goals. In sum, this study reinforces the value of a player-centered approach in innovative game design, emphasizing the role of inclusive onboarding and multi-method evaluation in crafting meaningful, motivating experiences.

Disclosure of Interests. The authors have no competing interests.

A   Appendix A: Interview Questions

Table 5. Semi-structured Interview Script

Main Question	Follow-up Question
General Experience	
Overall, how would you describe your experience playing the game?	
What was the most significant moment of the game for you?	Why? What was the [best/worst] moment of the game for you?
Game Elements	
Did the soundtrack have an impact on you at any point during the game?	Why? Was it positive or negative?
Did the visual aesthetics have an impact on you?	Was it positive or negative? Did any particular element stand out?
How would you describe the game's narrative?	
How would you describe the game's objectives?	
What did you think of the moment when you changed the game's perspective/camera angle?	
Experience Elements	
Did you feel challenged?	By what? By which part/element?
Do you enjoy feeling challenged?	Did you enjoy the type of challenge this game provided?
At what point in the game did you feel most engaged?	
Would you say you felt immersed in the game while playing?	Why? If you could, would you change anything to make the game more captivating?
Did any moment in the game bring you personal satisfaction?	And frustration?
Final Experience	
What was it like for you to stop playing?	Was it difficult to stop playing?
If you were playing this game outside of this evaluation context,	would you have continued to play on your own?
How was the end of the game for you (the part that you played)?	
Observations	
[Questions about specific observations from the player's gameplay]	
Closure	
If you could describe the game in one adjective, what would it be?	
And the main character?	

References

1. Abeele, V.V., Spiel, K., Nacke, L., Johnson, D., Gerling, K.: Development and validation of the player experience inventory: A scale to measure player experiences at the level of functional and psychosocial consequences. Int. J. Hum.-Comput. Stud. **135**, 102370 (2020). https://doi.org/10.1016/j.ijhcs.2019.102370, https://www.sciencedirect.com/science/article/pii/S1071581919301302
2. Alexiou, A., Schippers, M.C.: Digital game elements, user experience and learning: a conceptual framework. Educ. Inf. Technol. **23**, 2545–2567 (2018). https://doi.org/10.1007/s10639-018-9730-6
3. Andersen, E., et al.: The impact of tutorials on games of varying complexity. In: Proceedings of the SIGCHI Conference on Human Factors in Computing Systems. CHI '12, pp. 59–68. Association for Computing Machinery, New York, NY, USA (2012). https://doi.org/10.1145/2207676.2207687
4. Aranha, R., Nunes, F.: Player experience with Brazilian accent: development and validation of px-br, a summarized instrument in Portuguese. In: Anais do XVIII Simpósio Brasileiro de Sistemas de Informação. SBC, Porto Alegre, RS, Brasil (2022). https://sol.sbc.org.br/index.php/sbsi/article/view/21357
5. Aranha, R.V., Nunes, F.L.: Player experience with Brazilian accent: development and validation of px-br, a summarized instrument in Portuguese. In: Proceedings of the XVIII Brazilian Symposium on Information Systems, pp. 1–8 (2022)
6. Borges, J.B., Juy, C.L., de Andrade Matos, I.S., Silveira, P.V.A., Darin, T.d.G.R.: Player experience evaluation: a brief panorama of instruments and research opportunities. J. Interact. Syst. **11**(1), 74–91 (2020). https://doi.org/10.5753/jis.2020.765, https://journals-sol.sbc.org.br/index.php/jis/article/view/765
7. Bradley, M.M., Lang, P.J.: Measuring emotion: the self-assessment manikin and the semantic differential. J. Behav. Therapy Exp. Psychiatry **25**, 49–59 (1994). https://doi.org/10.1016/0005-7916(94)90063-9, https://www.sciencedirect.com/science/article/pii/0005791694900639
8. Braun, V., Clarke, V.: Using thematic analysis in psychology. Qual. Res. Psychol. **3**(2), 77–101 (2006). https://doi.org/10.1191/1478088706qp063oa, https://www.tandfonline.com/doi/abs/10.1191/1478088706qp063oa
9. Carneiro, N., Viana, W., Darin, T.: Valerie: a guide to qualitative evaluation of player experience in location-based games using interviews. In: Anais do XX Simpósio Brasileiro sobre Fatores Humanos em Sistemas Computacionais. SBC, Porto Alegre, RS, Brasil (2021). https://sol.sbc.org.br/index.php/ihc/article/view/19383
10. Choong, L.: Using AI-supported onboarding systems in video games to improve player experience. Master's thesis, University of Waterloo (2024). http://hdl.handle.net/10012/20444
11. Dahlström, C.: Impacts of gamification on intrinsic motivation (2017). https://api.semanticscholar.org/CorpusID:211116565. Accessed 16 May 2025
12. Delaney, M.L., Royal, M.A.: Breaking engagement apart: the role of intrinsic and extrinsic motivation in engagement strategies. Ind. Org. Psychol. **10**, 127–140 (2017). https://doi.org/10.1017/iop.2017.2
13. Denisova, A., Cairns, P.: Adaptation in digital games: the effect of challenge adjustment on player performance and experience. In: Proceedings of the 2015 Annual Symposium on Computer-Human Interaction in Play, pp. 97–101. ACM (2015). https://doi.org/10.1145/2793107.2793141

14. Doherty, K., Doherty, G.: Engagement in HCI: conception, theory and measurement. ACM Comput. Surv. **51**(5) (2018). https://doi.org/10.1145/3234149

15. Elson, M., Quandt, T.: Digital games in laboratory experiments: controlling a complex stimulus through modding. Psychol. Popular Media Cult. **5**(1), 52–65 (2016). https://doi.org/10.1037/ppm0000033

16. Hatzl, A., Hedberg, O., Keramidas, I., Mardunovich, D., et al.: Player onboarding in a low-complexity game favouring implicit instructions: a case study of the game *the social grip* (2024). https://www.uu.se/student/institution/speldesign/examensarbeten.html

17. Kanellopoulou, C., Giannakoulopoulos, A.: Engage and conquer: an online empirical approach into whether intrinsic or extrinsic motivation leads to more enhanced students' engagement. Creat. Educ. **11**(2), 143–165 (2020). https://doi.org/10.4236/ce.2020.112011

18. Krath, J., Altmeyer, M., Tondello, G.F., Nacke, L.E.: Hexad-12: Developing and validating a short version of the gamification user types hexad scale. In: Proceedings of the 2023 CHI Conference on Human Factors in Computing Systems (CHI '23), pp. 1–18. Association for Computing Machinery, New York, NY, USA (2023). https://doi.org/10.1145/3544548.3580968

19. Krath, J., Altmeyer, M. Tondello, G.F., Nacke, L.E.: Hexad-12: developing and validating a short version of the gamification user types hexad scale. In: Proceedings of the 2023 CHI Conference on Human Factors in Computing Systems. CHI '23. Association for Computing Machinery, New York, NY, USA (2023). https://doi.org/10.1145/3544548.3580968

20. Lalmas, M., O'Brien, H., Yom-Tov, E.: Measuring User Engagement, Synthesis Lectures on Information Concepts, Retrieval, and Services, vol. 6. Morgan & Claypool Publishers (2014). https://doi.org/10.2200/S00605ED1V01Y201410ICR038

21. Lopes, P., Fachada, N., Fonseca, M.: Closing the loop: a systematic review of experience-driven game adaptation, arXiv preprint (2025). https://arxiv.org/abs/2505.01351

22. Mekler, E.D., Bopp, J.A., Tuch, A.N., Opwis, K.: A systematic review of quantitative studies on the enjoyment of digital entertainment games. In: Proceedings of the SIGCHI Conference on Human Factors in Computing Systems. CHI '14, pp. 927–936. Association for Computing Machinery, New York, NY, USA (2014). https://doi.org/10.1145/2556288.2557078

23. Mekler, E.D., Brühlmann, F., Tuch, A.N., Opwis, K.: Towards understanding the effects of individual gamification elements on intrinsic motivation and performance. Comput. Hum. Behav. **71**, 525–534 (2017). https://doi.org/10.1016/j.chb.2015.08.048, https://www.sciencedirect.com/science/article/pii/S0747563215301229

24. Miranda, D., Juy, C.L., Darin, T.: UES-BR: translation and cross-cultural adaptation of the user engagement scale for Brazilian Portuguese. Proc. ACM on Hum.-Comput. Interact. **5**(CHI PLAY), pp. 1–22 (2021). https://doi.org/10.1145/3474705

25. Miranda, D., Li, C., Darin, T.: UES-BR: translation and cross-cultural adaptation of the user engagement scale for Brazilian Portuguese. Proc. ACM Hum.-Comput. Interact. **5**, 1–22 (2021). https://doi.org/10.1145/3474705

26. Nagpal, RameshKumar M.: Navigating teachers' adoption of artificial intelligence in English foreign language: uncovering inhibitors and drivers. SPAST Reports (2024). https://api.semanticscholar.org/CorpusID:270872344. Accessed 16 May 2025

27. Nipo, D., Gadelha, D., Silva, M.d., Lopes, A.: Game-based learning: possibilities of an instrumental approach to the fez game for the teaching of the orthographic drawings system concepts. J. Interact. Syst. **14**(1), 231–243 (2023). https://doi.org/10.5753/jis.2023.3190, https://journals-sol.sbc.org.br/index.php/jis/article/view/3190. acesso em: 17 maio 2025

28. Nunes, C., Darin, T.: Brazilian Portuguese version of intrinsic motivation inventory (imi-teq br): towards a digital well-being culture in Brazil. J. Brazil. Comput. Soc. **30**(1), 394–410 (2024). https://doi.org/10.5753/jbcs.2024.4305

29. Pereira Nunes, C., Darin, T.: Cross-cultural adaptation of the intrinsic motivation inventory task evaluation questionnaire into Brazilian Portuguese, pp. 1–11 (2024). https://doi.org/10.1145/3638067.3638083

30. Peterson, J.S.: Presenting a qualitative study: a reviewer's perspective. Gifted Child Q. **63**(3), 147–158 (2019). https://doi.org/10.1177/0016986219844789, Original Work Published 2019

31. Regalado, F., Ribeiro, T., Veloso, A.: Fez game - an heuristic evaluation (2021)

32. Ryan, R.M.: Control and information in the intrapersonal sphere: an extension of cognitive evaluation theory. J. Personal. Soc. Psychol. **43**(3), 450–461 (1982). https://doi.org/10.1037/0022-3514.43.3.450

33. Ryan, R.M., Deci, E.L.: Self-determination theory and the facilitation of intrinsic motivation, social development, and well-being. Am. Psychol. **55**(1), 68–78 (2000). https://doi.org/10.1037/0003-066X.55.1.68, https://psycnet.apa.org/doi/10.1037/0003-066X.55.1.68

34. Ryan, R.M., Deci, E.L.: Overview of self-determination theory: an organismic dialectical perspective. In: Deci, E.L., Ryan, R.M. (eds.) Handbook of Self-determination Research, vol. 2, pp. 3–33. University of Rochester Press, Rochester, NY (2002)

35. Ryan, R.M., Deci, E.L.: Self-determination theory. In: Maggino, F. (ed.) Encyclopedia of Quality of Life and Well-Being Research. Springer, Cham (2022). https://doi.org/10.1007/978-3-319-69909-7_2630-2

36. Santos, A.C.G., Muramatsu, P.K., Santos, W.O.d., Joaquim, S., Hamari, J., Isotani, S.: Investigação psicométrica da escala hexad para identificação de perfis de usuários de gamificação em português brasileiro. Anais estendidos (2024)

37. Smith, A.M., Nelson, M.J., Mateas, M.: A case study of expressively constrainable level design automation tools for a puzzle game. In: Proceedings of the 2012 Conference on the Foundations of Digital Games (FDG '12). ACM (2012).https://doi.org/10.1145/2282338.2282375

38. Tondello, G., Wehbe, R., Diamond, L., Busch, M., Marczewski, A., Nacke, L.: The gamification user types hexad scale (2016). https://doi.org/10.1145/2967934.2968082

39. Tondello, G.F., Mora, î, Marczewski, A., Nacke, L.E.: Gamification user types. In: Proceedings of the 2016 Annual Symposium on Computer-Human Interaction in Play, pp. 229–243. ACM (2016). https://doi.org/10.1145/2967934.2968082

40. Tyack, A., Mekler, E.D.: Self-determination theory in HCI games research: current uses and open questions. In: Proceedings of the 2020 CHI Conference on Human Factors in Computing Systems, pp. 1–22. ACM (2020). https://doi.org/10.1145/3313831.3376723

41. Xie, T., Cao, M., Pan, Z.: Applying self-assessment manikin (SAM) to evaluate the affective arousal effects of VR games. In: Proceedings of the 2020 3rd International Conference on Image and Graphics Processing (ICIGP '20), pp. 134–138. Association for Computing Machinery, New York, NY, USA (2020). https://doi.org/10.1145/3383812.3383844
42. Yáñez-Gómez, R., Cascado-Caballero, D., Sevillano, J.L.: Academic methods for usability evaluation of serious games: a systematic review. Multimedia Tools Appl. **76**, 5755–5784 (2017). https://doi.org/10.1007/s11042-016-3845-9

Author Index

© The Editor(s) (if applicable) and The Author(s), under exclusive license
to Springer Nature Switzerland AG 2026
T. Darin et al. (Eds.): WIPlay 2025, CCIS 2623, p. 201, 2026.
https://doi.org/10.1007/978-3-032-01426-9

The manufacturer's authorised representative in the EU is Springer
Nature Customer Service Centre GmbH, Europaplatz 3, 69115 Heidelberg,
Germany. If you have any concerns regarding our products, please
contact ProductSafety@springernature.com

Printed and bound by CPI Group (UK) Ltd, Croydon, CR0 4YY
28/04/2026
02098522-0001